Hong Kong Horror Cinema

For Paul & Lucie, and Ian & Eileen

Hong Kong Horror Cinema

Edited by Gary Bettinson and Daniel Martin

EDINBURGH
University Press

Edinburgh University Press is one of the leading university presses in
the UK. We publish academic books and journals in our selected subject
areas across the humanities and social sciences, combining cutting-edge
scholarship with high editorial and production values to produce academic
works of lasting importance. For more information visit our website:
edinburghuniversitypress.com

Edinburgh University Press Ltd
The Tun – Holyrood Road
12 (2f) Jackson's Entry
Edinburgh EH8 8PJ

Typeset in Monotype Ehrhardt by
Servis Filmsetting Ltd, Stockport, Cheshire,
and printed and bound in Great Britain.

A CIP record for this book is available from the British Library

ISBN 978 1 4744 2459 2 (hardback)
ISBN 978 1 4744 2460 8 (webready PDF)
ISBN 978 1 4744 2461 5 (epub)

Contents

Acknowledgements

Daniel would like to thank colleagues in the School of Humanities and Social Sciences at KAIST for their support of this project. The students of HSS217 in the autumn semester of 2016 are also due thanks for being so receptive to some ideas-in-progress on fantasy-horror, and for their thoughtful responses to films screened. Particular gratitude for their friendship and encouragement is due to Grant Fisher, Mark Morris and Mark Jancovich. Adoring distractions were provided, as always, by Hyunjoo, Montgomery and Errol; final thanks to Youngsook Ryu for providing immeasurably helpful bouts of babysitting.

Gary would like to thank Law Kar, Li Cheuk-to, Yvonne Teh, Bey Logan, Wing-Ho Lin, Timmy Chen, Yiping Lin, Kristof Van den Troost and Richard Rushton. Appreciation goes to Victor Fan and an audience at King's College London for their hospitality and insightful comments on horror cinema. Pang Ho-cheung gave generously of his time, deftly assisted by Veronica Bassetto. Special thanks are due to Robert and Shirley.

We would both like to thank our editor at Edinburgh University Press, Gillian Leslie, for her constant encouragement and enthusiasm for this project.

Lastly, we thank Eddie Clark for editorial support, and Lel Gillingwater for attentive copy-editing.

Notes on the Contributors

Gary Bettinson is Senior Lecturer in Film Studies at Lancaster University. He is the author of *The Sensuous Cinema of Wong Kar-wai: Film Poetics and the Aesthetic of Disturbance* (2015), editor of the *Directory of World Cinema: China* Volumes 1 and 2 (2012; 2015), co-author (with Richard Rushton) of *What is Film Theory? An Introduction to Contemporary Debates* (2010), co-editor (with James Udden) of *The Poetics of Chinese Cinema* (2016) and co-editor (with Tan See Kam) of *Asian Cinema*.

Felicia Chan is Senior Lecturer in Screen Studies at the University of Manchester, researching the construction of national, cultural and cosmopolitan imaginaries in film. She is also author of *Cosmopolitan Cinema: Cross-cultural Encounters in East Asian Film* (2017), co-editor of *Chinese Cinemas: International Perspectives* (2016) and founding member of the Chinese Film Forum UK.

Kenneth Chan is Professor of English and Director of Film Studies at the University of Northern Colorado. He is the author of *Remade in Hollywood: the Global Chinese Presence in Transnational Cinemas* (2009) and *Yonfan's Bugis Street* (2015). His essays have also appeared in numerous edited book collections and academic journals, including *Cinema Journal*, *Journal of Chinese Cinemas*, *Asian Cinema*, *Discourse: Journal for Theoretical Studies in Media and Culture* and *Camera Obscura*. His latest research focuses on the fantastic in contemporary global cinemas.

David Scott Diffrient is Professor of Film and Media Studies in the Department of Communication Studies at Colorado State University. His articles have been published in *Asian Cinema*, *Cinema Journal*, *Historical Journal of Film, Radio and Television*, *Journal of Film and Video*, *New Review of Film and Television Studies*, *Quarterly Review of Film and Video*, and other journals. He is the author of *Omnibus Films: Theorizing*

Transauthorial Cinema (Edinburgh University Press, 2014) and the co-author of *Movie Migrations: Transnational Genre Flows and South Korean Cinema* (2015). He recently served as the co-editor of the *Journal of Japanese and Korean Cinema*.

Andrew Grossman is the editor of the anthology *Queer Asian Cinema: Shadows in the Shade*, a regular contributor to *Bright Lights Film Journal* and *Popmatters*, and a contributor to numerous edited collections, including *Movies in the Age of Obama*, *Transnational Chinese Cinema: Corporeality, Desire, and the Ethics of Failure*, and *Clint Eastwood's Cinema of Trauma*. He is currently co-editing (with Brian Bergen-Aurand) *The Encyclopedia of Queer Cinema*. He also directed a documentary film, *Not That Kind of Christian!!* (2007), which was featured at the Montreal World Film Festival.

Enrique Ajuria Ibarra is Assistant Professor at Universidad de las Américas Puebla, Mexico. He has previously published several articles and book chapters on Gothic and horror cinema. He is the editor of the peer-reviewed online journal *Studies in Gothic Fiction*, and is currently preparing a monograph on the relationship between movement, Gothic and the horror film.

Vivian Lee is Associate Professor at the City University of Hong Kong. She is the author of *Hong Kong Cinema Since 1997: the Post-nostalgic Imagination* (2009; Chinese translation to be published in 2018) and editor of *East Asian Cinemas: Regional Flows and Global Transformations* (2011). Her current research interests include East Asian cinemas and visual cultures, cultural policy and the politics of heritage-making in Greater China and Asia. A co-authored volume on Hong Kong independent cinema and a book-length study on Hong Kong's left-wing studios are due to be published in 2018.

Liang Luo is Associate Professor of Chinese Studies at the University of Kentucky. She is the author of *The Avant-Garde and the Popular in Modern China* (2014). Her recent writings on intermediality, the politics of performance, and the dialectics of dancing and writing can be seen in *Modern Chinese Literature and Culture*, *Trans-humanities*, and *Frontiers of Literary Studies in China*. She is working on two projects, *The Humanity of the Non-human: Gender, Media, and Politics in* The White Snake (book and digital project) and *The International Avant-Garde and Modern China* (book and documentary film project).

Daniel Martin is Associate Professor of Film Studies in the School of Humanities and Social Sciences at the Korea Advanced Institute of Science and Technology (KAIST). His recent research concerns the international circulation of films from South Korea, Japan, and Hong Kong. He is the author of *Extreme Asia: the Rise of Cult Cinema from the Far East* (Edinburgh University Press, 2015), co-editor of *Korean Horror Cinema* (Edinburgh University Press, 2013), and has published articles in *Cinema Journal, The Journal of Film and Video, Continuum, Film International, Acta Koreana, Asian Cinema* and *The Journal of Korean Studies*.

Lisa Odham Stokes teaches Humanities and Film Studies at Seminole State College in Central Florida. She is co-author (with Michael Hoover) of *City on Fire: Hong Kong Cinema* (1999; rpt. 2001) and author of *The Historical Dictionary of Hong Kong Cinema* (2007) and *Peter Ho-Sun Chan's 'He's a Woman, She's a Man'* (2009). She has travelled extensively in China and Hong Kong, presenting papers at film conferences, and she has published numerous articles on film, literature and popular culture with a special interest in Chinese cinemas. She is a long-time programmer for the Florida Film Festival.

Raymond Tsang is a doctoral student in Cinema Studies at New York University. His areas of interest include cultural studies, postcolonial theory, Hong Kong cinema, Chinese-language cinema, and martial arts cinemas. He has also published cultural criticism and film reviews in various magazines and books in Hong Kong and China. His working dissertation is about the cultural formation of Chinese martial arts/martial arts cinema and the history of governmentality in Hong Kong during the Cold War. Forthcoming publications include an essay on Stephen Chow's movies in *Journal of Chinese Cinemas*.

Andy Willis is a Reader in Film Studies at the University of Salford and Senior Visiting Curator: Film at HOME (Greater Manchester Arts Centre). He is the co-author of *The Cinema of Alex de la Iglesia* (2007) with Peter Buse and Nuria Triana Toribo, editor of *Film Stars: Hollywood and Beyond* (2004), and co-editor of *Spanish Popular Cinema* (2004) with Antonio Lazaro Reboll, *East Asian Film Stars* (2014) with Wing-Fai Leung, *Chinese Cinemas: International Perspectives* (2016) with Felicia Chan and *Cult Media: Re-packaged, Re-released and Restored* (2017) with Jonathan Wroot.

Introduction

Gary Bettinson and Daniel Martin

The film industry of Hong Kong has long been associated with genre cinema. While the territory boasts a long and proud history of aesthetic experimentation and art cinema, and of incredible diversity in its crowd-pleasing hits, the cinema of Hong Kong is frequently seen as essentially defined by its association with various forms of action. For a vast majority of Western audiences, Hong Kong cinema is kung fu, epitomised by the perfection of Bruce Lee or the controlled chaos of Jackie Chan; for a different audience, John Woo's pioneering 'Heroic Bloodshed' bullet ballets symbolise the greatest achievements of Hong Kong film-makers. Horror has emerged as another of these iconic, kinetic modes of Hong Kong film-making, capturing the attention of global audiences and honouring a centuries-old tradition of ghost stories of the macabre and bizarre.

According to several domestic critics, the horror film reached its commercial and artistic peak in the 1980s, partially as a response from film-makers and audiences to the decline of the dominance of kung fu (Teo 1989: 41). Phrased in more poetic terms by the critic Sek Kei, kung fu was the 'flesh and blood' of Hong Kong cinema in the 1970s, while horror films 'have occupied its soul in the eighties' (Ibid.: 13). If this moment represents the peak for Hong Kong horror, the golden age was short-lived: for one journalist, the cycle sputtered out by the mid-1990s (O'Brien 2003: 5). This popular view of Hong Kong horror – as a brief and bright flame that lasted barely longer than a decade – discounts both the rich history of horror in Hong Kong, dating back as long as films have been made in the territory, as well as an enduring legacy that continues to inspire film-makers and thrill audiences today.

The 2013 film *Rigor Mortis* (directed by Juno Mak) was seen by many as a catalyst for a re-examination of Hong Kong horror's unique appeal. Premiering at the Venice Film Festival to an appreciative audience, the film represented both the old and the new, nostalgically incorporating references to Hong Kong horror's greatest achievements while acknowledging the shifting global market for East Asian cult cinema. *Rigor Mortis* was produced by Takashi Shimizu, well known for his horror films made in Japan (*Ju-on: The Grudge* (2002); *Marebito* (2004); *Reincarnation* (2005)) and Hollywood (notably 2004's *The Grudge*, an English-language remake of his own breakthrough hit). The film reimagines the iconic *Mr. Vampire* (Ricky Lau, 1985) with slick special effects and a somewhat more serious sense of dread, while retaining the tonal dissonance that made the original film so compelling (though the comedic elements of *Rigor Mortis* were pointedly hidden in its international marketing as an art-action-horror).

Rigor Mortis, though not quite triggering a full renaissance for Hong Kong horror, is a sure sign that the genre never disappeared; it only evolved. The contemporary Hong Kong horror film is both nostalgic and innovative, time-worn and modern, local and global: these are films expressing specific cultural values and local taste formations while appealing to universal values. The Hong Kong horror cinema is unlike any other, and its specific history, narrative morphology and integration of conflicting tones and subgenres set it apart from the frightful films of Hollywood, as well as the well-circulated horror of Asian neighbours such as Japan and South Korea.

The way that *Rigor Mortis* exhibits many nostalgic, even historical qualities is suggestive of features that are also intrinsic to the broader horror genre in Hong Kong. Ghost stories and tales of dread from the territory draw on a long tradition of mythology and folklore narratives, reflecting ancient and deep-seated superstitions and spiritual beliefs. The infusion of Hong Kong horror with prehistorical Chinese mythology is a manifestation of the way those tales have evolved over time. Historically, Chinese scholars did not typically record or preserve myths as distinct works of literature. As a result, mythic stories and oral folklore were fractured and redistributed, appearing as aspects of both supposedly real history and various forms of fiction, and Chinese mythology therefore has a 'diffuse and fragmentary' nature (K'o 1993: xii).

The Hong Kong horror film is thus one of many narrative forms to incorporate these myths, spiritual beliefs and fairy tales of Chinese history, and is one of the key factors accounting for the fundamentally hybrid nature of the genre. The legendary fable of the magical white snake (discussed in detail in Chapter Two of this collection), for example, exhibits the flexibility of this kind of mythological tale. This story of a magical snake who transforms into a human-looking woman and pursues a romance with a normal, mortal man is ripe with potential for expressing various tones. The story of the white snake can thus be told as a horror, intended to elicit fear and disgust, or as a romance, designed to appeal to the traditions of melodrama; most frequently, in the tradition of Hong Kong cinema's penchant for generic blends, the tale is both.

Pu Songling's literary masterpiece *Strange Tales from a Chinese Studio* is a collection of short stories written in the seventeenth century, many of which depict ghosts and spirits, fox-vixens and demons. These stories form an enduring prototype of the Hong Kong horror, and set out precisely the way subsequent writers, poets, artists and film-makers would use a variety of fantastic horror premises to comment on contemporary society and politics. A set of core recurring themes examine gender politics, the psychology of sexuality, corruption in the government and the hypocrisy of hierarchical society (Cass 2010: 12); these themes would be repeatedly exhumed by directors in many of the films considered in this volume. *Strange Tales from a Chinese Studio* was also instrumental in establishing Hong Kong horror's ambivalent depiction of the female ghost: she is neither completely an object of terror nor entirely harmless. Indeed, the seductive spirit offers her (typically) male lover/victim a 'lethal mixture of infatuation, fascination, and fear' (Minford 2006: xxii).

Alongside female ghosts, Chinese mythology – and, therefore, the Hong Kong horror film – also prominently features animals and beasts, both real and imagined. The most iconic example of this trend is manifest in the epic *Journey to the West*, a sixteenth-century novel widely circulated and frequently adapted; the heroic protagonist is an anthropomorphised monkey warrior-king. Many gods and spirits appear in folklore not as human in appearance, but as chimeric creatures, exhibiting the bodily features of various animals (Chen 2011: 1). This explains, to a large degree, the relatively high frequency with which Hong Kong horror features supernaturally potent animals, shape-shifters that can transform from humans to beasts, and bizarre creatures invested with psychological complexity. Reptiles, especially snakes, are an especially common motif, as evidenced by their inclusion as the central focus of two chapters featured in this collection. Foxes, too, appear often: the multiple-tailed *huli jing* can assume human form and often appears female in order to seduce a luckless male victim. Similar figures appear in Japanese and Korean horror (the *kitsune* and the *gumiho*, respectively), though the creature is far less frequently malevolent in its Chinese/Hong Kong iteration.

Another important facet of Chinese mythology is the nature of the connection between 'Heaven' (in the broadest sense, a magical realm in the sky) and the real world of mortal humans on Earth. According to the stories and beliefs of ancient China, characters can cross between these worlds with relative ease. Humans and gods can communicate and converse, and might even trade places (Chen 2011: 2). In short, the divine and magical exists on the margins of the real, and is practically accessible for many characters in these stories. The Hong Kong horror film regularly depicts this trope: divine warriors descend to Earth from Heaven to combat a great evil, or mortal men of everyday society stumble into a magical realm accidentally and easily. In the kitsch horror-romance-musical *The Snake Prince* (Lo Chen, 1976), for instance, the villagers can commune with the snake-gods who watch over their settlement simply by hiking up a mountain. The close proximity of the mythical and the real in the Hong Kong horror presents a serious danger yet, often, also offers salvation.

One significant aspect of this folklore and myth is the widespread cultural and social attitudes to spiritual beliefs in Hong Kong and China. For many people, the concepts of ghosts and magical spirits, and of supernatural factors influencing the 'good' or 'bad' destinies of individuals, are held as real, serious beliefs. This gives the Hong Kong horror film a distinct meaning for domestic audiences, and it inspires fear in a different way: for an American audience, the creatures of Hollywood horror, such as werewolves and vampires, are pure fiction, but the people of Hong Kong 'really believe these creatures existed' (Logan 1996: 101). Indeed, simply put, 'Hong Kong horror films reflect the genuine beliefs and fears of a superstitious people' (Ibid.). The prototypical Hong Kong zombie-panic 'hopping corpse' film, *The Spiritual Boxer, Part II* (Liu Chia-Liang, 1979), depicts re-animated dead bodies, ghostly spirits, and magic both malevolent and heroic. Yet the film begins with a short message informing audiences that while the film's premise is based on folklore, it's up to you, the viewer, to decide if the story is credible. Hong Kong horror's most outlandish imagery is often rooted in plausible beliefs; the line between the fantastic and the ordinary is perilously thin.

If we are to properly characterise Hong Kong horror cinema, then it is necessary to expand the category of 'horror' beyond standard Western definitions. Insofar as many Hong Kong horror movies depict multifarious demons, wraiths and reanimated corpses, they satisfy Noël Carroll's chief criterion for horror fiction: the presence of a scientifically inexplicable monster eliciting fear and disgust (Carroll 1990). Yet many other cases of what we would consider Hong Kong horror elude this definition altogether – think, for instance, of *The Untold Story* (1993) and *Dream Home* (2010), whose protagonists act monstrously but within the realms of scientific explanation. In contrast to Carroll, Cynthia Freeland (2000) identifies *evil* as the lynchpin of horror fiction; but Hong Kong cinema furnishes numerous cases wherein the 'evil' force is fundamentally benign, romantic or playful (recall the phantoms of *Rouge* (1988), *Where's Officer Tuba?* (1986), and *Friendly Ghost* (1985)). Moreover, Freeland's criterion admits films that would not typically be categorised as horror (for example, Johnnie To's crime drama *Election* (2005), which dramatises a secular form of evil). If attempts to define Western cinematic horror have proven unavailing – for such definitions tend to be either too restricted or too inclusive – the problem is exacerbated when applied to Hong Kong horror film, whose generic borders are even more porous than those within American and European cinemas.

Hong Kong cinema's generic hybridity obliges us to conceptualise the local horror genre in broad terms. Rare is the Hong Kong horror film that occupies unalloyed generic terrain. Horror-comedy and romantic horror are favourite local traditions, but Hong Kong film history also offers up instances of the horror-musical (*The Phantom Lover* (1995)) and kung fu-horror (*The Legend of the 7 Golden Vampires* (1974)). Perhaps inevitably, then, this book encompasses certain films whose status as 'horror' may be disputed. Are *Rouge* and *A Chinese Ghost Story* (1987) really horror films? Arguably not, by Western criteria. Yet within a local context these films exemplify the Hong Kong horror movie: they mesh 'traditional' horror elements with ingredients from other genres, fostering horror-film permutations quite unlike those in Western cinemas. Consequently, Hong Kong horror teems with generic anomalies that push cinematic horror beyond Western conventions.

For local critic Cheng Yu, genre hybridity is 'one more indication of the Hong Kong cinema's inability to establish a proper Horror genre' (Cheng 1989: 20). Cheng compares the domestic horror cinema unfavourably to that of Hollywood, which he argues is more efficiently compartmentalised. Whereas 'the Horror-Ghost movies of the Hongkong cinema are a mishmash of genres and other movies,' Hollywood horror films file neatly into discrete categories such as science-fiction horror (for example, *Alien* (1979)) and the vampire film (for example, *Dracula* (1958)). Notwithstanding Cheng's too-convenient characterisation of Hollywood horror (which underestimates Hollywood's degree of genre cross-fertilisation), it seems clear that 'a proper Horror genre' would, for Cheng, replicate or resemble Western horror traditions. Yet it is precisely the generic and cultural hybridity of Hong Kong's horror cinema – its tendency to defamiliarise rather than imitate Hollywood horror norms – that is this local tradition's unique contribution to horror cinema internationally. From sword-wielding zombies to 'big-head' babies, Hong Kong cinema serves up nightmares unimagined in Western cinemas.[1]

Just as Hong Kong horror yokes with other genres, so it permeates all modes of local film production. Horror is not solely the province of mainstream journeymen, who hone their craft directing formulaic supernatural and slasher movies. The horror film also attracts independent newcomers seeking to establish a fresh cinematic style. Director Soi Cheang launched his career with a string of indie horror movies because, he says, the genre enabled him to cultivate a distinctive visual 'atmosphere' (Bettinson 2008: 212). Nor is Hong Kong horror cinema reducible to exploitation cinema, even though a vibrant tradition of such film-making (known as Category III) thrives in the region. To the contrary, indigenous horror traverses both high and low culture. The foray into horror territory by Ann Hui (*Visible Secret* (2001)), Fruit Chan (*Dumplings* (2004)), Stanley Kwan (*Rouge*), Pang Ho-cheung (*Dream Home*), Tsui Hark (*Missing* (2008)), and Johnnie To (*My Left Eye Sees Ghosts* (2002)) is not mere carpet-bagging. Rather, these auteurs find artistic possibility in the local horror genre's malleability, which enables both the expression of signature themes and an innovative play with horror-film conventions. At the same time, the films of these directors have legitimised what was once locally considered an artistically disreputable genre.

Partly because Hong Kong horror cinema is generically diffuse and resistant to Western definitions, it has been slighted within English-language scholarship. While the field has produced invaluable knowledge about Hong Kong cinema's action traditions, it has made scant inroads into Hong Kong horror. Within broader studies of the Hong Kong film industry, horror is typically neglected. David Bordwell's lively and passionate *Planet Hong Kong: Popular Cinema and the Art of Entertainment* (in its second edition as of 2011) is one of the key academic texts on Hong Kong cinema, canvassing all major genres in close detail, with the glaring omission of horror. Stephen Teo's *Hong Kong Cinema: the Extra Dimensions* (1997) offers a brief schematic overview of horror in the context of a wider study encompassing Hong Kong cinema *in toto*, but lacks significant depth. It should be noted, however, that Teo has contributed further work on horror in other publications, not least of which was commissioned as part of a celebration of horror at the 1989 Hong Kong International Film Festival. *Phantoms of the Hong Kong Cinema* offers an outstanding collection of short critical essays on the history of horror in Hong Kong, and its publication coincided neatly with the widely acknowledged peak of the genre, a time when horror represented a major force in the industry.

More recently, Vivian P. Y. Lee's *Hong Kong Cinema Since 1997: the Post-Nostalgic Imagination* (2009) constitutes a superb historical survey conceived conceptually and theoretically, largely to the exclusion of genre. It therefore more often falls to publications concerned more broadly with horror as a global genre to engage with Hong Kong's output – though this still represents a small fraction of research. *Horror to the Extreme: Changing Boundaries in Asian Cinema* (ed. Jinhee Choi and Mitsuyo Wada-Marciano, 2009) is one of the few edited collections to consider East Asian horror collectively, and includes three chapters covering Hong Kong horror. Additionally, the non-academic but highly readable *Spooky Encounters: a Gwailo's Guide to Hong Kong Horror* by Daniel O'Brien (2003) captures some of the depth of Western fandom for Hong Kong horror, and reflects the diversity of titles that became known to a global audience.

Additionally, much of the work relevant to an understanding of Hong Kong horror is not directly about the genre at all. Monographs by Stephen Teo (2009) and Leon Hunt (2003) focusing on martial arts cinema contain scant reference to horror, but offer valuable insights into the hybrid nature of the Hong Kong kung fu-horror, a major staple of the genre. Likewise, a study of Category III films by Davis and Yeh (2001) considers the transgressive nature of Hong Kong's exploitation industry, yet the torture porn and morbidly grisly true crime stories they describe as 'pornoviolence' all broadly fall under the auspices of horror, as most critics would define the term.

Indeed, even the most fundamental definitions of horror as a film genre, as noted, prove problematic in the context of Hong Kong. One of the core debates in horror studies concerns the binary opposition between the 'restrained tradition' and 'body horror,' two subtypes of horror that inspire fear in radically different ways. The restrained tradition, as identified by Gregory A. Waller (1987) and Ivan Butler (1979), privileges the suggested rather than the explicit, and creates an intense sense of fear by misdirection: the principle being that the unseen monster lurking in the shadows, only fully formed in the imaginations of the audience, will always be more terrifying than the seen. In contrast, a cycle of body-horror films exemplified by the early work of David Cronenberg and celebrated in publications like *Fangoria* appeals to its audience in precisely the opposite way: using special effects to depict explicit violence and gore, giving visceral imagery to monstrous acts of violence and terrible creatures of fear (Martin 2015).

While posited as an irreconcilable contrast in terms of modes of horror, what both the restrained tradition and body horror share is a common desire to inspire dread and fear. The Hong Kong horror film often ignores even this supposedly fundamental, unifying attribute of the horror genre. Hong Kong horror frequently prioritises comedy over fear, and romance over terror; Hong Kong horror film-makers aim to make their audience laugh, rather than scream, to stir romantic sensibilities and evoke the heartbreak of melodrama, or the pure thrill of martial action. This broad range of emotional affect makes traditional Hollywood-based definitions of horror inadequate to fully appreciate the genre's manifestation in Hong Kong. Indeed, as Teo has noted, in the Hong Kong kung-fu horror film, there really isn't any horror (Teo 1989: 42).

The complex and often abstruse nature of Hong Kong horror might account for its relative neglect in English-language film studies, but those same cultural differences in genre formation presented no barrier to global circulation. Hong Kong cinema has enjoyed significant international visibility at least since the kung fu 'craze' of the early 1970s, which saw a raft of English-dubbed action films achieve unprecedented success at the US box office in 1973 (Desser 2000: 19). While it was Sammo Hung's *Encounters of the Spooky Kind* (1980) that was credited with instigating the horror boom of the 1980s in Hong Kong, with its pioneering fusion of martial arts, comedy and horror, the same film did not have an equal impact in the West. Instead, Ricky Lau's *Mr. Vampire* can be seen as the vanguard of Hong Kong horror for an international audience. The film was undoubtedly seminal in the domestic market, too, where it started the hopping-corpse (*gyonshi*) cycle (Charles 2000: 212). *Mr. Vampire* was subsequently shown on British television in the 1990s, alongside films like *A Chinese Ghost Story*, and attracted a devoted cult following. Fanzines offered videotapes via mail order, and by the end of the 1990s many of these titles were widely available on officially licensed video cassettes in the US and UK. Indeed, O'Brien noted that the publication of his book *Spooky Encounters* in 2003 came at a time when 'Hong Kong movies are growing in their North American accessibility.' *Mr. Vampire* in particular was seen as the prototypical film, not just of Hong Kong horror but of East Asia more generally.

In a 1997 publication, Thomas Weisser argued that the film 'has all the unique elements that distinguish oriental horror films from those of other countries' (Weisser 1997: 134). While the statement itself is a fatuous generalisation, it indicates the extent to which Hong Kong horror dominated perceptions of East Asian cult cinema. This was the era before the explosion of 'J-horror' and Korean thrillers, launched to British and American audiences almost entirely thanks to the shrewd marketing and distribution of Tartan Films and their 'Asia Extreme' brand. *Mr. Vampire* had little competition; few other East Asian horror films were available, save perhaps classic Japanese fare like Masaki Kobayashi's *Kwaidan* (1965). As awareness of Hong Kong cinema's distinctive qualities – its dissimilarities from Japanese and South Korean cinema – has grown, so too has the need for a devoted study of exactly what makes Hong Kong horror special.

Other compelling questions, too, remain unexplored or under-theorised.

What is Hong Kong horror's heritage in local literary, artistic and folkloric traditions? How has the genre developed over time? In what ways have new technologies transformed horror film-making? What thematic and stylistic motifs govern Hong Kong horror, and why have they proven so durable? How far does genre hybridity expand the parameters of the Western horror category? How have Hong Kong horror movies shaped the genre internationally? And – in the present era of both Sinicisation and PRC crackdowns on supernatural horror fiction – to what extent is Hong Kong horror cinema bound up with assertions of local identity? This book aims to explore such historical, empirical and theoretical issues, as well as other lacunae in the literature.

Hong Kong Horror Cinema sets out to chart the historical development of Hong Kong horror-genre film-making; to characterise the norms and conventions of this tradition; to specify the cultural distinctiveness of the genre; and to consider patterns of influence between Hong Kong's horror cinema and horror movies from other key film-making centres, including Hollywood. It provides unique perspectives on the most controversial and extreme horror films of recent years, and provides detailed case studies of landmark movies including *The Eye* (2002), *Mr. Vampire*, *The Bride with White Hair* (1993) and *Rigor Mortis*. At the same time, it introduces readers to less well-known yet historically important horror films. Most broadly, *Hong Kong Horror Cinema* bears witness to a variety of methodological approaches – culturalist, formalist, cognitive, transnational, industrial, historiographic – with the aim of demonstrating that Hong Kong horror cinema rewards attention from a range of critical angles.

The chapters in the first part of this collection cover trends and cycles of older films, providing an insight into the historical development of Hong Kong horror film and examining many seminal titles and overlooked classics of the genre. Raymond Tsang's chapter offers a valuable dissection of a little-discussed cycle of Cantonese-language ghost films of the 1950s. Indeed, while a great deal of scholarship on Hong Kong horror movies focuses on the other-worldliness of the ghost in relation to Hong Kong's identity crisis before and during the 1997 takeover by China, during the 1950s Hong Kong horror presented a remarkably different picture. This chapter argues that the ghost in the 1950s horror film has a pedagogical function, by considering two films in detail: *Beauty Raised from the Dead* (1956) and *Nightly Cry of the Ghost* (1957). Cantonese film-makers in the 1950s used the conventions of horror and the figure of the *neoi gwei* (female ghost) to tell moral tales about arranged marriage, superstition and social values. These films, denounced as cheaply made and vulgar, can be seen as an example of 'vernacular modernism', as they were rife with liberal agendas, addressing the contemporary horror of living conditions and the colonial governance, and the climate of the Cold War. This cycle stands in stark contrast to contemporary Hong Kong horror, yet it retains a heavy influence on modern films.

If the female ghost is the most enduring icon of Hong Kong horror, then the transforming and seductive snake is a close second. Liang Luo's chapter charts the historical development and transnational cross-pollination of one of China's 'four great folktales', the Legend of the White Snake. Considered one of the key narratives in the Chinese oral tradition, the Legend of the White Snake and its theatrical and popular cultural metamorphoses played an important role in the pre-cinematic origins of Hong Kong horror cinema. The story features two magical snakes, gifted with immortality and shape-shifting powers, who assume human form – usually as an older and younger sister – and must battle enemies while hiding their true identities in the pursuit of love. This chapter examines a series of films based on the White Snake legend produced or co-produced by Hong Kong film companies, including the lavish opera *Madam White Snake* (1962) as well as versions of the tale adapted in Japan and Taiwan. These films both challenge and enrich understandings of the horror genre, and pose important questions about national identity and gender politics.

While the various incarnations of the White Snake films typically embody a prideful sense of 'quality' cinema, Andy Willis' chapter on exploitation films considers a very different manifestation of monstrous snakes. Category III film-making represents the 'raw commercial concerns' of the industry, and is often associated with artless titillation. This chapter examines several auteurs of the exploitation industry to reframe their work in the context of thematically rich horror, expressing anger at social inequality and dissatisfaction with local politics. Centring on detailed analysis of *The Killer Snakes* (1974) and *The Untold Story*, Willis unpacks the meaning behind the monstrous murderers of these films, marginalised individuals whose sense of psychological despair and social alienation speaks to serious real-world issues.

While female ghosts and homicidal reptiles are the most frequently recurring apparitions of the Hong Kong horror film, another icon of misery and monstrousness is found in *The Bride with White Hair*. The eponymous woman warrior of Ronny Yu's cult classic has become emblematic of Hong Kong horror in a manner that reflects a high degree of generic hybridity. Daniel Martin's chapter considers the way different generic tropes and narrative frameworks have been fused to create a film epitomising horror, fantasy, *wuxia* (swordplay), and romance. A bleak moral landscape evokes horror while challenging traditional notions of chivalry, and the film's monstrous antagonist(s) exemplify the magical/fantastic while conforming to a problematic pattern of demonised depictions of disability. As one of the first and most prominent Hong Kong horror films to reach a Western audience, *The Bride with White Hair* deserves detailed attention.

The chapters of Part II examine an important and unique facet of Hong Kong horror: generic hybridity and the balance of (sometimes wildly different) tones and styles. Considering comedy-horrors and the fusion of kung-fu with horror, these chapters establish many of the most significant and culture-specific qualities of Hong Kong horror cinema. In an investigation of comedy-horror, Andrew Grossman posits instructive contrasts between this subgenre's Hong Kong and Hollywood variants. Though largely a marginal and disreputable category in the West, the comedy-horror has flourished as a staple of Hong Kong film production, spawning several of the region's 'classic' movies: *Mr. Vampire*, *The Dead and the Deadly* (1982) and *Spooky Encounters*. After surveying this local generic terrain, Grossman goes on to examine the figure of the *jiangshi* (reanimated corpse), tracing its kinetic traits to local and Western comedic traditions. These traditions, moreover, are premodern, as opposed to post-human: spectatorial engagement with the *jiangshi* relies upon a level of corporeal authenticity that digital technology cannot furnish. Grossman generalises the spectator's activity to Hong Kong comedy-horror per se, arguing that such films engage the spectator in an incongruous, 'bivalent' mode of viewing.

Felicia Chan approaches Hong Kong comedy-horror from a performative perspective, arguing that the subgenre's roots in theatrical traditions render diegetic verisimilitude a low priority – at least, in contrast to the 'realistic' diegeses constructed by Hollywood horror films. Taking *Rouge* and *A Chinese Ghost Story* as case studies, Chan unpacks these films' allegorical meanings; juxtaposes their negotiation of the cinematic 'real' against the verisimilitude of Hollywood horror; and re-examines the Hong Kong ghost film's distinctive relation to performance, catharsis and abjection. For Chan, the comic theatricality at the heart of *Rouge*, *A Chinese Ghost Story* and other 1980s Hong Kong ghost movies is no less evident in more recent genre entries such as *Visible Secret* and *Rigor Mortis*. Hong Kong's comedy-horror tradition, so vibrant in the 1980s, has not succumbed to ghostly disappearance; rather, Chan maintains, the tradition endures, adapting to industrial shifts, technological advances, and more or less dramatic social change.

The Hong Kong horror genre teems with recurring thematic and visual motifs, and David Scott Diffrient brings to light one of the most salient: the hand – a remarkably insistent and multivalent device in local storytelling.

Diffrient canvasses the Western literary and filmic texts that have ascribed hands special (not to say disconcerting) prominence, before adopting a comparative perspective on key Hong Kong examples. He plumbs the hand motif for hermeneutic significance in a range of horror movies, from Kuei Chih-Hung's *The Killer Snakes* and *Hex* (1980) to Tsui Hark's *We're Going to Eat You* (1980) and Sammo Hung's *Spooky Encounters*. The fugitive, autonomous, hideously severed hands in several Hong Kong horror films amply fulfil the genre's demands for diabolical imagery, but they also harbour crucial narrative, thematic and allegorical meanings. In a more recent context, Diffrient argues, the hand motif acquires symbolic resonance, chiming with Hong Kong's 'reattachment' to China and the fraught pro-democracy demonstrations that have ensued.

Kenneth Chan's chapter, concerning Tsui Hark's *Detective Dee* films (2010–13), illuminates the complex hybridity of Hong Kong horror cinema. If, prima facie, these films appear to reside outside the horror genre, this would be to deny the generic breadth of the Hong Kong horror category. Chan approaches the *Detective Dee* films as generic amalgams fusing supernatural horror, martial arts action and police procedural, the latter component traceable to a popular trend in recent US television drama. This generic fusion, Chan argues, reifies a thematic and cultural tension between tradition and modernity. At first glance, Tsui's *Detective Dee* films shrewdly promote Chinese nationalism and Chinese political power, which, Chan suggests, partly accounts for their domestic popularity at the mainland box office. But are the films' surface ideologies really so straightforward? Chan's close readings of the two films reveal Tsui Hark to be not only politically tactical but also, arguably, politically subversive.

The chapters assembled in the third and last part explore some of the most relevant and controversial Hong Kong horror films of the current generation of global distribution. These films are analysed in terms of their transgressive content, transnational dialogues and political provocations. In a chapter analysing *The Eye* franchise (2002–5), Enrique Ajuria Ibarra notes a millennial trend toward pan-Asian film production, which gained impetus with the founding of Applause Pictures (the producer–distributor of *The Eye*) in 2000. Coterminous with the rise of pan-Asian film production, Ibarra notes, was a putative transnational outlook and prospects for a 'global Southeast Asian identity'. Yet Ibarra's reading of *The Eye* trilogy registers cultural and regional tensions at the textual level. These tensions emerge through the central motif of vision, which in *The Eye* trilogy is gendered, politicised and uncanny. Ultimately, Ibarra argues, these tacit regional tensions belie and undercut the trilogy's apparent promotion of pan-Asian unity.

Local cuisine permeates many areas of Hong Kong culture, not least Hong Kong movies. As Lisa Stokes points out in her chapter, food in Hong Kong cinema often serves as a social adhesive, carrying positive associations of interpersonal bonding; it also often harbours culturally specific meanings (think of how food functions as both a sensual and a seasonal signifier in Wong Kar-wai's *In the Mood for Love* (2000)). In Hong Kong's horror cinema, however, food is consistently ascribed abject functions. Stokes examines the food motif in Fruit Chan's *Dumplings* and Herman Yau's *The Untold Story*, two films united by a stomach-churning trope of cannibalism. Both films, Stokes maintains, employ the transgressive food motif for commentative purpose, implicitly exposing male anxieties about the collapse of patriarchal society. Whether in the context of the impending 1997 handover (*The Untold Story*) or the post-handover impingement of Sinicisation (*Dumplings*), the horror-film plot is anchored to Hong Kong's real-world class disparities and inequities.

Part of the discomfort elicited by *The Untold Story* and *Dumplings* derives from the sympathy these films generate on behalf of their immoral heroes. Similarly, in Pang Ho-cheung's *Dream Home*, a slasher-killer protagonist becomes an ambivalent, even sympathetic, figure to whom the viewer's allegiance is directed. Gary Bettinson examines this controversial dimension of *Dream Home*'s narration, challenging the critical contention that Pang's structure of sympathy renders the film aesthetically and morally defective. Through a narratological and cognitive analysis, Bettinson examines how *Dream Home*'s flashback structure, internal moral hierarchy, affective tone, and tactics of subjective access and point of view shift the conventional stakes of allegiance, so that the viewer becomes allied with the female killer and justifies her blood-curdling crimes. Rather than constituting an artistic defect, Bettinson argues, *Dream Home*'s apparently perverse identifications 'cue and crystallise' a morally sound ideological critique.

Finally, Vivian Lee examines the politicisation of Hong Kong horror cinema in the postcolonial era. Since 2003 'high concept' Hong Kong-China co-productions have dominated the local production sector, relegating horror movies to the margins. As state censorship largely militates against cinematic horror, the genre has become a default site for self-conscious expressions of Hong Kong 'localness' – a site, Lee observes, of both local resilience and resistance (to Mainlandisation). Lee traces the ideological and industrial transformation of Hong Kong horror from the pre-handover period to the present, alighting on the long-running *Troublesome Night* series (1997–2007), the pan-Asian 'art-horror' movies directed by notable auteurs (Ann Hui; Peter Chan), and films such as

Juno Mak's *Rigor Mortis* which, Lee argues, have re-established horror as a 'local' genre. Recently revitalised, the Hong Kong horror genre satisfies commercial criteria while imparting urgent social comment. Though its ideological projections may be bleak, the Hong Kong horror cinema – deliriously pushing the boundaries of genre, cinematic style and bad taste – is (paradoxically) alive and well.

Note

1. Stephen Teo perceives an 'ambivalence' in Hong Kong's horror genre, which he ascribes to 'a refusal or an inability to recognise the integral boundaries of form' (Teo 1989: 41). Unlike Cheng, however, Teo concedes that 'this can be both a good and bad thing' (Ibid.: 41).

References

Bettinson, Gary (2008), 'New Blood: an interview with Soi Cheang', *Journal of Chinese Cinemas*, 2:3, pp. 211–24.

Bordwell, David (2000), *Planet Hong Kong: Popular Cinema and the Art of Entertainment*, Cambridge, MA: Harvard University Press.

Butler, Ivan (1979), *Horror in the Cinema* (3rd ed.), South Brunswick and New York: A. S. Barnes and Company.

Carroll, Noël (1990), *The Philosophy of Horror; or, Paradoxes of the Heart*, New York: Routledge.

Cass, Victoria (2010), 'Foreword', in Pu Songling, *Strange Tales from a Chinese Studio*, Singapore: Tuttle Publishing.

Charles, John (2000), *The Hong Kong Filmography, 1977–1997*, Jefferson: McFarland.

Chen, Lianshan (2011), *Chinese Myths and Legends*, Cambridge: Cambridge University Press.

Cheng, Yu (1989), 'Under a spell', in Li Cheuk-to (ed.), *Phantoms of the Hong Kong Cinema*, Hong Kong: Urban Council, pp. 20–3.

Choi, Jinhee and Mitsuyo Wada-Marciano (eds) (2009), *Horror to the Extreme: Changing Boundaries in Asian Cinema*, Aberdeen: Hong Kong University Press.

Davis, Darrell W. and Emilie Yueh-Yu Yeh (2001), 'Warning! Category III: the other Hong Kong cinema', *Film Quarterly*, 54:4 (summer), pp. 12–26.

Desser, David (2000), 'The kung fu craze: Hong Kong cinema's first American reception', in Poshek Fu and David Desser (eds), *The Cinema of Hong Kong: History, Arts, Identity*, Cambridge: Cambridge University Press, pp. 19–43.

Freeland, Cynthia (2000), *The Naked and the Undead*, Boulder, CO: Westview Press.

Hunt, Leon (2003), *Kung Fu Cult Masters: from Bruce Lee to Crouching Tiger*, London and New York: Wallflower.

K'o, Yuan (1993), 'Foreword', in Anne Birrell (ed.), *Chinese Mythology: an Introduction*, Baltimore and London: The Johns Hopkins University Press.

Lee, Vivian P. Y. (2009), *Hong Kong Cinema Since 1997: the Post-Nostalgic Imagination*, London: Palgrave Macmillan.

Logan, Bey (1996), *Hong Kong Action Cinema*, Woodstock: Overlook Press.

Martin, Daniel (2015), *Extreme Asia: the Rise of Cult Cinema from the Far East*, Edinburgh: Edinburgh University Press.

Minford, John (2006), 'Introduction', in Pu Songling, *Strange Tales from a Chinese Studio*, London: Penguin.

O'Brien, Daniel (2003), *Spooky Encounters: a Gwailo's Guide to Hong Kong Horror*, Manchester: Headpress.

Teo, Stephen (1989), 'The tongue: a study of Hong Kong horror movies,' in Li Cheuk-to (ed.), *Phantoms of the Hong Kong Cinema*, Hong Kong: Urban Council, pp. 41–5.

Teo, Stephen (1997), *Hong Kong Cinema: the Extra Dimensions*, London: British Film Institute.

Teo, Stephen (2009), *Chinese Martial Arts Cinema: the Wuxia Tradition*, Edinburgh: Edinburgh University Press.

Waller, Gregory A. (1987), 'Introduction', in Gregory A. Waller (ed.), *American Horrors: Essays on the Modern American Horror Film*, Urbana, IL and Chicago: University of Illinois Press.

Weisser, Thomas (1997), *Asian Cult Cinema*, New York: Boulevard Books.

Part I

Formations and Fragmentations: the Development of Hong Kong Horror

CHAPTER 1

What Can a *Neoi Gwei* Teach Us? Adaptation as Reincarnation in Hong Kong Horror of the 1950s

Raymond Tsang

Many Hong Kong horror films of the 1950s were pedagogical in nature, and subsequently had a great influence on the Hong Kong New Wave (1980–90). Much of the existing scholarship on Hong Kong horror focuses on New Wave films such as Ching Siu-tung's *A Chinese Ghost Story* (1987) and Stanley Kwan's *Rouge* (1988)[1] (Zou 2008; Lim 2009). However, scholarship less often pays attention to earlier Cantonese horror films. Without examining these earlier films, we cannot fully understand the practice of adaptation and the depiction of the female ghost in New Wave horror. These films are neither widely circulated in the West nor dubbed or subtitled in English, and limited attention is given to earlier Cantonese cinema in Western academia.[2] Even within Chinese-language scholarship, compared to studies of films in the Republican era (1911–49), Cantonese films before the New Wave are rarely studied. They are either characterized as *cu zhi lan zao* (roughly produced and hastily made) or *yue yu can pian* (dilapidated and valueless Cantonese films). Compared to the aesthetically advanced output of the more vertically integrated Mandarin studios such as the Shaw Brothers Studio and Motion Picture & General Investment Co. Ltd, Cantonese films were often criticised as inferior, backward and aesthetically underdeveloped. Because of the criticism from both intellectuals and cultural elites, Cantonese film-makers had tried to elevate Cantonese cinema since the 1930s, by the means of making films with 'healthy' themes of nationalism and anti-superstition. One of the means was adaptation of classic literary novels and folk tales. Interestingly, horror motifs or stories of female ghosts – forbidden themes in promoting Cantonese films – were often used and adapted so as to mount social and cultural interventions.

This chapter focuses on two Cantonese horror films, *Beauty Raised from the Dead* (1956) and *Nightly Cry of the Ghost* (1957), in order to examine the reincarnation of *neoi gwei* (female ghosts). I argue that the little-studied Hong Kong horror films of the 1950s can be understood as a site of political and cultural intervention. Most of these horror films are about reincarnation. The production of these films can also been understood as a process of 'reincarnation'. The practice and choice of adaptation are always a matter of politics. These film-makers not only gave new life to various literary sources,[3] but also created social interventions in the 1950s, exploring women's liberation, the enlightenment of science and socialist revolutionary potentiality. Alongside the two major case studies, several other significant *neoi gwei* films will be briefly discussed, including *Ghostly Wife* (1953), *The Voyage of the Dead* (1954), *Outcry of the Ghost* (1956), *Haunted Bridge* (1957), *The Dunce Bumps into a Ghost* (1957) and *The Beautiful Ghost's Grievance* (1959).

This chapter will focus on the question of how we theorise the practice of adaptation, how various literary sources are 'reincarnated', and how adaptation as reincarnation can be a site of cultural and political intervention in Cantonese films of the 1950s.

Adaptation/Reincarnation

Horror (*kongbu*) was not the only term to describe these ghostly films; the terms *shenguai* (gods/spirits and the strange/bizarre), *qi guai* (strange) and *shen hua* (godly story) were also used. These horror movies are neither shocking nor visually explicit, and are invested with a pedagogical function through a moral lesson that is typical of films featuring *neoi gwei* figures.

Bliss Cua Lim has explored spectral time exemplified in films from two 'New Cinemas' in Hong Kong and the Philippines, the aforementioned *Rouge* and Tony Perez's *Haplos* (1982) respectively, suggesting that the female ghost can be a site that critiques linear progression, homogenous time and historical chronology (Lim 2009:151). While this argument is convincing, it has some different implications in the case of the *neoi gwei* of the 1950s. Although spectral time is a political and cultural intervention, it does not always guarantee a radical change. The narratives of the horror movies under discussion are rigidly formed: most of these narratives begin with an encounter between a man and a *neoi gwei*. A long flashback reveals the identity of the *neoi gwei* and her cause of death. The ending will solve the conflict between the *noei gwei* and those who killed her or did her harm. It culminates in a happy ending in that she reincarnates and lives happily ever after with her loved ones. The spectral time is usually closed, with a romantic end.

Yet, the contribution of these horror movies lies in their political and cultural engagement within the interstices of popular culture. It was often a struggle for film-makers who had a progressive agenda to balance entertainment and pedagogy. In post-war Hong Kong, the practice of adaptation was an economical device to resolve this struggle. The adaptation of Chinese classics and various literary tales into film form can be entertaining on the one hand; they can be invested with cultural and political, if not ideological, intervention on the other.

In his guest lecture 'Hong Kong cinema of the 1950s: adaptation as a means of cultural formation' at the University of British Columbia in 2011, Leung Ping-kwan argued that the practice of adaptation in film and in literature in the 1950s created a unique sense of Hong Kong identity – a sense that Hong Kong culture is hybrid. The limitation inherent in this study of cinematic adaptation is the assumption that Hong Kong culture is separated from politics and that Hong Kong is a free 'processor' that enjoys laissez faire economy. Pointing to different adaptations of *Red Plum* (*hong mei ji*) in China and Hong Kong, Leung and Chan (2014) suggest that Hong Kong culture could emerge because its free and hybrid culture is distinct from political engagement in the People's Republic of China.

Cultural value, as an effect of the politics of power and social organisation, is always involved in social struggle and negotiation. Instead of simple separation between culture and politics, popular Cantonese horror movies of the 1950s were sites of political and cultural intervention and critique. Although they did not follow an ideological hard line, like that of Communist China, they progressively engaged with topics such as anti-feudalism, anti-superstition and revolution.

According to his rethinking of the theory and practice of adaptation, Robert Stam breaks away the theory of adaptation from fidelity to intertextuality, arguing that criticism of adaptation should not focus on notions of fidelity to the original text. Adaptation is a form of creation rather than imitation, a kind of 'reading, rewriting, critique, translation, transmutation, metamorphosis, recreation, trans-vocalization, resuscitation, transfiguration, actualization, trans-modalization, signifying, performance, dialogization, cannibalization, reinvisioning, incarnation, or re-accentuation' (Stam 2005: 25). Extending Stam's concept, my idea of adaptation as reincarnation also points to Buddhist tradition *lun hui* (*Saṃsāra*) and Chinese mythology. It is about the 'cyclicality of all life'. Every existence cycles life after life. In Chinese popular mythology, Meng Po is an old lady, guarding the *nai he* bridge (bridge of regret and helplessness), similar to the River Styx. She gives each soul a brew in order to let them forget their previous life and memories before reincarnation. Every adaptation is like this transfer of creative energy into multiple lives. Every text is crossing the *nai he* bridge, gaining a new life in every embodiment, and rereading and rewriting the source.

In short, adaptation as reincarnation means the practice of adaptation contains layered creative energy, but also is a political and cultural intervention that creates changes for societies. Given its difficult post-war circumstances, reincarnation signifies a rebirth for Hong Kong, offering new possibilities and hopes. That is why the theme of reincarnation is 'the backbone in all ghost stories, and it is the ghost story which defines Hong Kong's horror genre' (Teo 1997: 221). One of the main adaptation sources for film-makers in the 1950s is the May Fourth tradition (1919) and the New Culture Movement (mid-1910s to 1920s). In the following section, I will demonstrate that the *neoi gwei*'s reincarnation is a call for an end to the patriarchal family in favour of free love, individual freedom and women's liberation.

Anti-Feudalism: the Minor Struggles of Du Liniang

Beauty Raised from the Dead (*Yan shi hai yun ji*, 1956) was produced by Union Film Enterprises (*Chung-luen*) and directed by Lee Sun-fung. The story is a makeover of the *kunqu* opera *The Peony Pavilion* that was written as a fifty-five-scene play by Tang Xian-zu in the Ming Dynasty, and later adapted as a radio play in the 1950s.

Unlike the play, which starts from the perspective of the female protagonist Du Li-niang, who dreams about a romantic encounter with a scholar, *Beauty Raised from the Dead* opens with the male character Liu Meng-mei returning to his hometown. He arrives at a pavilion to seek shelter from the cold rain. There he meets Du, and they fall in love at first sight. They refrain from talking too much to each other because of the presence of Du's father. When they return to their homes they share the same dream, in which they play together in Du's garden. However, in reality, both of their fathers have already arranged their marriages. While Du's father forces her to marry her rich cousin, Liu's father agrees to wait three years for Liu to find the girl he dreamt about. After three years Du dies in distress and hopelessness while Liu is still searching for her. One day he accidentally comes to the abandoned house where Du used to live. Liu meets Du's spectre, and they promise not to leave each other. They clean the house, play together and compose poems; meanwhile, the old housekeeper informs Du's parents of the haunted house. While Du's mother feels pity for her daughter, Du's stern father wants to exorcise the ghost, and summons a Taoist to carry out the exorcism. Although the Taoist is ineffective in banishing the ghost, Du flees, fearful of her father; she promises Liu she will return soon.

Liu is exhausted and heartbroken, and swears he will never marry again. Sometime later Liu is informed that Du will soon be reincarnated in the body of a deathly ill young woman. Unlike the original play in which Du asks Liu to exhume her dead body for reincarnation, Liu marries the woman possessed by Du. The film ends happily with a pair of Chinese red candles signifying their reunion.

The problem of arranged marriage is the key element of the film's critical success. Unlike the play, which comments on the fate of the Song Dynasty (960–1279) and brings up philosophical questions of life and death, the film was celebrated for its theme of anti-feudalism. According to a film review in *Wah Kiu Yat Po*:

> The most successful part of this film is that although the story is about ghosts and souls, the mythic romance is moving and touching far beyond other films that feature romance drama. Also, it forcefully points out the problem of blind and dumb marriage. It accentuates the urge of the youngsters' free love and marriage. No matter how strong the pressures of feudal rites and society are, young people are willing to sacrifice and fight for it. This correct consciousness has struck a discordant note in those mean parents who take their children's marriage as trade and commodity. (Film Review of *Beauty Raised from the Dead*, 1956)

Although it is a ghost story and full of superstition, the film gained prestige among critics and scholars as it promotes anti-feudalism and the idea of free marriage and love. The success of the film can be attributed to the principles of the Union Film Enterprise, which was founded by a group of progressive film-makers and artists in 1952. Their objective was promoting 'better quality' and 'educational' Cantonese cinema. They adhered to the tradition of the May Fourth Movement, promoting scientific thinking, anti-feudalism, anti-arranged marriage and anti-traditional values such as Confucianism and superstitions. Accordingly, social realist melodramas were good vehicles to reflect social problems and mirror living conditions. In the *Union Film Illustrated Newspaper*, Wen Guang notes that the improvement and development of Cantonese films should be attributed to Union Film Enterprise, as film-makers and producers elevate the tastes of the audience from liking 'roughly produced and hastily made' films to more serious productions (Wen 1957).

Can *Beauty Raised from the Dead* really be considered progressive? Although it is about an anti-patriarchal society, feminists may criticise *Beauty Raised from the Dead* on the grounds that it reinforces the patriarchal system since the *neoi gwei* Du Li-niang is reincarnated in order to assume the role of housewife. She escapes her father's house only to go to her husband's house. The stereotypical division of labour in the film, showing Du cleaning and tidying the abandoned house and Liu lounging around, can also raise objections. However, *Beauty Raised from the Dead*, to a certain extent, responds to the predicament of modern women and the discussions held by the May Fourth intellectuals about women's liberation.

Among the key issues of these historical debates was the need for women to receive education and gain skills, and the uneven distribution of property between men and women/husbands and wives (Liu et al. 2013). Such ideas of communal property and economic independence stood against the ideas of those liberal idealists who agreed on the need for a new world on the one hand, but reproduced the uneven power relations and retained hierarchy in the emerging capitalist society on the other. Those idealist intellectuals and revolutionaries often dismissed struggling in a micro way like the independent economy of women. These notions suggest that greater nuance is required in interpreting the themes of anti-feudalism in *Beauty Raised from the Dead*. Apparently, Du Li-niang is not progressive enough because she asks Liu to marry the person into whom she will reincarnate as a human being, and returns to a restrictive role in a man's home.

However, her struggle is depicted in a subtle way. It is not a struggle directed from outside, but rather inside the patriarchal system. Instead of passively accepting and bemoaning her fate, Du actively takes control of her destiny. She is progressive in the sense that she is active in knowing, abiding by and making use of the rules of patriarchal society in fighting for her love. She asks Liu to follow traditional wedding rites, and all patriarchal rites and rules are followed. Liu can therefore marry a human being instead of a ghost, at once avoiding and accepting the barrier posed by the principle of the 'incompatible paths of human beings and ghosts' (*ren gui shu tu*). Second, filial Liu fulfils his father's greatest hope when he finally marries. Third, through reincarnation, Du becomes another girl, and she and Liu reunite. All this is attributed to the active struggle of Du.

Throughout the film, Du plays a more active role than Liu. In the scene in which they first meet, in the pavilion, Du's initial appearance is represented by the erotic close-up of her wet feet rubbing together. This invites Liu's attention. Later, in her garden, even though she cleans up and sews for Liu, she takes charge of decision-making, and thus builds her own liminal space between patriarchal society and women's liberation.

Despite this, her reincarnation has a great cost: the life of the young woman known only as Li Wing's daughter. We do not know her name or why she dies (or whether or not she is killed by Du?).[4] The success of Du's reincarnation and happy marriage seems to prove the importance of women's independence and determination. Yet, the sacrifice of another life may be the cost.

Two film reviews of *Beauty Raised from the Dead* were published in the leftist newspaper *Ta Kung Pao* a month after the premiere. The film was framed and celebrated as a fight against arranged marriage by reviewer Fang Jun, who contrasted Du's father's feudal and authoritative attitude with Liu's father's much more positive and progressive desire to give more freedom to his son. Neither of the film reviews mentions the subtle struggles Du has experienced. The progressiveness of the film lies not in the theme of anti-arranged patriarchy and Liu's father's open mindedness. The patriarchy and arranged marriage are questioned but not overthrown. Du's father may be the enemy of modern women, but Liu's father is no better. Liu's father also forces his son to marry; it is only because Du can capitalise on the rules of patriarchy that they can live happily ever after.

These leftist film-makers' concerns of anti-feudal practices are not without historical ground. In Hong Kong the abolition of the *mui tsai* system of indentured servitude of young girls as domestic servants, cheap labourers or as prostitutes in brothels only came to pass in the 1920s, and the Hong Kong government did not outlaw the Great Qing Legal Code that allows polygamy until 1971. Feudal practices like superstition, polygamy and arranged marriages in the 1950s prove that Hong Kong's enlightenment project remained unfinished, and highlighted the difficulties many progressive film-makers faced in intervening in social problems.

Scientism: Science and the Rule of Law

The Nightly Cry of the Ghost (*Gui ye ku*, 1957) was directed by Chun Kim and produced by the Kong Ngee Company, another important Cantonese film company at the time. Chun Kim, one of the members of Union Film Enterprise, was known for social realist works such as *For My Country* (*Man jiang hong*, 1949), *Infancy* (*Ren zhi chu*, 1951), *The Guiding Light* (*Ku hai ming deng*, 1953) and *Parent's Heart* (*Fe mu xin*, 1955).

Unlike *Beauty Raised from the Dead*, *The Nightly Cry of the Ghost*, loosely based upon the ghost story of Yu Yuan mansion in Yuen Long, is set in contemporary time and space. While Du Li-niang in the former film is a real ghost, the spectre in the latter is a hoax. Stephen Teo aptly notes that Cantonese ghost movies 'followed the traditional Radcliffian gothic model, indulging in the full panoply of supernatural thrills only to insist, in the end, on a rational explanation for the proceedings' (Teo 1997: 222). Or in Todorovian terms, *Beauty Raised from the Dead* is fantastic/ marvellous in that events 'are presented as fantastic' and 'end with an acceptance of the supernatural' (Todorov 1973: 52), while *The Nightly Cry of the Ghost* is uncanny in that the appearance of strange events can be accounted for by the laws of reason (Ibid.: 46).

In order to fight against the feudal family system and superstition, *The Nightly Cry of the Ghost* uses rational thought and modern technology to uphold justice. Fang Tao, a student of radio broadcasting, visits his cousin on a rural farm where he hopes to learn poultry farming. He tells his cousin and cousin's wife that on the way to the farm he met a *neoi gwei* named Ding Xiu-hua. His cousin does not believe in the supernatural, but the cousin's wife confirms to Fang that he has met a ghost. She tells him that the ghost has always wailed at the balcony of the mansion. Fang is confused as he thinks the girl he met is a human being, and holds strong to his belief that there are no supernatural spirits in the world. His cousin agrees, assuring him 'we, as scientific researchers, should use scientific thinking. If you believe in something, it seems to exist. If you do not believe, it doesn't exist at all.'

Fang later breaks into the abandoned mansion and finds the mysterious woman. She tells him how her stepmother and her cousin, Liu Mang, attempted to kill her. A long flashback sequence reveals the cause of her 'death'. She inherited a large sum of money from her dead father. In order to get the inheritance, Liu planned to marry her, but he was rejected. He tried to rape her but accidentally 'killed' her instead, and ended up throwing her body in a pool. However, Ding held her breath and her housekeeper, Uncle Wong, saved her. She then reveals to Fang that she disguises herself as a ghost with the help of Uncle Wong in order to enact her long-planned revenge.

Fang feels sympathy and agrees to help her. He and Ding ask his cousin, the cousin's wife and Uncle Wong to collaborate and trap the step-mother and Liu. Since the stepmother and Liu are afraid of ghosts, Fang plans to make use of his scientific knowledge and record their confession as evidence when they face Ding disguised as a *neoi gwei*. The plan is suc-cessful, and a police officer comes and arrests the guilty parties; Fang and his cousin are also subject to a stern lecture against engaging in investiga-tion without informing police officers.

The theme of *neoi gwei* as a hoax[5] can be seen in other Cantonese horror films such as Chow Sze-luk's *The Ghostly Wife* (*Gui qi*, 1953), Leong Sum's *Outcry of the Ghost* (*Li gui hu sheng*, 1956) and Wong Hok-sing's *Haunted Bridge* (*Meng gui qiao*, 1957). These films are set in the ancient past, and the female victims disguise themselves as ghosts and wait for a hero to come and take revenge against the landlord, the warlord or the stepmother who tried to kill her. Most of them are similar to martial arts films in which heroes join the victim and take revenge.[6] However, unlike in the case of these other films, in *The Nightly Cry of the Ghost* the char-acters are divided into good and evil by their belief in the law of science.

Through scientific thinking and the use of modern technology (such as the audio recorder), the virtuous characters take advantage of the weakness – superstitious beliefs – of the wrongdoers.

Throughout the film, the question of whether we should believe in science or the supernatural occupies the narrative. Many scenes are about rational thinking and planning. When Fang's cousin leads him around his production house of broiler chickens, this horror film suddenly turns to a non-diegetic sequence in which the voiceover explains poultry farming with a series of montages of different infrastructures. This sequence includes description of chicken husbandry, food portions, temperature control and the number of days involved in hatching. The only horror scene in the film is when Ding crosses through the wall of Fang's room and turns her disfigured face towards Fang. However, it becomes an uncanny scene as it happens only in Fang's anxious dream.

Science prevails over the supernatural, and rational thinking becomes a potent weapon in the fight against crime. A police officer tells Fang and Ding that they should have both witnesses and evidence of the attempted murder; otherwise, the police cannot charge the criminals. Ding discovers that her stepmother and Liu are running out of money. Fang says that they can bait them by offering them expensive jewellery.

This plan is inspired by the famous folk tale of Bao Zheng, a righteous government officer in the Northern Song Dynasty (960–1127). In order to prosecute a corrupt official, Guo Huai, Bao and other officials bring him to an 'underworld mansion'[7] and disguise themselves as 'Ox-Head' and 'Horse-Face,' two guardians of the underworld, to escort the newly dead to the underworld mansion in Chinese mythology. Guo is terrified, and confesses. The characters of *The Nightly Cry of the Ghost* modernise this scene by using an audio recording of Ding's voice to scare Liu and compel him to speak the truth. Fang's cousin concludes that ghosts do not exist, and only a person who does bad things would be superstitious enough to believe in the supernatural. The use of the scientific mind is thus moralised.

Here we can see how the director Chun Kim intervened in the debate on 'science and metaphysics', which had already been a hot topic among intellectuals since the early 1920s in China. Linking these debates to the subject of censorship and film aesthetics, Zhang Zhen argues that the prevalent critical rhetoric of science vs superstition and the eventual censorship of the popular genre cannot be disassociated from this extensive debate on the fate of the modernity project in China (Zhang 2005: 223). It is hard to ignore the fact that many historical movements in China, such as the New Life Movement, the Great Leap Forward and the Cultural Revolution, have employed similar political rhetoric to purge undesirable elements and political subjects in order to obtain a healthy, non-superstitious and hygienic body and nation.

Extending Zhang's observation to Hong Kong cinema, there is a similar practice of purging ghosts and undesirable elements in the Hong Kong Cleansing Movement in 1949. This was a third wave of 'cleansing' in the Hong Kong film industry.[8] Cantonese film-makers and actors resisted those capitalists who only invested in martial arts films and other popular genres that were dominant in the film industry (Feng 2010). In their view, in order to elevate Cantonese films and contribute to national cinema, film-makers have to stop making poisonous films that contradict the national interest. Chun Kim was therefore one of the signatories of the 'Manifesto of Cleansing Movement', published in *Ta Kung Pao* on 8 April 1949.

The ending of *The Nightly Cry of the Ghost* presents a legitimate use of science. The use of science is not only moralised, but also instructed and legitimised by the state apparatus. Using science and rational thinking to help Ding be 'reincarnated' is not enough; the crime must be reported to the police. The advocacy of science finally hands power to the criminal justice system, which becomes the legitimate and the neutral arbitrator of law and order. The police are the only legal authority to conduct the 'reincarnation' of Ding (since the audio recorder is the key evidence in the court), while Fang and his family are discredited as 'dangerous' because they work outside the rule of law. The sense of a neutral and authoritative police force in the film can be seen as an early sign of the ideology free position and legitimation of the Royal Hong Kong Police Force and the Colonial Hong Kong government in the late 1960s.

The marriage of the use of science and the rule of law prevails over not only the supernatural, but also the superstitions of Hong Kong. Both Yu Yuan and Lee Yuan, the site of the original ghost tale and the film location, respectively, are located in the New Territories, where agriculture and traditional ways of life were dominant at the time. Influenced by progressive intellectuals and film-makers who dismissed Hong Kong as bereft of culture, only a hub of commerce, Chun Kim let Fang, a student of radio broadcasting, and Fang's cousin, a poultry farmer, not only punish the criminal ghost-believers, but also promote and enlighten the people of Hong Kong on the importance of science and the rule of law.

Conclusion

This chapter has illustrated how Cantonese horror films in the 1950s, through adaptation viewed as reincarnation, became a site of cultural and political intervention. During the Cold War, even though the Hong Kong government adopted a liberal attitude to film censorship,[9] films were not able to directly depict ideas of revolution. In spite of this, stories engaging in any way with the concept of revolution became popular in the 1950s and were a frequently important aspect of horror movies. Yeung Kung-leung's *The Voyage of the Dead* (*Wan li xing shi*, 1954) and Lee Sun-fung's *The Beautiful Ghost's Grievance* (*Li gui yuan chou*, 1959) are remakes of Ma-Xu Weibang's *Song at Midnight* (*Ye ban ge sheng*, 1937),[10] and Lee Wo's radio play[11] respectively. Both of them are about revolutionary comrades fighting against evil landlords. Like *The Nightly Cry of the Ghost*, the ghosts in these films are hoaxes. What is different from the previous film is that they actively use the identity of ghosts to empower the unity of comrades; they are like ghosts, living miserably under a tyrant's rule. In both stories, 'ghosts' are political agents that use masquerade as a revolutionary means to disguise themselves in order to cross borders during curfew and plan their revolution. Unlike 'ghosts' in China, which were representatives of the victims of the old China and the need to be transformed into revolutionary subjects in the new China (as, for example, in Shui Hua and Wang Bin's *The White Haired Girl* (1951)), the masquerade of ghosts is not the political ends but the means in Hong Kong horror.

In *The Beautiful Ghost's Grievance*, there is an interesting scene worth mentioning. Lee Sun-fung constructs a plot with a play within a play (*xi zhong xi*). The scene starts with the theatre curtain opening. Tension escalates when the warlord finds the Cantonese opera performance re-enacting his crime. The five-minute scene includes a medium shot zooming in and out on the players on the stage, and a wide shot of the mass audience and a close-up of the conscience-stricken warlord. These reflexive shots solicit the attention of the general audience who can participate in the diegetic narrative of the film. This is a moral questioning and rupturing of the condition of spectatorship that reproduces the passivity of identification. In this way, this play-within-a-play device may break away the violent gaze of passivity that was a serious cultural question raised by Lu Xun, one of the advocates of the May Fourth Movement.[12] What I want to show is that film-makers not only used script-writing to intervene politically and culturally, but also made interventions in the filmic forms that generated new possibilities and interventions for the audience.[13]

However, while these interventions open up new possibilities, they cannot lead to the radical critique of homogenous time and political engagement proposed by Bliss Cua Lim. Because of film censorship and commercial needs, the formulaic and hastily made nature of these productions limit their impact. Nevertheless, these adaptations of horror films tell us *how* to render the cliché, as Carol Clover explicates the remakes of horror film that 'a particular example may have original features, but its quality as a horror film lies in the way it delivers the cliché' (Clover 1989: 94).[14] Adaptation as reincarnation in Hong Kong horror of the 1950s is a site of political and cultural intervention: the *neoi gwei* can have a minor feminist struggle in *Beauty Raised from the Dead*; a ghost story can impart ideas of scientism and the rule of law in *The Nightly Cry of the Ghost*; the identity of the *neoi gwei* in *The Beautiful Ghost's Grievance* can be a political means to overthrow landlords and warlords.

Some Cantonese horror films of the 1960s came closer to detective thrillers, films in which a detective or a revolutionary investigate a strange case and reveal a ghost as a hoax or a criminal scheme, as is the case in Cheung Ying and Choi Cheong's *The Bride from the Grave* (1964). Within the interstices of popular culture, political and cultural intervention invested in Cantonese films cannot be separated and dismissed as meaningless. The horror films discussed in this chapter do not represent a comprehensive list that can present a full picture of this phenomenon,[15] but suggest at least that the practice of adaptation in Hong Kong horror offers creative energy, critiques and interventions.

Notes

1. In principle the Pinyin transliteration system for Chinese words is used. However, exceptions are made with respect to historical and regional circumstances. For institutions and names of film-makers in Hong Kong, Cantonese terms will be used. For example Stanley Kwan instead of Guan Jin-peng. Also, because *neoi gwei* is my key term to talk about Hong Kong horror films, this will remain in Cantonese instead of *nü gui*.
2. Some valuable works in English are exceptions; see Jarvie 1977; Fonoroff 1988; Teo 1997; Bordwell 2000; Chu 2003; Law and Bren 2004; Fan 2015 and 2016.
3. Literary sources include radio drama, folk tales, comedy, Western literary classics, Chinese literary classics, Chinese opera plays and popular martial arts fiction.
4. The scene does not indicate if Lee Wing's daughter is killed by Du. Lee Wing's daughter faints in the bride's sedan. A special effect of superimposition and a dissolve cut was used to indicate Du's success of reincarnation.
5. The female-ghost-as-hoax story is not exclusive to Hong Kong horror. The South Korean film *The Devil's Stairway* directed by Lee Man-hee in 1964 is a psychological thriller in which a woman poses as a ghost to torment and expose the man who tried to kill her.
6. The relationship between horror films and martial arts films is important. Both of them employ visual effects and experiment with different use of the

medium. However, both of them also face criticisms from scholars and critics for their risqué content. Chen Huan-wen's *Magical Flying Swordsman (Yuan zi fei jian xia*, 1951) is a good example of how martial arts film marries with horror. The film employs a lot of visual effects such as when a decapitated vampire wakes up and picks up its own head, and a Taoist fires animated flying swords and casts a magic spell to stop the vampire and burn it.

7. Underworld mansion (*difu*) is an imaginary place derived from Taosim, Buddhism and traditional folk religion. It serves to punish evil spirits before their reincarnation.

8. In 1935 there was the first Cleansing Movement, advocated by Xu Di-shan, a Chinese professor at the University of Hong Kong and one of the key figures in modern Chinese literature, who joined members of the Society of Hong Kong Overseas Education and called for a cleansing movement in order to boycott poisonous films of magic and superpower and supernatural. In 1938 Luo Ming-you, the founder of the Lianhua Film Company, and other producers advocated the second Cleansing Movement with Christian organisations in Hong Kong.

9. Terms of reference were quoted in a file of censorship in 1947: (1) Offend or bring into contempt the accepted rules of morality or decency; (2) Provoke feelings of racial or national hostility or any resentment on religious grounds; (3) Exacerbate political rivalries; (4) Prejudice unfavourably relations with friendly powers; (5) Tend to corrupt the minds by examples of gross depravity or obscenity or sordidness; (6) Glorify crime, the use of violence and criminal methods; (7) Encourage the use of firearms or other lethal weapons to commit crimes of violence (or terrorism) or overthrow the rule of law and order or established government. See HKRS41-1-2254.

10. *Song at Midnight* is considered the first Chinese horror film, and was adapted from Gaston Leroux's *Phantom of the Opera*.

11. Lee Wo is a famous radio jockey whose series of 'Air-Wave' novels were popular in Guangzhou before 1948. After 1949 he continued his career in Hong Kong. His air-wave novels were broadcast in Radio Rediffusion, Commercial Radio and Radio Vilaverde Lda. *The Beautiful Ghost's Grievance* was broadcast in Radio Vilaverde Lda. See Ng 1997a, 1997b.

12. That the theme of passivity of gaze is a violent act can be seen in much of Lu's work; citizens are interested in watching the beheading of revolutionaries in *The True Story of Ah Q* and *Medicine*; people see the tragedies of others in *Kong Yiji, New Year Sacrifice*.

13. Other films like Wong Toi's *The Dunce Bumps into a Ghost* (1957) and Chow Sze-luk's *The Ghostly Wife* (1953) are comic-horrors from the 1950s. Although these adaptations look average and simple, some filmic devices are used to elicit attention from the audience. Influenced by Cantonese opera and local singing tradition (like *Namyam*), they include a multilayered frame story, direct address to the camera and parody of common representations of ghosts.

14. Meaghan Morris's (2013) account of cliché as a modern concept that involves active participation and change is helpful too in explaining the rigidity of this cycle of Cantonese films.
15. Films about snake demons were also popular in the 1950s. Hong Kong had imitated films about snake demons from the Philippines. Gerardo de Leon's *Sanda Wong* (1955) and Wong Tin-lam's *The Serpent Girl's Worldly Fancies* (*She nü si fan*, 1958) were coproduced by Hong Kong and the Philippines. Also, local film-makers make use of snake legends to recount the folk tales of *The Legend of the White Snake* (Ng 2008).

References

Anon. 'Film Censorship in Hong Kong – Request for Information Concerning 21.04.1947 – 12.05.1948', HKRS41-1-2254, Government Records Service of Hong Kong, Hong Kong.

Anon. (1956), 'Film review of *Beauty Raised from the Dead*', *Wah Kiu Yat Po*, Hong Kong, 3 August.

Bordwell, David (2000), *Planet Hong Kong: Popular Cinema and the Art of Entertainment*, Cambridge, MA, and London: Harvard University Press.

Chu, Yingchi (2003), *Hong Kong Cinema: Coloniser, Motherland and Self*, London: Routledge Curzon.

Clover, Carol J. (1989), 'Her body, himself: gender in the slasher film,' in James Donald (ed.), *Fantasy and the Cinema*, London: British Film Institute, pp. 77–89.

Fan, Victor (2015), *Cinema Approaching Reality: Locating Chinese Film Theory*, Minneapolis: University of Minnesota.

Fan, Victor (2016), 'Poetics of parapraxis and reeducation: the Hong Kong Cantonese cinema in the 1950s', in Gary Bettinson and James Udden (eds), *The Poetics of Chinese Cinema*, New York: Palgrave Macmillan, pp. 167–183.

Fang, Jun (1956a), 'On the two old men in *Beauty Raised from the Dead*', *Ta Kung Pao*, 17 July.

Fang, Jun (1956b), '*Beauty Raised from the Dead* – Is it sexy romance? Fantastic?', *Ta Kung Pao*, 20 July.

Feng, Quan (2010), 'On the clean-up campaign of Hong Kong film', *Contemporary Cinema*, 4, pp. 91–4

Fonoroff, Paul (1988), 'A brief history of Hong Kong cinema', *Rendition*, 29–30, pp. 293–308.

Jarvie, I. C. (1977), *Window on Hong Kong: a Sociological Study of the Hong Kong Film Industry and Its Audience*, Hong Kong: Centre of Asian Studies, University of Hong Kong.

Law, Kar and Frank Bren (2004), *Hong Kong Cinema: a Cross-cultural View*, Lanham: Scarecrow Press.

Leung, Ping-kwan (2011), 'Hong Kong cinema of the 1950s: adaptation as a means of cultural formation' [also referred to as 'Literary adaptation and cultural negotiation in Hong Kong cinema of the 1950s'], The University of British Columbia, YouTube, 7 October, <https://www.youtube.com/watch?v=_sShnA-jlm8> (last accessed 29 May 2016).

Leung, Ping-kwan and So-yee Chan (2014), 'Cultural politics of red flowering plum', *Journal of Modern Literature in Chinese*, 12:1, pp 158–66.

Lim, Bliss Cua (2009), *Translating Time: Cinema, the Fantastic, and Temporal Critique*, Durham, NC: Duke University Press.

Liu, Lydia, Rebecca E. Karl and Dorothy Ko (eds) (2013), *The Birth of Chinese Feminism: Essential Texts in Transnational Theory*, New York: Columbia University Press.

Morris, Meaghan (2013), 'Transnational glamour, national allure: community, change and cliché in Baz Luhrmann's *Australia*', in Jan Shaw, Philippa Kelly and L. E. Semler (eds), *Storytelling: Critical and Creative Approaches*, Basingstoke: Palgrave Macmillan, pp. 83–113.

Ng, Ho (1997a), 'Radio plays and the Cantonese cinema', in C. Li (ed.), *Cantonese Melodrama: 1950–1969 (Revised Edition)*, Hong Kong: Urban Council of Hong Kong, pp. 59–61.

Ng, Ho (1997b), 'A case study of Li Wo', in C. Li (ed.), *Cantonese Melodrama: 1950–1969 (Revised Edition)*, Hong Kong: Urban Council of Hong Kong, pp. 65–6.

Ng, Ho (2008), 'Snake demon and heart demon: on cross-border films of coproduction of Hong Kong and the Philippines in the 1950s', *Gu Cheng Ji: Lun Xianggang Dian Ying Ji Su Wen Xue* (Legend of a lonely city: on Hong Kong film and mass culture), Hong Kong: Sub-Culture, pp. 86–115.

Stam, Robert (2005), 'Introduction: the theory and practice of adaptation', in Robert Stam and Alessandra Raengo (eds), *Literature and Film: a Guide to the Theory and Practice of Film Adaptation*, Malden: Blackwell, pp. 1–52.

Teo, Stephen (1997), *Hong Kong Cinema: the Extra Dimensions*, London: British Film Institute.

Todorov, Tzvetan (1973), *The Fantastic: a Structural Approach to a Literary Genre*, Cleveland: Press of Case Western Reserve University.

Wen, Guang (1957), 'Cantonese films adapted from famous novels', *Union Film Illustrated Newspaper*, 20 June.

Zhang, Zhen (2005), *An Amorous History of the Silver Screen: Shanghai Cinema, 1896–1937*, Chicago: University of Chicago.

Zou, John (2008), '*A Chinese Ghost Story*: ghostly counsel and innocent man', in Chris Berry (ed.), *Chinese Films in Focus: II*, Basingstoke: Palgrave Macmillan, pp. 56–63.

CHAPTER 2

The White Snake in Hong Kong Horror Cinema: from Horrific Tales to Crowd Pleasers

Liang Luo

The White Snake Films: Complicating 'Hong Kong Horror Cinema'

Considered one of the four great folktales in the Chinese oral tradition, the legend of the White Snake and its theatrical and popular cultural metamorphoses played an important role in the pre-cinematic origins of Hong Kong horror cinema. This chapter first analyses the horror elements in the White Snake tale from its earliest written versions onwards, with an emphasis on male sexual encounters with a snake woman and their horrifying aftermaths. It then surveys the changing representation of gender and horror and the transformation of the 'demonic love' of the snake woman to the 'pure love' between her and her human husband in a series of films based on the White Snake legend from the 1920s to the 1970s. The films include early Japanese and Chinese experimental films *The Lust of the White Serpent* (*Jasei no in*, directed by Kurihara Kisaburō, 1921) and *Lakeshore Spring Dream* (*Hubian chunmeng*, directed by Bu Wancang, 1926); the commercial trilogy *The Righteous Snake* (*Yiyao Baishe zhuan*, directed by Runje Shaw, 1926–7) made by the parent company of Shaw Brothers in Shanghai in the 1920s; the Japanese-language Hong Kong–Japan co-production *The Legend of the White Serpent* (*Byaku fujin no yoren*, Toyoda Shirō, 1956); the 1962 Shaw Brothers' *Huangmei diao* film *Madam White Snake* (*Baishe zhuan*, directed by Yueh Feng); and the Hong Kong-Taiwan co-production *Love of the White Snake* (*Zhen Baishe zhuan*) of 1978, made by a director (Li Han-hsiang) who connects Hong Kong, Taiwan and Mainland Chinese film-making through his illustrative career.

Centred on a very horrific concept (a monstrous snake disguised as a beauty and married to a human male), these films nonetheless enrich or even challenge our understanding of the genre of horror cinema in their service to a wide range of other genres: operatic performance, romantic melodrama, fantasy adventure, slapstick comedy, and social and political commentary. In addition to challenging the very concept of horror, this cluster of White Snake films poses further challenges to the idea of Hong Kong cinema, as they range from a Tokyo production, a Shanghai production, a Hong Kong–Japan co-production, to a production based in Hong Kong with South Asian distributors, and a Hong Kong–Taiwan co-production with a Shaw Brothers director, Taiwanese actors and distributors, Japanese crew members and outdoor scenes shot in South Korea and Taiwan.

In this context, it is instructive to trace a possible 'Shaw Brothers connection' in the White Snake films, from the Shaw Brothers' parent company in Shanghai, to its co-producing efforts with Japan, to its *Huangmei diao* film inspired by traditional Chinese theatre, and then to the impact of Hong Kong film-making in Taiwan and Southeast Asia. Although the films are neither entirely produced in Hong Kong, nor exclusively by the Shaw Brothers, the Shaw Brothers factor and the location of Hong Kong serve as key components in linking the past, present and future of the White Snake films (Bai 2013). As a result, these White Snake films, with their strong connections to the Shaw Brothers in Hong Kong, not only manifest the linkage between the evolution of the White Snake legend and the changing representation of gender and horror in Hong Kong cinema, they also illuminate Hong Kong cinema's deep and dynamic cultural ties to Japan, the Chinese Mainland, and East and Southeast Asia throughout the long twentieth century.

Horror in the White Snake Tales: Sexual Encounters and Their Aftermaths

Originated in tales from the seventh century, the legend of the White Snake took shape in the sixteenth century. Popular versions of the tale recount how a white snake and a green fish (later a green snake), disguised as two beautiful maidens, meet a handsome young man by the enchanting West Lake. The White Snake forms a sexual relationship with the young man. Her transgressive sexuality attracts the attention of a Buddhist monk, who is determined to prevent such dangerous liaisons between a human male and a snake woman. Feng Menglong's seventeenth-century vernacular tale, one of the most popular retellings of the legend, repudiates the lust of the snake woman while upholding the monk as a defender of natural human relations. The early iterations of the White Snake tale are thus about the horrifying aftermath of having sexual encounters with a snake woman, about male fears and anxieties towards female transgression, and the need to contain that transgressive power.

Over time, the tale of the White Snake has been creatively manipulated in many ways and through different media to serve various political,
cultural and social needs. In the twentieth century the tale has been used
to promote themes as diverse as freedom to marry, women's rights, grassroots revolutionary spirit, homosexual love and transgender rights. Today
the legend is the basis for Chinese tourist sites and theme parks that connect a fantastic tale to a global neo-liberal economy.

One of the first written accounts of the tale involves a certain Mr Li's
horrible death after enjoying three days of ultimate sexual pleasures with
a mysterious 'girl in white' (*baiyi zhishu*). Mr Li returns home, smelling
like stinking rotten fish. He becomes bedridden. Although he can still
speak, he feels his body vanishing under the quilt. When others lift the
quilt and look at his body, it has turned into a pool of water, only his head
remaining.[1] Originated in the Tang Dynasty from the seventh century
onwards, and included in the tenth-century Northern Song dynasty collection *Taiping guangji*, this early version of the tale clearly sets it up as a
horror story for the male protagonist as well as his male readers, warning them to be fearful of transgressive sexuality embodied by monstrous
female/animal bodies.

The horror elements of the tale continued into Feng Menglong's retelling in the seventeenth century, as 'a gust of foul-smelling wind sprang up
from the deserted interior of the house' when the male protagonist, now
surnamed Xu, goes back to look for the woman in white whom he had met
the night before (Feng 1624: 483). Later, when a snake-catcher is hired
to deal with the snake woman, a chilly wind again springs up, and, 'as it
blew past, a python with a body as thick as a water bucket thrust fiercely
at him,' then, 'the python lunged forward as if to bite him, its blood-red
mouth wide open, showing its snow-white fangs' (Ibid.). These popular
accounts again emphasised the animal nature and the dangerous qualities
of the snake woman, as well as the devastating aftermath of having had
bodily and sexual contacts with her/it.

Horror in Early Experimental White Snake Films: Tokyo and Shanghai Connections

The Japanese writer Ueda Akinari based his now-canonised eighteenth-
century collection *Ugetsu Monogatari* (*Tales of Moonlight and Rain*) on
Feng Menglong's seventeenth-century version of the White Snake tale,
on which the modernist writer Tanizaki Jun'ichirō again based his film
scenario *The Lust of the White Serpent* (Ueda 1776; Tanizaki and Kurihara
1921). Tanizaki's highlighting of the dangerous lustfulness of the White

Snake image had much to do with the cultural milieu of Taishō Japan, when the Tokyo showing of *The Cabinet of Dr. Caligari* (1920) became a sensational event in the history of Japanese film-making. Thomas Kurihara (Kurihara Kisaburō), a Japanese actor–director returned from Hollywood and a friend of the Chinese writer Tian Han,[2] had just begun shooting Tanizaki's scenario *The Lust of the White Serpent* when *Caligari* premiered in Tokyo in the early 1920s. *Caligari* provided Tanizaki and Kurihara with a timely stimulus for producing an adaptation of the White Snake legend by way of Ueda Akinari's Japanese adaptation.[3] A contemporary Japanese film scholar commented on the connection between *The Lust of the White Serpent* and *Caligari*: 'The grotesque film about the snake-woman haunting a man and his wife can be seen as the Japanese reproduction of the uncanny German cinema' (Yamamoto 1983: 135).

Inspired by Tanizaki's film scenario *Jasei no in* (1921), the Chinese writer Tian Han conceived a film story, *Hubian chunmeng* (*Lakeshore Spring Dream*), featuring the psychological hallucination of a male narrator and his 'spring dream' involving a modern femme fatale, in the spirit of the White Snake.[4] In the film, the 'vampire' woman and sadistic femme fatale abuses the male protagonist for sexual enjoyment.[5]

Early experimental cinema in Japan and China celebrated the transgressive power of the femme fatale and its continued threat to the forging of a modern masculinity. However, rather than focusing on the animal nature and physical horrors closely associated with the snake woman's serpentine qualities, the films instead took on the elements of the grotesque and the uncanny, and a resulting sense of psychological horror. Only a few years after Freud published his piece on the 'Uncanny', these cinematic experiments in both Japan and China from the 1920s echoed well the spirit of that essay by laying bare the roots of horror. As according to Freud, the uncanny 'is actually nothing new or strange, but something that was long familiar to the psyche and was estranged from it only through being repressed' (Freud 2003: 148). Repressed female sexuality, as well as an emerging modern femininity, proved to be more horrifying and threatening than the monstrous animal bodies and physical horrors of the past.

The White Snake in Early Commercial Feature Film: Tianyi Film Company, Shanghai, 1926–7

Tian Han's modernist experiments in *Lakeshore Spring Dream* coincided with the first Chinese commercial feature film of the White Snake tale. On 11 July 1926 *The Righteous Snake*, a two-part feature film starring Hu Die as the White Snake, premiered at the Central Grand Theatre in

Shanghai. Although the film is no longer extant, its plot summary, published in a contemporary newspaper, listed the following scenes: White
Snake descends to the human realm to repay her debt towards Xu Xian;
she encounters Xu at the West Lake and borrows his umbrella; the two get
married in her residence; White Snake gives Xu stolen silver and causes
trouble; Xu moves to Suzhou and practises medicine there; White Snake
transforms into her original shape and scares Xu to death after taking
medicinal wine; White Snake steals a magic herb to bring Xu back to life;
Monk Fa Hai intervenes and takes Xu to the Golden Mountain Temple;
White Snake floods the Temple; Fa Hai suppresses her under the Leifeng
Pagoda.[6]

Such a dramatic tale is bound to be a visual feast and seems full of cinematic potential. In particular, the promotional stills of the famed actress
Hu Die in traditional costume posing as the White Snake, published
in contemporary illustrated magazines, add to the spectacular cinematic
allures of the White Snake tale. *Tuhua shibao* (*Pictorial Times*) featured
such a still in 1926, with a full body portrait of Hu Die as the White Snake,
fully made up with elaborate head pieces and traditional costumes of the
type favoured by young maidens of a respected family. However, her
inquisitive eyes, instead of looking sideways or downwards, gaze straight
into the camera. In addition to the daring gaze that might have betrayed
her true identity, the only other detail that would have spoken to her
magical power as a snake spirit after thousands of years of cultivation, is
the *hossu* she prominently holds behind her back. The *hossu*, a wooden or
bamboo staff, has served as a significant prop on the Chinese theatre stage,
as it signals Daoist cultivation or Buddhist teaching, often with strong
implications on its owner achieving high martial or magical skills.[7]

Another surviving still of the lost 1926 film confirms such an implication, as here the White Snake figure is shown dressed in exactly the same
costume and adorning the same head pieces, except that she is raising
her *hossu* high in mid-air in one hand, and holding tight to the tail of it in
another, in a pose suggesting imminent fighting.[8] A third contemporary
archival document further supports the unique contribution of Tianyi
Film Company's rendering of the White Snake tale. Comparing the White
Snake tale with such literary classics as *The Dream of the Red Chamber*, the
writer advocated for the value of the White Snake tale as it represented
the popular (*tongsu*) spirit of the Chinese people. Tianyi Film Company
should be commended for its unique and grand vision of making the tale
into a film, concluded the writer (Tao 1926: 60–1).

The company behind one of the first commercial film adaptions of the
White Snake tale was the Shanghai Tianyi (Unique) Film Company, with

Runje Shaw heading the company and directing the films. Runje is the older brother of Runde, Runme and Run Run Shaw. Under his leadership, his younger brothers established branches of Tianyi in Hong Kong and Singapore, of which the Shaw Brothers Studio came to dominate film-making in Hong Kong.

The very first Chinese commercial feature films based on the White Snake tale, as a result, ushered in the image of the White Snake as a female warrior. Although the snake woman embodied threats from alien species and hybrid identities, her reformed identity of being a 'righteous demoness' (*yiyao*), as highlighted in the title of the films, largely diluted the horror elements in this initial attempt at commercial feature film-making. The box office success of the two-part film in 1926 even warranted a third instalment in 1927, and laid a solid foundation for the Hong Kong revival of the White Snake films by Tianyi's branch company, the Shaw Brothers. This Shanghai episode of early commercial film-making centred on the White Snake theme illuminates a transformative moment in the popularisation and humanisation of the horrific tale and signals an important shift towards commercial success.

Hong Kong–Japan Co-production: *The Legend of the White Serpent*, Tokyo, 1956

Before the Shaw Brothers took up the White Snake tale in the early 1960s in Hong Kong, there were a few important cinematic endeavours in Japan that warrant attention.[9] In particular, the Japanese costume film *The Legend of the White Serpent* starring the illustrious Japanese actress Yamaguchi Yoshiko (Li Xianglan) reminds us how competing cinematic representations of the White Snake theme shaped political life and popular culture in post-war East Asia. As a co-production between the Toho Film Company in Tokyo and the Shaw Brothers in Hong Kong, the film attempted to use beautiful imagery to dissolve political conflicts, and in it, gender transgression became the art of reconciliation. *The Legend of the White Serpent* ends with the White Snake flying away with her human lover to live happily ever after in their afterlives, symbolising Japan's goodwill for peaceful development at its post-war moment of cultural rejuvenation.

Directed by Toyoda Shirō, *The Legend of the White Serpent* is representative of the Japanese film industry's co-production efforts with Hong Kong, Taiwan and South Korea in many post-war films. Sangjoon Lee (2011) has written on this history of post-war co-production in East Asian film industries, in particular, between the Shin Films in South Korea, the

Shaw Brothers in Hong Kong and the GMP (Guolian) in Taiwan, all of which co-produced films on the White Snake tale from the late 1950s to the late 1970s.

In this 1956 Japanese-language cinematic rendition, in one particular scene, White Snake instructs her companion Green Snake to poison water sources in order to save her human husband Xu Xian's medical business. 'Why are we doing such evil (*daidu*) things?' rendered the official Chinese subtitle of Green Snake's questioning of White Snake's order. The Chinese compound word *daidu* implies both treacherous (*dai*) and poisoning (*du*), quite fitting for a description of the deeds of two horrifying snake spirits. The physical and psychological horrors of poisoning the people in order to sell them medicine remain in this post-war Japanese reinterpretation, very much echoing Feng Menglong's seventeenth-century version of the tale emphasising the monstrosity of the animal spirit and the consequences of its poisoning action.

Throughout the film, the strongest sense of horror derives from the male protagonist Xu Xian's constant feeling of suspicion towards the White Snake. In the scene in which the White Snake's magnificent residence transforms into a ruined house, the non-diegetic music fosters a haunting sensation, again evoking Feng's story. Moreover, when the camera discloses how, amidst the debris in the abandoned house, the snake woman is sitting by herself on the bed, and the camera zooms in on a pile of stolen silver by her side, the psychological impact on the contemporary audience would have been quite strong. Then, when she disappears into thin air in the next instance, thanks to Tsuburaya Eiji's special effects (laudable for the 1950s), such a horrifying effect would have been further intensified.

In another dramatic encounter in the 1956 film, the White Snake triumphs over a Daoist snake-catcher with her magical skills, although the whole affair is tainted, or salvaged, by a comical touch. During the initial encounter, a series of close-ups suggest White Snake's possible transformation into a python under her quilt, after being affected by the Daoist's magical talisman brought home by her husband. This scene of 'horror under the quilt' strongly echoes Mr Li's horrifying death, turning into a pool of water under his quilt, in the *Taiping guangji* version of the tale from the tenth century. However, when the White Snake confronts the Daoist with her magical power, he is quickly blown up in mid-air and, thanks to special effects, he is seen hanging upside down from the eaves of majestic buildings, like a miniature clown.

The climatic horror moment in the film follows the climax of the original story, when the White Snake is forced to drink medicinal wine, transforms into her original form and frightens her human husband to death. The shocking facial reaction of the husband upon witnessing such a transformation, intensified by extreme close-ups, brings about a chilling sense of psychological horror. Another iconic moment of horror is none other than the 'Flooding Golden Mountain Temple' scene, again aided by Tsuburaya Eiji's special effects, when a long tracking shot discloses the devouring of fields, crowds, and finally the temple by the flood initiated by the snake women.

Special to the 1956 Japan–Hong Kong co-production was its leading actress, Yamaguchi Yoshiko. At the beginning of the film in a scene featuring the White Snake and Xu Xian's encounter by the lotus pond inside her garden residence, the camera lures the audience into an extreme close-up of White Snake's face with heavy make-up, full scarlet lips, dark and heavy eyeliner, and meticulously outlined dark eyebrows. White Snake's tortuously painful facial expression when Xu Xian grabs her throat out of frustration of his poor background and inability to accept her marriage proposal, dominates the screen. This physical interaction unexpectedly turns on both of their desires and results in one of the most explicit 'kiss and bed' scenes in the White Snake repertoire for its times. Again, physical and sexual encounters with the White Snake could be terrifying, especially when the original audience was aware of how such desires could result in the psychological horror and bewitchment of both parties involved.

Given the leading actress Yamaguchi Yoshiko's past association with China, putting her in Chinese robes and having her impersonating an exotic and erotic snake spirit from a Chinese legend must have invited a complex range of psychological identifications and misrecognitions for movie-goers, both inside and outside Japan. Jennifer Coates, in her article on Yamaguchi, borrows from a Japanese scholar's articulation of Yamaguchi's 'realism' and notes how that realism adds a thrilling aspect of threat to her portrayal of monstrous or excessive female characters (Coates 2014: 33), in addition to highlighting the actress's fitting exoticism. Coates focuses on the dialectics of nature and deception in the character of the White Snake in this film starring the enigmatic Yamagushi, emphasising how, as a spirit with the ability to control the wind and water, White Snake is intimately associated with nature. However, Yamaguchi's performance amplified by the cinematic language of the film manifests her deception and highlights her demonic nature (Ibid.: 34).

The 1956 White Snake film made international news by winning a prize at the Berlin Film Festival for its use of colour. Hong Kong's English-language newspaper *South China Morning Post* repeatedly reported on the film's Berlin win, from late June to early July in 1956. One of the reports praised its enchanted atmosphere of gardens and landscapes (in fact mostly studio shots), the high-calibre acting from the film's cast, its magnificent scenes of 'magical happenings' (special effects), in addition to the film's use of colour (SCMP 1956).

More than ten years after the 1956 film's initial run in Hong Kong, the *South China Morning Post* again reported in March 1970 the opening of '*The Legend of the White Snake*, A Toho Production', in the Oriental Theatre. The profound impact of the 1956 White Snake film lingers on in Hong Kong and throughout East and Southeast Asia, as shown in its multilocational and multilingual commercial posters and advertisements in Chinese, English and Thai for screenings in Malaysia, Singapore and Thailand.

This episode of post-war Japan–Hong Kong co-production complicates our understanding of Hong Kong horror cinema in a number of important ways. Hong Kong's unique political situation in Cold War East Asia conditioned its privileged position as a Cold War commercial and cultural powerhouse, serving as an important commercial partner and key cultural consultant for the Japanese reinvention of its film industry and reaffirmation of its peaceful nation-building process at the crucial post-war moment. At the same time, Japanese special effects and use of colour technology enriched its Hong Kong partner's technical know-how and provided important inspirations for the development of special effects in Hong Kong horror cinema (Bordwell 2009).

Made in Hong Kong: the Shaw Brothers' *Madam White Snake*, 1962

The feminine genre of the *Huangmei diao* film, an invented tradition from Hong Kong that repackaged traditional Chinese theatre in a softer and more popularised version in film, made possible the transmission of the White Snake tale and its feminine aesthetics to Southeast Asia and globally, from the early 1960s onwards. Indeed, Shaw Brothers' 1962 film *Madam White Snake* should be considered together with a cluster of *Huangmei diao* films originated from Hong Kong in the 1960s.[10] In these opera films, feminine re-enchantment, as embodied by the glamorous and humane White Snake, the romantic Butterfly Lovers, and other iconic images, could be read as expressions of the charm offensive of the People's Republic of China's far-reaching 'soft power', which was already prominent in the early 1960s as mediated through Hong Kong.

The 1962 film opens with White Snake and Green Snake singing 'in order to pursue happiness we are going to the human realm' (*yao kuaile dao renjian*). White Snake's red silk handkerchief resembles the key symbol of desire and danger in the 1956 Japanese film, and remains an important plot device throughout different climaxing scenes in the *Huangmei diao* film.

In the Shaw Brothers' recreation in Hong Kong in the 1960s, some of the central horror elements of the film derived from Green Snake's magic powers, rather than that of the White Snake's. In fact, in contrast to the more humane image of the White Snake, it was the maid/sister figure, Green Snake, who was often seen on screen to showcase a demonic spirit, including the episode focusing on her dealing and fighting with the Daoist snake-catcher. It appears that the Green Snake has long been more horrifying than the White Snake, as already highlighted in the Broken Bridge scene from different renditions in Peking Opera and various local opera genres.[11]

Music again plays an essential role in fostering and strengthening the atmosphere for horror. Almost all versions of the White Snake films, the Shaw Brothers' 1962 version is no exception, highlight the other-worldly atmosphere fostered by the meticulously arranged background music when White Snake's magnificent residence transforms into a ruined courtyard house on the screen, accentuating White Snake's ghostly identity and her power to disguise and seduce. The visual and audio cues in these scenes were largely inherited from the strange tales from Pu Songling's early eighteenth-century short story collection *Strange Tales from a Chinese Studio*, and the horror is fostered by the beautiful appearance of humans and their surroundings transforming back into their horrible 'original' forms after deceptions are uncovered.

Although the narrative of the film still follows the logic of repaying Xu Xian's debt of saving the White Snake in her previous life, the film does emphasise the honesty and sincere quality of Xu's words upon their first encounter at the West Lake, which bears traces of some of the exact wordings from Tian Han's Peking Opera version of the tale finalised in the 1950s in Beijing. Following the same trajectory of humanising White Snake and making Xu Xian a more likeable character, the film omits the episode of stealing silver, and as a result, the two marry right away. Instead of Xu Xian being exiled to Suzhou, White Snake suggests their move voluntarily in order to create better business for her husband. The episode of poisoning water in order to sell medicine was also omitted.

Jean Gordon, in her *South China Morning Post* piece, characterises *Madam White Snake* as a 'charming screen comedy-fantasy of an age-old Chinese legend' (1962a). Gordon considers the special effects of the film 'cleverly achieved,' and best of all, 'the attractive story never loses sight of the underlying comedy' (Ibid.). In an earlier report, Gordon had already emphasised the comical elements of the film, especially Chao Lei's nice sense of comedy in his role as Xu the husband. Gordon gives the example of one of the charming scenes when Chao's character Xu almost plunges everyone into water in his effort to be polite in the narrow boat they share upon their first encounter at the West Lake (Gordon 1962b: 4). In another article by Gordon on other films, *Madam White Snake* is mentioned as the previous first-week box office record holder for Chinese pictures in Hong Kong (1963: 4).

In a 1965 *Variety* review of this 1962 Shaw Brothers' rendition of the White Snake tale, the Japanese cameraman Nishimoto Tadashi is mentioned as a weak effort from Shaw Brothers to seek outside help, and the film is criticised as having not made a real effort to reach out to non-Chinese audiences (Robe 1965). The reviewer commented that the Eastman colour used in the film is 'too brightly hued', and that it gives the characters a 'porcelained look' which shows that 'Nishimoto had little actual control' (Ibid.). The small studio sets also limited the cameraman's imagination, according to the review. The physical limit of Hong Kong and the resulting lack of outdoor locations were listed as major flaws, while the film music was considered something Chinese film must change in order to develop with the times, as the Japanese have.

Mixed reviews aside, more than ten years after the film's initial run, the 1962 *Huangmei diao* film *Madam White Snake* is again listed as showing at 11:30 p.m. for the Midnight (Horror) Show in June 1976 in Hong Kong under the Shaw Brothers logo. On the same page there is another advertisement for *Madame White Snake*, 'a family picture winning Silver Bear Award', apparently referring to the 1956 Japan–Hong Kong co-production. The fact that both White Snake films are still showing in Hong Kong theatres in 1976 demonstrates their relevance to and lasting impact on Hong Kong cinema and the Hong Kong market in general.[12]

The case of the Shaw Brothers' production of the *Huangmei diao* White Snake film is a complicated one in the history of Hong Kong horror cinema. On the one hand, it forms one of the most celebrated classics in the repertoire of *Huangmei diao* films as well as White Snake films. On the other hand, it continues, rather remarkably, the key shift made in Shanghai by its parent company Tianyi, in popularising and commercialising the White Snake theme. In the process of humanising the White Snake, comedy proved to be the most effective strategy and many of the horror elements still visible in the Japan–Hong Kong co-production from the 1950s were left out. The film's use of a Japanese cameraman and its technical advances, as well as limitations evaluated against Japan by an American film reviewer, illustrates Hong Kong's complicated relationship with Japan and America, among other cinematic giants, in its history of film-making.

Connecting Hong Kong and Taiwan: *The Love of the White Snake*, 1978

Similar to the Shaw Brothers version, Green Snake was often seen on screen displaying her magic powers in *Zhen Baishe zhuan*, or, *The Love of the White Snake*, made in Hong Kong by First Films in 1978. The film is directed by Li Han-hsiang, a legendary director who started his career with the Shaw Brothers in the 1950s, moved to Taiwan in the 1960s to establish the GMP (Guolian) Film Company, and returned to Hong Kong in the 1970s and then to Mainland China in the 1980s to continue making films, especially costume dramas.[13] In the 1978 film, Green Snake's magic powers included making rain and changing rocks and leaves into two male servants and four maids. The gender implication of the humanity of the non-human (rocks into males and leaves into females) is significant here, especially in the context of the snake women's newly acquired humanity linking animals and humans. In addition, the two rock-turned-male servants are named *Baifu* (White the Rich) and *Baigui* (White the Noble), further engraving human values onto non-human objects.

Comical elements abound in this late 1970s reinvention of the White Snake tale from Hong Kong and Taiwan. When the Green Snake uses magic to make rain as an excuse to make Xu Xian stay, it is interpreted as even Heaven was trying to make the guest stay (*tian liu ke*). When the White Snake needs the Green Snake to be her matchmaker, she promises to share 10 per cent of her future husband Xu Xian with her, while Green Snake wants to have at least 30 per cent instead. After seven days of waiting, Green Snake is excited about having Xu Xian for herself for three days; however, White Snake is simply making empty promises (using a honeymoon as an excuse, she keeps delaying Green Snake's 'share' of her husband) and this results in a series of incidents resembling a slapstick comedy.

Instead of White Snake 'repaying life-saving debts' from Xu Xian (*bao en*) as in earlier renditions, Green Snake hopes to be 'holding Xu Xian's legs' (*bao datui*, the two phrases share the same Chinese character *bao*). White Snake's explanation on delaying and finally rejecting Green Snake's advances on Xu, supposedly, has to do with Green Snake's 'demon spirit' – that is, since she has not yet been cleansed of her 'evil spirit as a demon' (*yaoqi weichu*), having intimate contact with her will poison Xu Xian (*guanren zhongdu*). What a horrifying thought for the loyal wife of a human male! No wonder she must protect her sexual monopoly of her husband.

The most impressive character in the 1978 film, however, is the previously unimpressive human husband, Xu Xian. In this version he not only does not buy into Monk Fa Hai's words attempting to separate husband and wife, he is also always squarely on the side of the White Snake, very much unlike the cowardly, wavering figure he was often portrayed as in earlier renditions. He is tricked by the *mi* (confused) character written down in his palm and follows the Daoist sent by the monk to the temple, against his free will, unlike in previous film renditions in which he is easily persuaded by the monk. By making Xu Xian an even more likable character, the film is able to further humanise the White Snake character and seems to have moved away from elements of horror.

Still, the 1978 film finds other ingenious ways of rendering horror. One example of this is the employment of Sichuan Opera theatrics. Instead of zooming in on Xu Xian's shocking facial expression after witnessing White Snake's transformation into her serpentine form after drinking medicinal wine, through split screen and time-lapse technology, the film shows Xu imagining Green Snake and White Snake's faces changing into frightening masks, as often seen in Sichuan Opera performances. After Xu recovers from the shock of witnessing her transformation, White Snake has to create a fake White Snake, and calls it *canglong* (dragon of the storage) in order to get rid of Xu's suspicion. The auspicious 'dragon of the storage', which according to White Snake's explanation to Xu, is a good omen and only appears to bring prosperity to the household. Such an explanation echoes folk beliefs throughout East Asia, and Xu's buying into it so willingly adds a sense of comedy to the previous scene of horror.

Compared to the lack of outdoor scenes in earlier versions, the 1978 film is a truly international big-budget production in that it was shot on location in South Korea and Taiwan, especially for realistic outdoor locations.[14] The stealing of the magic herb episode and the water battle scene, among many others, were fully shot with realistic outdoors scenery for the first time. The film's use of special effects also reaches a new level, but at the same time, it shows a prominent resemblance to the special effects employed for the 1956 version. In particular, after giving birth to her child, White Snake is shown as in a miniature version and entered into Fa Hai's golden bowl as she promised, effortlessly.

From the demonic love (*yoren*) of the 1956 Japan–Hong Kong co-production *The Legend of the White Serpent* to the true (*zhen*) love in the 1978 *The Love of the White Snake* connecting Hong Kong and Taiwan, the desire of the White Snake has metamorphosed from horrific to romantic. The actress who impersonated the White Snake in the 1978 film, Lin Ching-Hsia (Brigitte Lin), was indeed the goddess of Taiwanese romance films and TV soap operas from the 1970s onwards. Lin's crowd-pleasing screen persona had a lasting impact on bringing the romantic image of the

White Snake into mainstream popular culture in the Chinese-speaking world and beyond.

Conclusion

As shown in the cluster of White Snake films surveyed in this chapter, the 1920s' experimentalist renditions of the uncanny demoness and modern seductress in Tokyo and Shanghai creatively echoed the spirit of the snake woman and its horrifying effect in various versions of the White Snake tale from the seventh century onwards. From the late 1920s onwards, the White Snake films further demonstrated a 'Shaw Brothers connection', which linked early commercial film-making on the White Snake theme from Shanghai of the 1920s to Hong Kong and Tokyo in the 1950s and 1960s, and to Hong Kong and Taiwan in the 1970s, among other locations in East Asia and beyond.

Furthermore, the charming form of the *Huangmei diao* film, popularised by the Shaw Brothers in Hong Kong in the 1960s, was inherited, to an extent, by the 1992 Taiwanese TV series *The New Legend of the White Snake* (*Xin Bainiangzi chuanqi*), which brought the White Snake tale to the level of a household name in Mainland China from the 1990s onwards. Most recently, during the National Day holiday season in October 2016, a brand new White Snake film based on the 1992 Taiwanese TV series, featuring actors aged eight to ten years, again became an instant sensation, and the *Huangmei diao* singing by the child actors was again part of the central attraction of the newest instalment in the White Snake cinematic canon.

Thematically, the horror of the Green Snake, originated in its androgynous identity and expressed as a range of ambiguous sexualities in the contemporary reinventions of the White Snake tale represented by Lilian Lee's novel, Tsui Hark's film, and Tian Jinxin's stage play, among others, echo the psychological horror expressed in early White Snake films from Tokyo and Shanghai, inspired by Freud's theory of the uncanny and German expressionist film-making of the early 1920s.[15] Transgressive sexuality in contemporary popular cultural renditions of the White Snake tale, highly comparable and intricately connected to repressed femininity in early cinema, speaks to the heart of the making of horror: encountering the unknown and the unfamiliar in something seemingly known and familiar.

The changing representations of the snake women in Hong Kong honor cinema demonstrates how the White Snake legend is so flexible, so ripe for appropriation and reinterpretation in different geopolitical locations and at changing historical moments, for a wide range of aesthetic and political purposes. These hybrid images of animal, woman and human speak to some of the deep-rooted fears and desires of the human psyche, the strangeness and newness they embodied were at the centre of cultural and political debates from the early twentieth century onwards, and are still truly relevant at the time of this writing, when the new administration in the US is busy with getting rid of 'alien' elements in order to form its coherent 'humanity'.

The power of the snake women to pose challenging political questions on-screen as well as to remain the leading site for contemporary popular cultural reinvention pose a fundamental attraction to any serious researcher of cinematic and cultural history. Even more intriguing is the snake women's power to traverse political divides and geographical boundaries, in Japan, Hong Kong, South Korea, Taiwan, Mainland China, and across Southeast Asia, throughout the twentieth century and beyond. The snake women do embody horrific concepts and alien existences; however, their increasing politicisation, humanisation, romanticisation and commercialisation also make them crowd-pleasing eternal motifs in contemporary popular cultural productions across East Asia and beyond.

Notes

1. See 'Li Huang,' in Li Fang (ed.), *Taiping guangji wubaijuan* (Shanghai: Saoye shanfang, 1924), vol. 458, 'she san' (third chapter on snakes); translations and paraphrases from the Chinese and the Japanese originals are my own, unless otherwise noted.

2. Tian would rewrite the White Snake tale into a Peking Opera in the 1950s in Beijing, and his version became one of the most frequently adapted texts for later local operatic, cinematic, as well as contemporary stage experimentations in mainland China, Taiwan, Singapore, and elsewhere. For more on Tian Han's experiments with the White Snake tale in the 1950s, see 'A White Snake in Beijing: re-creating socialist opera,' in Liang Luo, *The Avant-Garde and the Popular in Modern China: Tian Han and the Intersection of Performance and Politics* (Ann Arbor: University of Michigan Press, 2014), Chapter Five.

3. See Joanne Bernardi, *Writing in Light: the Silent Scenario and the Japanese Pure Film Movement* (Detroit: Wayne State University Press, 2001), p. 165; Nobuo Chiba, *Eiga to Tanizaki* (Tokyo: Seiabō, 1989), p. 150; and Thomas LaMarre, *Shadows on the Screen: Tanizaki Jun'ichirō on Cinema and 'Oriental' Aesthetics* (Ann Arbor: Center for Japanese Studies, University of Michigan, 2005).

4. Bu Wancang, dir. *Hubian chunmeng* (*Lakeshore Spring Dream*). Conceived and with inter-titles written by Tian Han, Mingxing, 1927, non-existent.

5. I discussed this film in detail in a previous study, in which I treat the female figure in the film as an incarnation of the image of the White Snake, an image mediated by Tanizaki's 1921 film scenario for *Jasei no in* and one that combines the mysterious folk spirit with the image of a modern seductress. See Liang Luo, *The Avant-Garde and the Popular in Modern China: Tian Han and the Intersection of Performance and Politics* (Ann Arbor: University of Michigan Press, 2014), pp. 90–1.

6. 'A plot summary of "Yiyao Baishezhuan"', published in the 'local supplement' of *Shenbao*, 4 July 1926.

7. The caption to the image reads 'Ms. Hu Die as the White Snake in the costume drama *The Legend of the White Snake* by Tianyi Film Company', and the image is entitled 'A Scene from *The Legend of the White Snake*', in *Tuhua shidao* (*Pictorial Times*), 1926, no. 301, p. 4.

8. The caption reads 'Hu Die as Madame White' and the photograph is entitled 'Tianyi Film *The Legend of the White Snake*'. It was marked as a gift from a certain Li Yuanlong in the 'Yingju tekan' (special column on film and theatre) section of *Zhongguo sheying xuehui huibao* (Journal of the Chinese Photographers' Association), 1926, no. 40, p. 317.

9. *Byaku fujin no yoren*, directed by Toyoda Shirō, starring Yamaguchi Yoshiko (Li Xianglan), Toho and Shaw Brothers, 1956; and *Hakuja den*, directed by Yabushida Taiji and Okabe Kazuhiko, Toei Animation, 1958. The 1958 Japanese animation, not discussed in this chapter, premiered in the US as *Panda and the Magic Serpent* in 1961, with the Chinese-American actress Lisa Lu (Lu Yan) as the English voice actor for Bai-Niang (White Snake) and the Japanese American Actress Taka Miiko as Xiaoqing (Green Fish).

10. Influential *Huangmei diao* films from the Shaw Brothers include *Huatian cuo* (1962), *Liangzhu* (1963), *Feng huan chao* (1963), *Yu meiren* (1965) and *Sanxiao* (1969), among many others.

11. *Duanqiao*, or 'The Broken Bridge' scene, has long been one of the most performed highlights in the White Snake repertoire in Peking Opera and local operatic traditions. Green Snake has a dominating role in this scene, in which she is fiercely angry with Xu Xian, the husband of the White Snake, who in most versions, followed the Monk Fa Hai to the Golden Mountain Temple and deserted a pregnant White Snake out of suspicion.

12. *South China Morning Post*, 2 June 1976, p. 17.

13. For more on Li Han-hsiang's film career connecting Hong Kong and Taiwan, see Emilie Yeh Yueh-Yu, 'From Shaw Brothers to grand motion picture: localisation of *Huangmei Diao* films', in *Li Han-hsiang, Storyteller*, edited by Wong Ain-ling, Hong Kong Film Archive, 2007.

14. See 'Lin Ching Hsia was followed by an Indonesian merchant Mr Chen Tzu Hsing to Korea', in *Yingse shijie* (Cinemart), no. 96, December 1977, not

paginated; and 'Love of the White Snake', in *Yingse shijie* (Cinemart), no. 103, July 1978, pp. 54–5.

15. Lilian Lee (Lee Pik Wah), *Ching Se* (Green Snake), Taipei: Huangguan, 1993; *Ching Se* (Green Snake), directed by Tsui Hark, starring Maggie Cheung and Joey Wong, Hong Kong: Film Workshop, 1993; and *Qing She* (Green Snake), stage play, directed by Tian Qinxin, starring Qin Hailu and Yuan Quan, premiered at the 41st Hong Kong Art Festival, March 2013.

References

Anon. (1956), 'Japanese film success: most effective use of its colour, Berlin Festival', *South China Morning Post*, June 26.

Anon. (1977), 'Lin Ching Hsia was followed by an Indonesian merchant Mr Chen Tzu Hsing to Korea', *Yingse shijie* (Cinemart) 96, December, not paginated.

Bai, Huiyuan (2013), 'The Shaw Brothers tradition in the White Snake films – centered on the 1926 *Yiyao Baishezhuan* from the Tianyi Film Company', *Dianying yishu* (Film Art), 5:352, pp. 119–22.

Bernardi, Joanne (2001), *Writing in Light: the Silent Scenario and the Japanese Pure Film Movement*, Detroit: Wayne State University Press.

Bordwell, David (2009), 'Another Shaw production: anamorphic adventures in Hong Kong', <http://www.davidbordwell.net/essays/shaw.php> (last accessed 18 February 2017).

Chiba, Nobuo (1989), *Eiga to Tanizaki*, Tokyo: Seiabō.

Coates, Jennifer (2014), 'The shape-shifting diva: Yamaguchi Yoshiko and the national body', *Journal of Japanese and Korean Cinema* 6:1, pp. 23–38.

Feng, Menglong (comp.) [1624] (2005), 'Madam White is kept forever under Thunder Peak Tower', in *Stories to Caution the World: a Ming Dynasty Collection*, Shuhui Yang and Yunqin Yang (trans.), Washington, DC: University of Washington Press, vol. 2, p. 483.

First Films (1978), 'Love of the White Snake', *Yingse shijie* (*Cinemart*) 103, July, 54–5.

Freud, Sigmund (2003), *The Uncanny*, David Mclintock (trans.), London: Penguin Books.

Gordon, Jean (1962a), 'A fairy tale from old Cathay', *South China Morning Post*, 3 October, p. 4.

Gordon, Jean (1962b), 'The East prevails this week', *South China Morning Post*, 6 October, p. 4.

Gordon, Jean (1963), 'Films of suspense and novelty', *South China Morning Post*, 2 February, p. 4.

LaMarre, Thomas (2005), *Shadows on the Screen: Tanizaki Jun'ichirō on Cinema and 'Oriental' Aesthetics*, Ann Arbor: University of Michigan Press, 2005.

Lee, Sangjoon (2011), *The Transnational Asia Studio System: Cinema, Nation-state, and Globalization in Cold War Asia*, PhD Dissertation, New York University.

Luo, Liang (2014), *The Avant-garde and the Popular in Modern China: Tian*

Han and the Intersection of Performance and Politics, Ann Arbor: University of Michigan Press.

Robe (1965), 'Film reviews', *Variety*, 3 November.

Tanizaki, J. and Kurihara, T. [1921] (2001), 'The lust of the White Serpent', in Joanne Bernardi (ed.), *Writing in Light: the Silent Scenario and the Japanese Pure Film Movement*, Detroit: Wayne State University Press, pp. 300–4.

Tao, Fengzi (1926), 'The value of *The Legend of the White Snake* and *The Pearl Pagoda*', in *Tianyi tekan* (Special Issue of Tianyi Films) 8, pp. 60–1.

Ueda, Akinari [1776] (1983), *Ugetsu monogatari; Harusame monogatari*, M. Takada and H. Nakamura (eds), Tokyo: Shōgakkan.

Yamamoto, Kikuo (1983), *Nihon eiga ni okeru gaikoku eiga no eikyō: hikaku eigashi kenkyū*, Tokyo: Waseda Daigaku Shuppanbu.

Yeh Yueh-Yu, Emilie (2007), 'From Shaw Brothers to grand motion picture: localisation of *Huangmei Diao* Films', in *Li Han-hsiang, Storyteller*, Ain-ling Wong (ed.), Hong Kong: Hong Kong Film Archive, pp. 114–25.

CHAPTER 3

From Killer Snakes to Taxi Hunters: Hong Kong Horror in an Exploitation Context

Andy Willis

From the Shaw Brothers genre production line to the cycle of clones of Bruce Lee films that appeared in the wake of the superstar's death, Hong Kong cinema has long been seen as driven by raw commercial concerns. Like many other commercial film industries, most notably Hollywood, production in the Hong Kong film industry has also been focused on popular cycles of production. These have included phases when family melodramas, historical swordplay and kung fu films, screwball comedies and Triad-based crime films have all proved successful at the domestic and regional box office. As with other commercially focused film industries there has also been a low-budget sector within the Hong Kong business. Within this arena producers and directors have fashioned energetic, populist films that were designed to appeal to audiences' desire for works that contained sex and violence. The horror genre is an ideal vehicle to satiate these needs. This chapter will explore the work of film-makers who worked at this 'rougher' end of Hong Kong horror in the 1970s, 1980s and 1990s. As well as placing them into this exploitation context of production, it will discuss their excessive content and the visual style employed by directors such as Kuei Chih-hung (*The Killer Snakes*, 1974, the *Hex* series beginning in 1980), Danny Lee and Billy Tang (*Dr Lamb* (1992)) and Herman Yau (*The Eight Immortals Restaurant: The Untold Story* (1993), *Ebola Syndrome* (1996)) to deliver their exploitative content.

Pete Tombs has noted that the 1970s saw a shift in the type and style of horror films produced within the Hong Kong film industry. He argued that in previous decades stories that revolved around ghosts and spirits had been prevalent but, 'The arrival of the horror film in Hong Kong in the seventies coincided with a more explicit depiction of sex in locally produced movies. Several films explored the connection between the two in a uniquely Hong Kong fashion' (Tombs 1997: 29). One of the ways in which that arrival was distinct was the fact that some of the rawer films – such as those of Kuei Chih-hung discussed below – were produced by one of the territory's major producers, the Shaw Brothers studio. In an interview about working in this era, actor Kam Kwok-leung, who appeared in *The Killer Snakes*, suggests that the studio's 'attitude was rather shameless; they threw in nude scenes or sex scenes regardless of the genre [. . .] As long as they could insert these scenes, they didn't mind throwing logic out of the window. *The Killer Snakes* was no exception' (Li and Tse, 2011: 49). It is due to this attitude that it is possible to argue that Shaw Brothers were working concurrently both sides of the Hong Kong film, producing on the one hand the more respectable and lavish costume dramas that they are famous for while not being averse to embracing a more exploitation driven sensibility when they thought it might result in a profit. It is through examples such as *The Killer Snakes* that we can concretely see that during this period Shaw Brothers worked in both the top end of production but also the more commercial, exploitation side of the industry.

Kuei Chih-hung: Working on the Edge of the System

Director Kuei Chih-hung had spent most of the early 1970s making a number of successful action-orientated films for Shaw Brothers. These included the contemporary set *The Teahouse* (1974) and *Big Brother Cheng* (1975), two films that in their urban settings clearly spoke to the economic conditions in Hong Kong at the time and sought to bring to the screen a more realistic representation of the city's working class communities. Wong Chi-fai argues that Kuei:

> has always taken the perspective of a social critic whenever possible, making his films expressions of his concern, love and hatred towards the happenings around him. His films reflect the reality of current affairs, with a focus on social incidents that affect people's livelihood. (Wong 2011: 75)

Alongside these films, which are now seen as some of his most significant works, Kuei would operate within recognisable genres such as the historical martial arts film, most clearly with *Killer Constable* (1980), and the horror film. Matthew Cheng has argued that 'Kuei was one of the few Hong Kong directors to specialize in horror. His subversive films explored three major themes: contemporary social problems, the sexual exploitation of women and the worlds of the supernatural' (Cheng 2011: 88). The horror genre was an arena where these concerns could be explored in a commercially viable form, keeping the director within the Hong Kong film system even if on its more interesting fringes.

Kuei's first horror film, *The Killer Snakes*, brings together the social conscience of his contemporary urban dramas with the use of a more explicit set of horror codes and conventions. Pete Tombs acknowledges that:

> *The Killer Snakes* was a Shaw Brothers production and one of their darkest ever films. Although inspired by the Hollywood hit *Willard*, *The Killer Snakes* entirely lacks the sentimentality of the American film in its depiction of urban underbelly poverty and sexual frustration leading to violence. (Tombs 1997: 29)

Like *The Teahouse* and *Big Brother Cheng*, both notable for their settings outside the glitzier side of Hong Kong life, '*The Killer Snakes* is a downbeat look at life in the back alleys of Hong Kong. No modern skyscrapers and glistening shopping malls here' (Ibid.). In a similar vein Wong identifies the film as being one that displays a clear social conscience, stating that it touches 'upon the issues of the livelihood of immigrants and adolescent crime' (Wong 2011: 75). At the core of the film is the idea of exploitation, both as a style of film-making and as a central issue that drives the film's narrative.

As I shall explore later in this chapter, the idea of an exploitation cinema from Hong Kong is often reductively linked to the Category III films of the late 1980s and 1990s. There is, however, clear evidence that an earlier Hong Kong exploitation cinema existed in the 1970s, and closer to the mainstream than many critics writing of the period acknowledge. Certainly, one must begin to see films such as *The Killer Snakes* clearly operating in that arena if one accepts Mark David Ryan's definition that:

> Exploitation filmmaking is generally characterised by gratuitous or 'excessive' nudity, extreme violence, gore, explosions and so on, driven by sensational marketing, and generally regarded by 'high-brow' critics as 'bad film' rather than quality or serious cinema. (Ryan 2010: 845)

The Killer Snakes: Revenge of the Exploited

The transgressive potential of *The Killer Snakes* is apparent from its opening scenes. A young boy is at a desk, perhaps doing his homework, while off-screen we at first hear and then, when the film cuts, see a close up of a woman's mouth as she says, 'hit me, hit me again – hit me as hard as you can.' This shot is accompanied by the crack of a whip on the soundtrack. In response to what he hears, the boy takes a snake from a box on the desk and the camera zooms in on his hand gently stroking its head. That shot dissolves to the title *The Killer Snakes* which appears superimposed on a shot of a pile of writhing snakes and accompanied by discordant music on the soundtrack. From the outset, with these sounds and images *The Killer*

Snakes lays out the exploitation territory it will explore. Following this opening, the titles fade and the image of the snakes changes from being in a washed-out colour palette to one that contains much more vibrant colours. After the title we are shown a man confidently handling snakes and cutting out their gall bladders whilst his hands are bitten, suggesting some kind of an immunity to their bites. A longer, wider shot reveals the interior of a small store with a couple sitting at a table waiting to drink the liquid that is drained from the snake's gall bladder. They are clearly signalled as wealthier than the workers in the store by their smart and modish fashion. As their outfits seem expensive when compared to the simple clothes of the shop worker the use of costume here clearly marks them out as outsiders from the poorer milieu of the shop.

This sequence in the shop is followed by a long, wide shot of a rundown district of Hong Kong, indicated by refuse piled up on the streets, and buildings that are clearly in a state of disrepair. A man appears from what seems to be some kind of corrugated iron shack and walks across a piece of wasteland to dispose of more rubbish. In a sequence of closer shots we see this man intercut with brief shots of the neighbourhood showing people going about their daily business on street stalls, selling goods and offering services such as haircuts. The couple from the snake store then appear on the street and the character carrying the rubbish turns and accidentally collides with them, falling on top of the woman. In retaliation, the well-dressed man beats him. This is the first of a number of sequences in which the character of Chi Hung is beaten by those who see themselves as his betters or who wish to exploit him. Ultimately, it is these beatings that set in motion the film's narrative of revenge. However, it is important to highlight the film's use of social/class distinctions here, which are shown to drive Chi Hung's feelings of being an outsider, marginalised by the wider, aspirational society.

The film then cuts to the interior of a shack where Chi Hung is lying on a bed, blood on his face from the beating. The sequence that follows shows the run-down place where he sleeps, with makeshift furniture and surrounded on the walls by pictures of women tied up with rope and other images of a sadomasochist nature taken from pornographic books and magazines. The *mise en scène* within these images links Chi Hung to the boy in the pre-credit sequence. In doing so there is a suggestion that the character has not recovered from the traumas of his childhood witnessed in the pre-credit sequence, hinting that these moments contributed to his being a psychologically troubled adult marginalised by mainstream society and often unable to articulate his inner feelings. This is anchored when the film next utilises a montage of the S&M images on the walls and magazines accompanied by female moaning and a discordant score on the soundtrack. The sequence progresses from using these still images of women to shots of Chi Hung with a naked woman, then of him whipping her. The way in which the sequence is constructed, with images of the couple superimposed over those of him lying down on the bed as its opening shot, suggesting this is his fantasy rather than a concrete memory. This series of shots creates the impression of a disturbed character who we later learn has no qualifications and suffers from a stammer, both further positioning him as an outsider. *The Killer Snakes* is a film that suggests that this social environment is something that contributes to Chi Hung's personal problems. By linking the environment and the actions of its lead character, *The Killer Snakes* is a work that challenges those watching to try and understand what made Chi Hung what he is and not just dismiss his actions simplistically as that of a clichéd generic monster.

One way in which this is done is through Chi Hung's various attempts at a 'normal' life. For example, he attempts to develop a relationship with Hsiu Chuan, a young woman who works on one of the stalls near where he lives. It is his inability to navigate this potentially positive relationship that is one of the factors that drives him to the verge of a psychological breakdown, which in turn leads to his uncontrolled desire for revenge. The pressures of 'normality' are further exposed when he takes a job as a restaurant delivery person only to encounter some street thugs loitering at a brothel. They make fun of him and then, in the street, attack him, strip him, steal his money and break his delivery tray – thus taking his livelihood away from him. When he further attempts to act within the norms of society and arranges a visit to the cinema with Hsiu Chuan, she misses the meeting due to her father's terminal illness. Given his fragile state, her non-appearance sends him into a rage that sees him destroy the stall where she works during the day. Not realising her father has died, his impotent frenzy is directed at the wrong place, ultimately destroying the environment in which he lives and making the chance of his finding happiness with Hsiu Chuan even more unlikely.

Frustrated, psychologically fragile and socially isolated, Chi Hung befriends a snake that has escaped from the store next door. Talking to it as if it is human, he enlists its help as he begins to take revenge on those who have exploited him due to his social situation. The snakes become the way he can resist the poverty and exploitation that he has to live with and become the organ through which he is able to rebel against the situation he is placed in. They help him battle and kill the street thugs who attacked him, see off Hsiu Chuan's mean-spirited landlady who evicts her when she cannot pay the rent due to her father's death, and take revenge on the cruel snake-store owner, who is clearly represented as a capitalist exploiter who does not respect his workers, or for that matter the snakes that his livelihood depends upon.

Following the relative success of *The Killer Snakes*, Kuei would continue to return to horror, making a variety of films in this genre such as *Ghost Eyes* (1974), *Hex* (1980), *Hex vs Witchcraft* (1980), *Hex After Hex* (1982), *Curse of Evil* (1982), and *The Boxer's Omen* (1984). *Hex* is good example of this work. It is a period piece shot entirely in the studio and is designed to appeal to its audience by combining horror elements with soft-core titillation through its relatively risqué content. For example, in the latter stages of the film the character of Leung Yi Wah, played by Chan Sze-Kai, is seen naked and tattooed with esoteric symbols. *Hex* and its sequels were once again made for the Shaw Brothers studio and are further examples of how Hong Kong's exploitation cinema rubbed shoulders with more mainstream productions in the 1970s and 1980s. However, as it is not set in a contemporary reality the film's ability to deal with social issues within the horror genre is more limited.

Despite their attempts to deliver classic horror tropes combined with audience pleasing elements of sex, the likes of *The Killer Snakes, Hex* and its sequels would be swept aside in the late 1980s by the rise of an even rawer form of exploitation cinema that drew on real-life stories, ripped them from the headlines and represented them to audiences in graphic detail. Many of these films were to find themselves clustered within a new category of Hong Kong films, Category III, so called because of the 'adults only' censorship label the authorities stamped on their release. However, there can be little doubt that films such as those of Kuei Chih-hung, that is works that combined classic exploitation elements such as sex and violence, laid the groundwork for these future exploitation trends within the Hong Kong film industry. What is noteworthy regarding Kuei's work in particular are the ways in which the films are explicitly set in a milieu inhabited by an often marginalised and economically brittle Hong Kong working class and begin to suggest that the transgressive behaviour of their characters is at least partially caused by the social and economic conditions they find themselves in. This is something that would be repeated by directors such as Herman Yau who would come to prominence in the era of the Category III film.

Category III: Definitions and Contexts

Introduced in 1988 through the 'Movie Screening Ordinance Cap.392', Category III films are those that are 'Approved for Exhibition Only to

Persons who Have Attained the Age of 18 Years'. Products made for the
market that quickly developed for Category III films can clearly be seen
to be part of a burgeoning Hong Kong exploitation sector. These films,
as exploitation films did elsewhere around the world and as noted above,
offered audiences 'cheap' thrills usually based on images that contained
sex or violence – and often both. Category III films were also quickly
made and released to create an immediate impact and attract audiences
looking for something illicit, possibly dangerous, and most of all offering
perspectives that were different from those found in the mainstream. As
Darrell W. Davis and Yeh Yueh-yu have noted, these productions quickly
became a significant part of Hong Kong film production. Writing in 2001
they argued that:

> Category III occupies a dominant place in the Hong Kong film market; it takes up
> an inordinate amount of screen time compared to its built-in age restriction and
> its miniscule coverage by critics. This 'adult' fare represents a huge share of the
> film entertainment in Hong Kong, and even more when small-screen formats are
> accounted for. (Davis and Yeh 2001: 13)

Typical Category III films include soft-core offerings such as *Sex and Zen*
(1991) and its sequels, and often imported the titillation of soft-core into
other cycles, for example the more action orientated, but, as its title suggests, still titillating *Naked Killer* (1992).

Whilst the majority of Category III films simply reflected troubling
aspects of Hong Kong society, this content also enabled many of them to
be read as potentially subversive works. Alongside this, the low production values of many of these films meant that they did not suffer from
the excesses of higher budget productions. Davis and Yeh put it thus:
'Category III films are a microcosm of Hong Kong cinema as a whole,
and they reveal the tug-of-war between transgression and control at work
throughout Hong Kong media' (Ibid.). While Julian Stringer argues:

> In being more indicative of social trends sidestepped by more 'respectable' Hong
> Kong films, the genre serves a distinct political function. It is 'adult' enough to deal
> with taboo subject matter and popular enough to provide an airing for repressed
> social issues. (Stringer 1999: 363)

As with other forms of exploitation cinema, Category III films were able to
speak to burning issues within Hong Kong society in the 1990s and 2000s
and some film-makers, like earlier examples such as Kuei Chih-hung,
were able to find space within the form to address contemporary social and
political concerns. For Stringer:

Shocking subjects combined into new commercial hooks, the better to squeeze the last dregs out of an uncertain economic situation. In the countdown to Mainland China's resumption of sovereign control over Hong Kong on July 1 1997, Category 3 films testified to a severe loss of confidence in the city's political stability. In these films serial killers are pursued at night by corrupt and incompetent cops, families break up, the media is ineffectual, triads control all businesses, and prostitutes hang out on every street corner. Such representations of eroticism and cruelty can be read as the death dance of a wicked, economically decadent city. (Stringer 1999: 362)

Within this argument is a vision of Category III films as transgressive social commentaries which is particularly useful when one is interested in seeing some of them as the successors to the likes of *The Killer Snakes*. In this context, the space of exploitation, where explicit content is all that producers demand in their search for profit, clearly allows for space to create social commentary. At the core of some of the most interesting examples of Category III films that attempt this is an exploration of class in Hong Kong, a city that in many ways offers an example of a hyper-extenuated version of raw capitalism and where the economic structures seem almost designed to leave behind those who cannot contribute to its success.

It is therefore perhaps not surprising that some of the most insightful writing about Category III films has attempted to move beyond a simple celebration of their excess and perceived transgressive nature and links their 'outsider' and marginal status to their use of working–class characters and settings. In doing so these writers create a politicised reading of the Category III films of the 1990s, works that were produced at a time of great social anxiety as Hong Kong moved towards a unification with the People's Republic of China (PRC). For example, Tony Williams, who has written perceptively about a range of Hong Kong films, argues that some of the key Category III films, *Dr Lamb, The Untold Story, Underground Banker* and *The Untold Story 2* are 'all set in a lower-depths environment representing the dark side of the Hong Kong economic miracle' (Williams 2002: 62). In a similar fashion, Julian Stringer has argued that 'the city's most graphic films are everywhere bearing witness to and exploiting the class resentments of its detritus – that is to say, of those who have resolutely failed to work its economic miracle' (Stringer 1999: 363–4). Both of these writers explore *Dr Lamb* as a film that is typical of this trend. On the surface this is clear exploitation material: the story focuses on a taxi driver who is questioned by the police after a photo shop worker is alarmed by the content of some of the pictures he processes and reports them. In police custody the driver confesses to a series of brutal killings of women which are then shown in flashback. In this instance, as in other films based on 'true-life' incidents, such as *The Eight Immortals Restaurant: The Untold Story* (better known by its abbreviated title *The Untold Story*) and *Taxi Hunter* (1993), the link to the horror label comes from the excessive violence and sadistic blood-letting of the serial killer central characters that is present rather than an all-out utilisation of familiar horror genre codes and conventions. The result is something of a lurid hybrid of social melodrama and gory violence, the excess of which has led to more fan-focused commentators having no problem in labelling them as horror films. For example, in an article titled 'Can you stomach these Category III gross-out horror films?' the *Dazed Digital* website states that *Dr Lamb* is 'a weird and wonderful slice and dice sickie about a taxi driver who has sex with dead bodies' (Waddell, n.d.). The definition of what might be considered horror films may be stretched in such instances to incorporate these violent examples of Category III works that on the surface may at first seem to exist in other genres.

Herman Yau: Category III's Social Commentator

One of the most distinctive film-makers to gain attention for his work in the Category III arena in the 1990s was Herman Yau. Yau first emerged in the late 1980s as a director of low-budget films as well as being a cinematographer of some note on Category III films such as *Sentenced to Hang* (1989) and bigger budget, more mainstream projects for the likes of director Tsui Hark. Since then he has balanced a developing profile in both roles with contributing to the scripts for a number of his own films. In the mid-1990s Yau would make a series of films that cemented his status as one of the most prolific and interesting directors working in the horror/ social commentary sphere of Category III, producing work that offered both images of excessive gore and strong elements of social critique. In doing so, Yau is a director whose work intersects with the potential political readings of Category III offered by Williams and Stringer. Indeed, the latter discusses Yau's *The Untold Story* in some detail, arguing that it is a film where 'those who live on the outer margins of Hong Kong's neon postmodern utopia are the ones doomed to suffer' (Stringer 1999: 370). Such an observation, combined with his rigorous analysis of the film's exploration of class, clearly identify Yau's horror work as being of some note. This point is echoed by Williams who argues that, 'Despite its graphic violence, *The Untold Story* is not to be dismissed as a sleazy, gratuitous production. It also deals with real-life social issues involving violence and exploitation in Hong Kong society' (Williams 2002: 65).

While May 1993 saw the release of Yau's *The Untold Story*, a film often labelled as a work of horror due to its fetid atmosphere and 'in your face' levels of gore, October of that year also saw the opening of another of his Category III films, *Taxi Hunter*. This film is less obviously a work within the horror genre particularly as its main narrative drive is the revenge of its central character on the cruel world around him. However, the blood-spattered deaths and the manic actions of the film's central character does, it can be argued, push the last hour of the film in that direction. Once again, as in *The Untold Story*, the lead in *Taxi Hunter* is performed by Anthony Wong. In this instance he plays Ah-Kin, a mild mannered mid-level worker for an insurance company whose world collapses when his pregnant wife is killed by a taxi driver. Whilst the class milieu of the central character in this instance is firmly that of the lower middle-class, white-collar worker, Yau and his collaborators once again bring a strong level of social critique to the film. Here, once more we are presented with Hong Kong's cut-throat capitalism running amok, in this instance in the form of the city's taxi industry. Drivers are represented as characters with no respect and who are not averse to ripping off their customers, behaving rudely and refusing point-blank fares they can't be bothered to take. At its crudest the film shows the city's taxi drivers as part of a basic, and extremely ruthless, supply and demand economy. This results in the fact that they can behave as they like even though their profession is, at least on the surface, one that provides a service for the public. However, *Taxi Hunter* offers a level of complexity beyond this simple picture.

Ah-Kin works for an insurance company and that equally cut-throat and exploitative world is also presented within *Taxi Hunter* in an unsympathetic way. Following his slide into depression due to the death of his wife and unborn child, Ah-Kin is warned by his boss for not hitting his targets, told that he will not now be considered for promotion and has it unsympathetically explained that he needs to pull himself together and not bring the outside world to work. The boss's response to Ah-Kin's situation recalls the earlier words of his colleague 'Fatty' who warned him about his closing a high number of contracts as he is raising the boss's expectations and may not be able to keep up these numbers. By foregrounding two equally problematic representations of basic capitalism *Taxi Hunter* manages to offer a logical image of an uncaring, inhumane system that cares little for individuals and their needs. As Tony Williams puts it, 'Social Darwinist influences in the tiger economy eventually lead to a violent cataclysm' (Williams 2002: 68). By anchoring Ah-Kin's violent action with a sense of it being in some way a logical, if exaggerated, response to the world around him and how the system spits out its victims, *Taxi Hunter*'s social concerns can be linked to the likes of *The Killer*

Snakes, once again showing how Hong Kong exploitation cinema offers a rich space for film-makers who wish to do more within their work than achieve simple commercial success.

Conclusion

Film-makers who are interested in making social comments within their work have often found an accommodating space within the field of exploitation films. This has been the case in a range of international contexts from Roger Corman's New World Pictures in the US in the early 1970s to the boom in horror film co-production that took place in Spain during the same decade (Willis 2003, 2005). The work of Kuei Chih-hung in the 1970s and Herman Yau in the early days of Category III in the 1990s shows that horror films produced on the exploitation fringes of the Hong Kong film industry were also able to engage critically with the social structures of the city of those times. These films are inhabited by working-class characters living on the edge of poverty, and in these low-budget horror films film-makers are able to explore the extremes of this and the way in which many of Hong Kong's inhabitants are on the verge of destruction due to their economic vulnerability which leads to psychological problems or drives them to extreme acts of violence. This form of politicised film-making that is driven by a desire to explore social inequality shows that some of the most distinctive voices within the Hong Kong film industry could be heard on the margins not within the mainstream. For this reason, it is always vitally important to revisit these outer fringes as well as the mainstream successes of particular eras when one seeks to understand the impact of genres such as horror in particular historical moments.

References

Cheng, Matthew (2011), 'Twilight zone – evil in the atheist world of Kuei Chih-hung', in Sam Ho and Li Cheuk-to (eds), *Kuei Chih-hung, the Rebel in the System*, Hong Kong: Hong Kong Film Archive, pp. 88–91.

Davis, Darrell W. and Yeh Yueh-yu (2001), 'Warning! Category III: the other Hong Kong cinema', *Film Quarterly*, 54:4 (summer), pp. 12–26.

Li, Cheuk-to and Alvin Tse (2011), 'Romancing the snakes: an interview with Kam Kwok-leung', in Sam Ho and Cheuk-to Li (eds), *Kuei Chih-hung, the Rebel in the System*, Hong Kong: Hong Kong Film Archive, pp. 46–50.

Ryan, Mark David (2010), 'Towards an understanding of Australian genre cinema and entertainment: beyond the limitations of 'Ozploitation' discourse', *Continuum: Journal of Media and Cultural Studies*, 24:6, pp. 843–54.

Stringer, Julian (1999), 'Category 3: Sex and Violence in Postmodern Hong Kong', in Christopher Sharrett (ed.), *Mythologies of Violence in Postmodern Media*, Detroit: Wayne State University Press, pp. 361–79.

Tombs, Pete (1997), *Mondo Macabro: Weird and Wonderful Cinema Around the World*, London: Titan Books.

Waddell, Calum (no date), 'Can you stomach these Category III gross-out horror films?' *Dazed*, <http://www.dazeddigital.com/artsandculture/article/27110/1/can-you-stomach-these-category-iii-gross-out-horror-films> (last accessed 28 February 2017).

Williams, Tony (2002), 'Hong Kong social horror: tragedy and farce in Category 3', *Post Script: Essays in Film and the Humanities*, 21:3 (summer), pp. 61–71.

Willis, Andy (2003), 'Spanish horror and the flight from 'art' cinema 1967–1973', in Mark Jancovich, Antonio Lazario-Reboll, Julian Stringer and Andy Willis (eds), *Defining Cult Movies*, Manchester: Manchester University Press, pp. 71–83.

Willis, Andy (2005), ' *La semana de asesinio*: Spanish horror as subversive text', in Steven J. Schneider and Tony Williams (eds), *Horror International*, Detroit: Wayne State University Press, pp. 163–79.

Wong, Chi-fai (2011), 'From the studio to the streets', in Sam Ho and Li Cheuk-to (eds), *Kuei Chih-hung, the Rebel in the System*, Hong Kong: Hong Kong Film Archive, pp. 72–5.

CHAPTER 4

The Enduring Cult of *The Bride with White Hair*: Chivalry and the Monstrous Other in the Hong Kong Fantasy-Horror

Daniel Martin

The Hong Kong horror film is replete with a variety of monstrous murderers, from ghosts and ghouls, demons and snakes, hopping corpses and vacuous vampires, to psychotic assassins and vengeful killers. None, however, are quite like the eponymous woman warrior of *The Bride with White Hair* (1993), a character full of contradiction: sympathetic and terrifying, brutal and tender, merciless and righteous; a fascinating anomaly in the canon of Hong Kong horror's wronged women and vindictive spirits.

The Bride with White Hair, based on a popular novel serialised in Hong Kong in the 1950s, tells the tale of a heroic swordsman's ill-fated love affair with his ferocious enemy, a woman raised by wolves and transformed by hatred into a white-haired killer. Ronny Yu's influential 1993 film, alongside its sequel (released the same year), has elevated the figure of the frosty-follicled executioner into one of the most enduring icons of the Hong Kong horror film. The timelessness and mysticism of the story lends itself to a highly hybridised type of horror, offering *wuxia* (swordplay), magical fantasy, romance and erotic scintillation alongside bloody fights and savage violence in a deeply ambiguous moral landscape.

The generic fusion evident in the film results in a profound challenge to traditional notions of chivalry, especially for its honourable swordsman protagonist, who finds his loyalty divided and is often aghast at the cruelty of both his enemies and allies. The magical elements present are, too, a source of horror, in the form of the film's ultimate malevolent antagonist, a pair of conjoined twins who use sorcery as a weapon of domination and manipulation. The monstrous depiction of the twins as a horrifying genetic 'other' is problematic, particularly in the context of wider debates on disability in the horror genre.

The Bride with White Hair reflects and repackages traditional genre patterns for audiences in Hong Kong and around the world. Indeed, *The Bride with White Hair* was one of the first Hong Kong cult/horror films to find an international niche audience, appealing to fans for its supposedly transgressive and erotic content in a way that anticipated Tartan Films' influential 'Asia Extreme' brand. This chapter therefore analyses the film in terms of its generic hybridity, its relationship to traditions in Hong Kong and East Asian horror, its representations of morality and disability, and its international marketing and reception in the context of broader trends in the global circulation of cult Hong Kong horror of the 1990s.

The Good, the Bad and the Ugly: Morality, Disability and Otherness

One of the core themes of *The Bride with White Hair* is morality; characters struggle to do the right thing in complex circumstances, and every wicked deed has a rationale. The plot of the film revolves around individuals who feel alienated in their own social worlds. Swordsman Cho Yi-hang is the favoured disciple of the Wu Tang warrior clan, yet his impulsive and kind-hearted nature often puts him at odds with leadership, and his peers. His encounter with a mysterious nameless 'Wolf Girl' leads to a passionate romance, and his decision to become a clanless recluse. The Wolf Girl, meanwhile, is beholden to an evil cult who oppose Wu Tang; she must endure a torturous ritual to obtain her freedom. The cult's leader is a pair of conjoined twins: the brother desires the Wolf Girl, and, driven by petty jealousy, the siblings slay the Wu Tang's master and frame the Wolf Girl in the process. Yi-hang's trust in his lover wavers, and the two are divided. The Wolf Girl's sense of betrayal is so intense it triggers a physical transformation: as her hair turns white, she slaughters Yi-hang's remaining allies and aids him only briefly, in a final showdown with the monstrous twins, before departing.

The emotional journey of the 'Wolf Girl', from warrior to lover to vengeance incarnate, is symbolised by her name. The character is initially nameless, referred to simply as 'Wolf Girl' as a way to describe her ferocity and abnormality, but also diminish her humanity. First seen in a dreamy sequence, as a young girl, she is instantly coded as different, magical, like a spirit of the forest, and she commits an act of simple kindness, saving young Yi-hang from bloodthirsty wolves. When the two meet again as adults, it is only after the Wolf Girl has experienced love (and sex) with Yi-hang that she becomes a 'complete' person, gifted with a name: Lien Ni-chang. This identity, too, is discarded, however, in the bitter transformation of the character into the eponymous avenger: the loss of her name symbolic of her regression to a feral killer, both superhuman in her magical/martial power and inhumane in her disregard for other life.

The Bride is a deeply conflicted character, driven by passion and often

restrained by her sense of obligation. Her violent acts of aggression are
frequently justified, however, by the bleak moral landscape of the film. In
her first appearance as an adult, the Wolf Girl swoops into a chaotic battle-
field and brutally slaughters enemy soldiers – bisecting her enemies with
a single crack of her whip. Rather than being positioned as a symbol of
fear, in this sequence the Wolf Girl functions as a force of just retribution.
In the preceding moments, the soldiers she butchers were shown committing unforgivable atrocities: attacking a civilian village, unarmed men
were killed, women were raped and a child was beheaded. Thus, while
the soldiers themselves fear the Wolf Girl as an other-worldly 'witch', she
clearly has the sympathy of the audience, generating a very different sense
of terror: righteous, rather than frightful.

In the climactic battle, however, and at the moment of her irrevocable
transformation into the merciless white-haired 'Bride', the character's violent retribution has far less moral authority. Pitted against her lover's clan
due to the machinations of her former master, the Bride lashes out indiscriminately, massacring all who stand against her, in spite of Yi-hang's
fruitless attempts to restore peace. The Bride's sense of betrayal is acute,
and while her anger is justified, her victims are largely innocent. The killings that follow depict the character as a monstrous other, as a seemingly
fatal stabbing triggers her transformation into an undead and undying
avenger. She weaponises her newfound telekinetic power, and uses long
strands of her newly white hair as impossibly powerful prehensile tendrils,
beheading scores of enemies simultaneously.

This physical and moral transformation leaves Yi-hang aghast, as the
Bride's insurmountable difference, or 'otherness', is made visually literal. The character thus joins a long tradition of supernatural women in
the Hong Kong and broader East Asian horror genre; female characters
set apart from 'normal' humans by some monstrous aspect. Similar figures have appeared in Hollywood horror, from the eponymous *Bride of
Frankenstein* (James Whale, 1935) to the progressively more terrifyingly
transformed Regan of *The Exorcist* (William Friedkin, 1973). To a much
larger degree, however, the vengeful female ghost is iconic of East Asian
horror, a cycle that became most prominent in the West following the
release of the Japanese movie *Ring* (Hideo Nakata, 1998). Similar figures
appear in South Korean and Hong Kong horror, too, with some significant deviations.

The ghostly spirit of Hong Kong horror is typically female, as the gender
of the 'other' reflects the diminished social rights of women, historically
(Yu 1989: 22). Younger, unmarried women are more likely to become
ghosts (O'Brien 2003: 7), adding a tragic dimension to their premature

passing. There is no sense that these female spectres are any less powerful than men; indeed, equality of gender is a core value of the depiction of undead and immortal spirits (Teo 1989: 43). These qualities are intrinsic to the Wolf Girl: she lacks autonomy, unable to pursue romance without incurring the wrath of her cult master. However, the character's vengeful nature sets her apart from many of Hong Kong cinema's female ghosts, who are frequently depicted as lovelorn and often harmless figures: the pitiful courtesan of *Rouge* (Stanley Kwan, 1988) haunts a young couple only to enlist their aid in finding her long-lost lover, while the amorous ghost of *Mr. Vampire* (Ricky Lau, 1985) chooses to free her hapless quarry from her enchanting bonds rather than do him harm. These ghosts stand in sharp contrast to their counterparts in Japanese and South Korean horror, who typically favour violent retribution: while Japanese virgin ghosts like *Ring*'s Sadako lash out from the afterlife with indiscriminate rage, the Korean *wonhon* chooses her victims carefully, enacting a brutal but entirely justified revenge on guilty sinners (Lee 2013).

The Wolf Girl of *The Bride with White Hair* is an oddity in this tradition: far more violent than many ghosts of Hong Kong cinema, she also kills arbitrarily, much like many of Japan's undead avengers. Yet, crucially, the Wolf Girl, even in her supernatural final form of the white-haired bride, is not properly a ghost: her death and rebirth is figurative, not literal. The Hong Kong horror offers many varieties of female ghoul, however, and the 'vixen' is another. Described as more playful and sexually voracious than the female ghost, the fox-spirit vixen is further removed from humanity, a magical spirit with more malevolent intentions (Lam 1989: 59). The Wolf Girl hardly fits this description, either, in spite of her association with vulpine predators and the passionate lovemaking scenes that cement the relationship between her and Yi-hang. Instead, the Wolf Girl/Bride must be understood as anomalous: an odd figure combining aspects of the ghost, the vixen, and drawing further on traditions from magical fantasy, rather than horror.

While the bride herself represents a morally complex anomaly, in the context of Hong Kong horror, her lover, Yi-hang, can be understood as morally conflicted in a manner that expresses some of the core characteristics of the *wuxia* hero. *Wuxia* films are part of a long-standing tradition in literature and film that reached a peak of popularity in Hong Kong cinema from the 1950s to the 1970s, and are more recently a mainstay of Mainland Chinese film production. These are action films of swordplay and impossible feats of heroism, showcasing the staunch dedication to justice of chivalrous errant knights (Teo 1997: 109). Yet while the *wuxia* protagonist typically behaves in a 'supermoral' way, righteous beyond expectation (Hunt 2003: 203), they often encounter opposition from allies, or are branded outlaws. This type of hero is 'rebellious and non-conformist' in nature (Teo 2009: 99) and demonstrates an ethical code best described as 'situational justice' (Schroeder 2004: 15). The *wuxia* hero will disobey laws, break rules and betray allies if it serves the greater good. The extent to which *The Bride with White Hair* must be understood as a generic hybrid of both *wuxia* and horror is reflected in its depiction of this trope.

Honourable Yi-hang is the film's moral compass: early scenes depict him protecting a family from their own brutal patriarch and literally saving a lamb from slaughter. These actions, however, elicit the wrath of his clan leadership, and he is scolded and punished for committing the crimes of theft and murder. Unrepentant, Yi-hang's defence is to remind his superiors that he was taught to be chivalrous, regardless of the context. Although he is a skilled fighter, Yi-hang has a gentle nature, and desires nothing more than a life of peace; in one scene, he uses a blade of grass as a weapon, rather than a sword, signalling his distaste at killing.

Indeed, Yi-hang seems especially out of place in his bloodthirsty peer group, and constantly questions orders, becoming more and more appalled at the cruelty of his supposedly virtuous warrior clan. The Wu Tang clan are frequently as monstrous as their enemies, brutally and sadistically murdering defenceless victims like the marauding hoodlums of an American horror film like Wes Craven's *The Last House on the Left* (1972). One of Yi-hang's senior allies orders a group of suspected infiltrators executed, mercilessly claiming it is 'better to wrongly kill one hundred' than let a single guilty party escape. One of Yi-hang's many acts of compassion involves sparing a desperate fleeing family, helping to deliver the baby of the injured wife (who dies in childbirth), and giving the surviving father and infant a valuable piece of jewellery as a gesture of financial support. When Yi-hang's jealous, vindictive ally Lu Hua discovers his act of kindness, she slaughters the innocent man (and, presumably, his hours-old baby) for no other reason than spite.

Yi-hang's disgust with the immorality of his allies leads to his decision to leave his clan and live as a recluse with the Wolf Girl, Ni-chang. His masters object, especially since Yi-hang is their favoured protégé, being groomed for leadership, but Yi-hang refutes their expectations that he acts against his convictions, declaring he 'can't believe being kind-hearted is a fault'. The Wu Tang clan is therefore positioned in a morally contradictory way: a proud and supposedly honorable clan of warriors, upholding order in a chaotic world, yet actually as brutal and heartless as any of their enemies. The final confrontation with the Wolf Girl as 'Bride' presents a massacre in which both sides have the moral conviction of preserving justice, yet both can rightly be described as merciless and monstrous.

Indeed, the horror genre is, in the broadest sense, fundamentally concerned with the opposition between normality and monstrosity (Sutton 2014: 76). *The Bride with White Hair* represents this not just through the reprehensible brutality of the Wolf Girl and the Wu Tang clan, but most effectively – and problematically – through its depiction of the evil conjoined twins as the ultimate antagonist. Inspired partially by the notorious carnival horror *Freaks* (Tod Browning, 1932), the twins were created by director Ronny Yu for the film, a major deviation from the original novel on which the story is based (Teo 2001). Described by one reviewer as 'the strangest of villains' (Odham Stokes 2015: 221), the monstrous twins embody a number of persistent tropes in the depiction of disability and genetic abnormality in the horror film.

The twins are a brother–sister pair, conjoined at the spine; they rule as 'Lord of the Supreme Cult', and, oddly, have only one name: Chi Wu-shuang. Their lack of discrete names indicates their status within the film: neither sibling is treated entirely individually, and thus neither is quite regarded as completely human. The male twin clearly dominates the pair, functioning as leader and decision-maker, with his sister primarily offering sardonic commentary; both are cruel and vindictive. The brother murders one of their own followers with a single magical gesture as punishment for coughing during a speech. The twins resent being exiled by the warrior clans twenty years earlier, and use the Wolf Girl as an instrument of revenge. Frequently in the horror film disability/abnormality is associated with sin (Sutton 2014: 76), and the extent to which the twins are justified in their campaign of vengeance against the Wu Tang clan is unclear, since both parties are shown capable of merciless violence. Nonetheless, the twins are consistently positioned as beyond redemption, as a great evil that must be banished.

Horror films consistently express a desire to 'eject or eradicate the monstrous and disabled body' (Sutton 2014: 74), and a significant number of slasher film antagonists exhibit some form of disability or physical difference. Freddy Krueger, first introduced in Wes Craven's *A Nightmare on Elm Street* (1984), is disfigured due to severe burns; Jason Voorhees of the *Friday the 13th* film series is mentally disabled and facially deformed. Both characters frequently embark on murderous rampages, indiscriminately targeting teenage victims. Interestingly, *The Bride with White Hair*'s director, Ronny Yu, would himself direct both characters in the Hollywood franchise crossover horror-action film *Freddy vs. Jason* (2003).

In Hollywood and Hong Kong, the disabled individual is an object of pity and fear, exhibiting rage and depravity (Sutton, 2014: 88).

Since the first marketing materials for *Freaks* elicited the curiosity of audiences by posing the question 'Do Siamese twins make love?', the horror film has expressed fascination with the sexuality of people with disabilities (Sutton 2014: 80). One of the major narrative threads of *The Bride with White Hair* concerns the male twin's unrequited sexual longing for the Wolf Girl. The sister cackles sadistically at her brother's infatuation and goads him to express his romantic desire violently. The subtext of the twins' relationship is undoubtedly sexual: the sister jealously tells her brother, 'I'm the only woman you need,' conveying a desire not just incestuous, but also quite literally a physical impossibility. The self-destructive psycho-sexual oddities of the twins are sharply contrasted with the passionately committed lovemaking of Yi-hang and Ni-chang, the former a subject of clear disgust, the latter a source of erotic scintillation central to the film's marketing appeal.

The otherness of the twins extends to their entire cult: their camp is depicted as tribal, primitive, hedonistic, indicative of a trope in horror whereby disability signals the greater corruption of a group or place (Sutton 2014: 77). The entire culture of this evil collective is presented as exotic and morally repugnant, even by the drastically contradictory standards of the world of Yi-hang's martial clan. In terms of Confucian deference to a master, the othering of the twins is stark: while Yi-hang feels deep loyalty to his clan master, an obviously parental figure, the Wolf Girl feels only revulsion and shame in dealing with the twins, to whom she is in indentured servitude.

The twins are ultimately detestable even to themselves, a prime example of the deeply problematic 'obsessive avenger' archetype: characters assumed to be angry and bitter about their disability (Sutton 2014: 79). The male twin rejects his sister's solicitous pleas with equally impossible rhetoric, uttering a frustrated 'Why do you always follow me? I don't want you!' – a moment expressing self-loathing and implicit of the notion that were he 'normal', the male twin could perhaps consummate his lust for the Wolf Girl. The monstrousness of the twins is made literal in the final battle scene, as is their desire for separation. Transforming briefly into snake-human hybrids (it is unclear if this is the 'true form' of the twins, or a quirk of their shape-shifting power), the twins are defeated by a sword blow that bisects and fatally separates them. At the moment of their death, they express only relief: the 'burden' of disability finally lifted.

Swords and Sorcery: the Generic Hybridity of Fantasy *Wuxia* Horror

The Bride with White Hair can clearly be understood as a horror film, drawing as it does on numerous conventions of the genre and creating an atmosphere of fear, dread and disgust. However, the film is also a contradiction, breaking away from many of the genre's tropes. For many critics, the horror film of Hong Kong is synonymous with the ghost film, yet *The Bride with White Hair* has no ghost. The film is a combination of disparate generic elements that are never entirely incompatible; indeed, *The Bride with White Hair* can be understood as a progression of the combined storytelling modes of horror, fantasy, *wuxia* and romance.

The Hong Kong *wuxia* film has frequently contained elements of the magical and impossible. While the kung fu film showcases the power of the human body, *wuxia* cinema displays power *beyond* the physical (Schroeder 2004: 16): a prowess with mystical energy, inhuman athletic displays and supercharged weapons. Following the release of *Zu: Warriors from the Magic Mountain* (Tsui Hark, 1983), which used sophisticated special effects technology to achieve more outlandish fantasy action, the *wuxia* genre has increasingly embraced the fantastic and bizarre. Kenneth Chan's chapter in this collection also addresses this trend, a distinct and significant subgenre known as *wuxia shenguai*: swordplay and martial arts films of gods, spirits and creatures of the imagination. Such films certainly fit with broader definitions of 'pure' fantasy cinema, too; a genre eliciting, at its core, a sense of wonder through 'elements of the supernatural or impossible' (Mathews 2002: 2).

The Bride with White Hair features sorcery as telekinesis, used by both the twins and the eponymous avenger, depicting wild abilities common to the *wuxia shenguai* film. The Bride's viciously enchanted hair, used to decapitate her victims, recalls the whimsical absurdity of *Zu: Warriors from the Magic Mountain*, in which Sammo Hung's character, a wizard-like monk, holds a demon spirit at bay by using his impossibly long eyebrows as binding tethers. Yet while *The Bride with White Hair* incorporates many of the magical elements of *wuxia shenguai*, it never fully embraces the form. Yi-hang, for instance, is not gifted with any magical abilities, and supernatural feats are exclusively the province of evildoers: the malevolent twins are the only members of their cult to master sorcery and shapeshifting, and the Bride only achieves truly magical skills at the moment of her monstrous rebirth.

The restriction of magic in this way suggests an interpretation of the film specifically as an 'intrusion' fantasy. Farah Mendlesohn's influential study on the rhetorics of fantasy proposes a subdivision of the genre into four categories, based on the nature of the relationship of the protagonist to the fantasy world (Mendlesohn 2008). In the 'intrusion' fantasy, rather than presenting an imagined world full of magic, the fantastic 'enters the fictional world' and intrudes on the life of the protagonist, in positive and/or negative ways (Ibid.: xiv). *The Bride with White Hair* centres on Yi-hang, an intelligent and skilled warrior who nonetheless is entirely unprepared for his encounters with the fantastic. The horror of the film, and its fantasy, come precisely from Yi-hang's depiction as a thoroughly relatable, realistic character, continually challenged to negotiate the moral and magical complexities of his environment.

Another way to explore the film in terms of traditions in the fantasy genre was suggested by its marketing materials. On its release on DVD format in the US, *The Bride with White Hair* was advertised with the tagline 'A Classic Chinese Tale of Swords and Sorcery'. The choice of words here is hardly accidental, and invites an interpretation of the film as an example of the 'Sword and Sorcery' subgenre of American fantasy-action film and literature, a category exemplified by the muscular hero-ics of *Conan the Barbarian* (John Milius, 1982). While Leslie Cheung's graceful, feminine physical stature in this film is far removed from Arnold Schwarzenegger's bullish build, there are substantial parallels between the sword and sorcery template and the core characteristics of *The Bride with White Hair*.

The central conflict of sword and sorcery pits a physically strong but entirely non-magical hero against a villain with potent supernatural powers (Clute et al. 1999: 915), in exactly the way Yi-hang must conquer and placate the twins and his lover, respectively. The setting of sword and sorcery tales is typically a 'land of fable' that exists somewhere between the real historical past and the imagined worlds of high fantasy, a dangerous and usually lawless place (Ibid.) that finds clear expression in the nihilistic world of *The Bride with White Hair*. The paradigmatic protagonist of sword and sorcery is strong, impulsive, romantic and loyal, yet indifferent to larger issues in society, embarking on a quest that is typically personal (Ibid.: 916). Yi-hang fulfils these characteristics completely, pursuing romance with an initially impulsive, wolfish sense of fun, and ultimately rejecting all community concerns in favour of a deeply personal desire to achieve love and redemption: the film begins and ends with a framing narrative, in which a profoundly regretful Yi-hang stands watch over a supposedly magical flower that he believes can reverse his lover's grotesque transformation. It is a mission to him more important than all others.

Thus, the suggestion made by the marketing of *The Bride with White Hair* that the film be considered within the parameters of a predominantly American fantasy subgenre is ultimately appropriate, and suggestive of the fluid nature of the film's genre identity. At once a horror, a *wuxia* and a fantasy, *The Bride with White Hair* expresses a generic hybridity absolutely typical of Hong Kong horror, and, indeed, contemporary Hong Kong cinema more broadly.

The Bride's Reception: the Global Cult of East Asian Horror Cinema

The Bride with White Hair deserves consideration not just for its themes and generic melange, but also for its relative significance in the global Hong Kong horror cycle. While the Asia Extreme brand of the mid-2000s represented a watershed moment in the mainstream visibility of cult East Asian cinema in the UK and US (Martin 2015), *The Bride with White Hair* formed part of a cycle of Asian cinema, focused specifically around Hong Kong content, that anticipated much of the rhetoric of that market. This cycle included Hong Kong horror films such as *Mr. Vampire* and *A Chinese Ghost Story* (Ching Sui-tung, 1987), alongside Category III sexploitation films like *Naked Killer* (Clarence Fok, 1992) and numerous examples of 'Heroic Bloodshed' films epitomised by John Woo's *The Killer* (1989) and *Hard Boiled* (1992). Thus, a broader concept of 'cult' cinema is a more accurate collective term, than strictly and exclusively horror.

DVD editions of *The Bride with White Hair* and its sequel, *The Bride with White Hair 2* (David Wu, 1993), were released in the US in 1998. In the UK, VHS editions came out in 2000, followed by DVDs in 2001. These releases shortly predated the mainstream breakthrough of Chinese martial arts cinema triggered by the release of *Crouching Tiger, Hidden Dragon* (Ang Lee, 2000), and were thus well placed to capitalise on the wave of renewed interest in the genre that followed.

An interesting aspect of the marketing of these home media releases of *The Bride with White Hair* is the way in which the film's generic hybridity was promoted. The UK VHS release emphasises the martial arts aspects of the film above all others, leading with a cover quote describing the film as a 'chop-chop actioner' – understandable, given the relative visibility and cult popularity of the kung fu films of Jackie Chan, Bruce Lee and Sammo Hung. The US DVD release of the film, on the other hand, privileges the fantasy elements with the aforementioned tagline promising 'a classic Chinese tale of swords and sorcery'; the other major feature promoted here is the film's sexual content, stressed through liberally capitalising the word 'erotic' in a (misattributed) quote from a printed review. A trailer produced specifically for the American release of the film repeats this emphasis on the film's erotic nature, and includes a description of the film's setting as 'a land of tyrants and slaves, of ghosts and demons, or warriors and witches' that effectively hits the three key genre points – fantasy, horror, *wuxia*.

The repeated centralisation of sexual titillation in the North American marketing of the film might belie the relatively tame scenes of lovemaking in the film, but it is a marketing strategy that makes sense in the context of Hong Kong cinema's status among US audiences at the time. The erotic comedy *Sex and Zen* (Michael Mak, 1991) had become something of an underground hit in the 1990s, and *Naked Killer* was the first Category III film released theatrically in New York (Stringer 1999: 378), with home video releases following in 1996. The obvious Orientalist dimension of the way these films were marketed positions Hong Kong as a distant exotic other, as a source of scintillating sexual content unavailable in Western media. The promotion of *The Bride with White Hair* as erotic runs counter to how the same film was framed in its domestic market, where a more tender sense of love and romance was emphasised. Indeed, one of the core marketing materials for Hong Kong audiences was the official song, a gentle romantic ballad performed by leading man Leslie Cheung.

The romantic facets of the film did not escape the notice of reviewers in the West, however, with *Variety* commenting that the film is 'as much a tragic romance' as an action film (Elley 1994). Yet other reviewers were predisposed to focus on the film's sexual content; a brief entry in the fan-focused book *Sex and Zen & A Bullet in the Head: the Essential Guide to Hong Kong's Mind-Bending Films* praises the film specifically for being 'darker and more erotic than most' (Hammond and Wilkins 1996: 17). Indeed, the review in *Variety* noted that 'Hong Kong costume actioners' constituted a 'crowded market' at this point in the mid-1990s (Elley 1994), and it was precisely the multifaceted and multivalent nature of *The Bride with White Hair* that allowed it to attract attention, appealing variously as a horror film, a fantasy, *wuxia* action, romance or erotic excess.

Conclusion: the Immortal Bride

The Bride with White Hair has an enduring legacy, and forms part of a multimedia narrative telling and retelling the same story both before and after the 1993 film. The original source is a novel by the influential writer Liang Yusheng, a pioneer of *wuxia* literature in the twentieth century. First published in the 1950s, the original story has remained popular, and

Ronny Yu's *The Bride with White Hair* is far from the only adaptation of the material. The first adaptation, *Story of the White-Haired Demon Girl*, was released as an epic trilogy in 1959 and directed by Lee Fa. *Sorceress' Wrath*, a Mandarin-language musical version, followed in 1980 (directed by Cheung Sing-yim). Numerous television series have also adapted the tale, and more recently, a Mainland Chinese production, *The White Haired Witch of the Lunar Kingdom* (Jacob Cheung, 2014) achieved modest success in the domestic market as well as international distribution on home media formats (as *The White-Haired Witch*).

The story and characters are both iconic and flexible, open to reinterpretation based on differing creative visions and the social mores of the time. Ronny Yu's 1993 version is undoubtedly the most visible, and the film embodies an important moment in the development of Hong Kong hybrid-horror, and the industry more generally. The film is in many ways emblematic of the way Hong Kong cinema of this period celebrated individual creative expression alongside special-effects driven action scenes with calculated popular appeal. Many auteurs of Hong Kong cinema articulated anxiety at the then-imminent handover of the colony to the Mainland Chinese government. It is certainly tempting to read *The Bride with White Hair* in these terms, and see in the film's protagonist, devastated at the object of his love and loyalty becoming twisted and unfamiliar, dangerous and uncaring, a reflection of wider cultural apprehension.

The Bride with White Hair's lasting iconic status is inexorably tied to its generic hybridity. The film represents an evolution for horror, *wuxia* and fantasy, in a manner that fascinated audiences both at home and abroad. The impact and influence of the film is considerable, and its place in the canon of Hong Kong cult cinema assured.

References

Clute, John, David Langford and Roz Kaveney (1999), 'Sword and sorcery', in John Clute and John Grant (eds), *The Encyclopedia of Fantasy*, New York: St Martin's Griffin.

Elley, Derek (1994), 'Review: Jiang-Hu: between love & glory/*The Bride with White Hair*', *Variety*, 9 May, <http://variety.com/1994/film/reviews/jiang-hu-between-love-glory-the-bride-with-white-hair-1200437288/> (last accessed 10 January 2017).

Hammond, Steffan and Mike Wilkins (1996), *Sex and Zen & A Bullet in the Head: the Essential Guide to Hong Kong's Mind-Bending Movies*, London: Titan Books.

Hunt, Leon (2003), *Kung Fu Cult Masters: from Bruce Lee to Crouching Tiger*, London and New York: Wallflower.

Lam, Michael (1989), 'Earthly delights', *Phantoms of the Hong Kong Cinema*, The 13th Hong Kong International Film Festival, pp. 58–62.

Lee, Hyangjin (2013), 'Family, death and the *wonhon* in four films of the 1960s', in Alison Peirse and Daniel Martin (eds), *Korean Horror Cinema*, Edinburgh: Edinburgh University Press, pp. 23–34.

Martin, Daniel (2015), *Extreme Asia: the Rise of Cult Cinema from the Far East*, Edinburgh: Edinburgh University Press.

Mathews, Richard (2011), *Fantasy: the Liberation of Imagination*, New York and London: Routledge.

Mendlesohn, Farah (2008), *Rhetorics of Fantasy*, Middletown, CT: Wesleyan University Press.

O'Brien, Daniel (2003), *Spooky Encounters: a Gwailo's Guide to Hong Kong Horror*, Manchester: Headpress.

Odham Stokes, Lisa (2015), 'The Bride with White Hair / The Evil White Haired Lady', in Gary Bettinson (ed.), *Directory of World Cinema: China 2*, Bristol and Chicago: Intellect.

Schroeder, Andrew (2004), *Tsui Hark's Zu: Warriors from the Magic Mountain*, Aberdeen: Hong Kong University Press.

Stringer, Julian (1999), 'Category 3: Sex and Violence in Postmodern Hong Kong', in Christopher Sharrett (ed.), *Mythologies of Violence in Postmodern Media*, Detroit: Wayne State University Press, pp. 361–79.

Sutton, Travis (2014), 'Avenging the body: disability in the horror film', in Harry Benshoff (ed.), *A Companion to the Horror Film*, Chichester: Wiley Blackwell, pp. 73–89.

Teo, Stephen (1989), 'The tongue: a study of kung fu horror movies', *Phantoms of the Hong Kong Cinema*, The 13th Hong Kong International Film Festival, pp. 41–5.

Teo, Stephen (1997), *Hong Kong Cinema: the Extra Dimensions*, London: British Film Institute.

Teo, Stephen (2001), '*The Bride with White Hair* film notes', *The Bride with White Hair* DVD, Metro-Tartan, UK.

Teo, Stephen (2009), *Chinese Martial Arts Cinema: the Wuxia Tradition*, Edinburgh: Edinburgh University Press.

Yu, Cheng (1989), 'Under a spell', *Phantoms of the Hong Kong Cinema*, The 13th Hong Kong International Film Festival, pp. 20–3.

Part II

Genre Hybridity: Comedy and Kung Fu in the Hong Kong Horror

CHAPTER 5

Animated Pasts and Unseen Futures: on the Comic Element in Hong Kong Horror

Andrew Grossman

Introduction: the Comic Sense of Horror

In the midst of filming *The Shining*, Stanley Kubrick faced a crisis both aesthetic and philosophical. A staunch non-believer, Kubrick began to wonder why stories of ghostly possession should horrify the jaded audiences of a more or less secularised culture. If anything, the presence of ghosts, malevolent or not, should instil us with hope, assuaging our anxieties about impending mortality and providing spiritual meaning in a nihilistic age. Kubrick probably worried that his usual highbrow audience, too sophisticated for fairy tales, would see the content of *The Shining* as laughable, despite its mannered, haute stylistics and grave, unwaveringly straight-faced presentation. Certainly, the original storyline by Stephen King, a devout believer, would seem silly to rationalists unwilling to suspend disbelief. Beyond the particularities of a single film, our scepticism broadens: if ghosts exist, why would they haunt houses or burial grounds rather than roam free? Must ghosts observe socially constructed geographical boundaries? And why should a roaming spirit, freed from its bodily prison, inject itself into the petty affairs of humanity when it presumably exists as a new, supra-human consciousness? Of course, the arbitrary conventions of generic horror – and of religious dogma – were never meant to withstand the force of logic. To foster the most extreme forms of belief, spiritual dogmas must be so irrational as to require miraculous leaps of faith by those who believe they are specially chosen to make such leaps. Horror films that exploit and adapt established conventions of supernatural belief thus stumble into a kind of burlesque, reverently treating the most arbitrary (and ridiculous) aspects of irrational faith.

In the cold light of scepticism (not to mention epistemology), *The Shining* should scare us less than some of life's more mundane travails, such as overcoming cancer, initiating a divorce, or amortising a mortgage. *The Shining* unnerves mainly for Kubrick's objectivised sense of the surreal and the Freudian uncanny, not for its intellectually dubious subject matter. Yet Kubrick's fears were partly unfounded: the very experience of watching a ghost story is *always* simultaneously horrific and absurd. Typically, audiences naively identify with spooked characters while also critically positioning themselves above risible narratives that call for absurdly irrational belief. Through this position, comically incongruous in itself, spectators negotiate a desire for mythic transcendence of the ego (the existence of ghosts) and the need to assert a disbelieving logos in a culture still susceptible to irrationality. At least since Plato, countless philosophers have addressed this conflict generally, but in the particular terms of spectatorship, Arthur Koestler's notion of 'bisociation' perhaps best reflects the subject's dual desires for fantasy and reason. In *The Act of Creation*, Koestler argues that both creativity and comedy emerge when a subject perceives one idea through the interaction of 'two independent matrices of perception or reasoning', resulting in 'either a collision ending in laughter, [. . .] their fusion in a new intellectual synthesis, or their confrontation in an aesthetic experience' (Koestler 1964: 45). Depending on one's intellectual perspective or even 'emotional climate', the same dually perceived or 'bisociated' idea can 'produce comic, tragic, or intellectually challenging effects' (Koestler 1964: 45). Though a dead-end dialectic could well provoke tragic – or tragicomic – realisations, for the present we will focus on the 'comic' premises and outcomes arising from intellectual and perceptual incongruities, which are the wellspring of nearly all comedy.

Though Koestler's phrase 'emotional climate' seems deliberately vague, it does embrace the mental framework of horror film-goers, allegedly rational agents who, at least temporarily, willingly open their minds, suspend disbelief and treat ridiculous supernatural antics as earnestly affecting. In these instances, sceptical spectators – though not unswerving, monovalent atheists – take seriously the content (not only the style) of a film like *The Shining*, using it as a framework for metaphysical daydreams they would otherwise rationally suppress. For Koestler, this incongruous position is a font of comedy, though if pushed further, a creative synthesis might occur, should the horror spectator discover a novel way to dialectically splice – and not merely rationalise – the seemingly irreconcilable tendencies of belief and disbelief. Bivalent (or ambivalent) spectators surely will be self-conscious of their positions, comically switching between a rational critique of the ridiculous and an irrational (or infantile, in the psychoanalytic view) submission to it. Monovalently logical minds, like Kubrick's, would probably scoff at such an indulgence of irrationality, but the fostering of bivalent subject positions is clearly one of horror's primary goals and effects. Admittedly, even ambivalent spectators enter the bargain with a healthy dose of irony, but we might remember the words of Kierkegaard, who wondered if 'real irony were not essentially a concealed enthusiasm in a negative age' (Kierkegaard 1962: 47).

If juggling irreconcilable views of a horror film engages the incongruities at the heart of comedy, horror spectators themselves become kinds of comic figures, consciously or otherwise. That this comic predicament should arise from the experience of horror should not surprise us, however, for comedy and horror trade in similar fantasies – especially fantasies of immortality. In their respective forms of pathos, both daredevil clowning and ghost tales differently manifest the ways in which spectators engage a denial of death (to borrow Ernest Becker's phrase). Just as undying zombies and reincarnated ghosts violate the natural laws of mortality, so do charmed clowns and holy fools defy death through miraculous stunts, native cunning or inexplicable fortune.

But so far we've only considered the ironic perception of horror films meant to be taken seriously. What happens when we address the hybrid horror-comedy, which transfers the comic element from the consciousness of the spectator to the text itself? In our present study of the Hong Kong horror-comedy hybrids of the 1970s and 1980s, we will keep in mind that the supernatural comedy-horror construct is not so much a 'novel' hybrid but the embodiment of the 'normal' way we look at supernatural horror. (We will put aside non-supernatural horror, which doesn't automatically engage metaphysical aspirations and therefore doesn't require a spectator's ambivalence between reason and unreason.) The horror-comedy hybrid pushes to the level of text the comic incongruity already present in the 'bisociating' mind of the spectator, who absurdly desires horror cinema's metaphysical fantasy but eventually reverts to logos, either to maintain a rationalistic ideology or to conform to societal expectations.

For Koestler, bisociated incongruities create the opportunity for dialectical creativity in the minds of subjects, who hopefully can synthesise conflicting perspectives into a personalised synthesis (creating a 'trivalence' that completes the tripartite dialectical process). Clearly, Koestler's notion privileges the inner workings of the subject more than the dialectical intentions of any given text. Whereas the colliding images of Eisenstein's dialectical montage, for instance, aim to produce particular synthetic associations for the viewer, the bisociating spectator of horror is not hostage to a film-maker's intentions. The horror-comedy hybrid apparently complicates this relationship, objectifying the comic element by moving it from the viewer's mind into the text itself. However, the viewer may also bisociate from a negative perspective, imagining how the horror-comedy might (or might not) be taken seriously were the comic element removed. In either case, the horror-comedy hybrid doesn't exist so much 'after' its constituent genres but rather manifests textually the absurd conflict that otherwise transpires in the viewer's ambivalent subjectivity. Presenting not two sides of the same coin but one side doubly, the horror-comedy engages the dual perspectives required of the secular age, in which the unquenchable desire for an afterlife, haunted or otherwise, clashes ridiculously with mortal realities.

I: the Horror-Comedy in Hong Kong Cinema

With a few auteurist exceptions, such as Whale's *The Invisible Man* (1933), Browning's *Mark of the Vampire* (1934), Polanski's *The Fearless Vampire Killers* (1967) or Romero's *Dawn of the Dead* (1978), the horror-comedy has suffered an unfortunate, vulgar reputation. This reputation partly stems from Hollywood's hoary supernatural farces of the 1940s, which saw Bela Lugosi engage in sad self-parody (for example, *Zombies on Broadway* (1945)) or had Abbott and Costello continually flee a threadbare array of mummies, werewolves and vampires. There is nothing inherently funny in seeing grossly inferior characters scream into the night or having a cowardly watchman bulge his eyes when stumbling across a skeleton. Even lowbrow audiences of the 1920s probably yawned through horror-comedies like *Habeas Corpus* (1928), which finds Laurel and Hardy as graveyard interlopers contending with rogues dressed in 'ghostly' sheets. At most, such lowbrow comic-horror tropes merely engage a childishly sadistic gaze that elevates invulnerable audiences above unrealistically stupid comic foils. As a subgenre, the horror-farce has been mostly stuck in a vicious cycle. Because they seldom hold ambitions greater than tasteless shocks, horror-farces rarely attract the legitimising cultural work of postmodern analysis and interpretation, and because they lack such analysis, horror-farces are rarely encouraged to mature beyond a perpetual adolescence. Here we should distinguish the horror-farce from the satirical horror film, however, which has undergone a more concentrated process of maturation, at least since the rise of cult cinemas and the crossover popularity of Romero's *Dawn of the Dead*. Arguably, the American horror-comedy only matured thematically with the resurrection (and overuse) of the zombie as an allegory for the dehumanisation endemic to late capitalism's spiritual vacuum.

In Hong Kong, however, the horror-farce came to occupy a central place during the New Wave's second phase in the mid- and late 1980s, when gruesome horrors such as *Devil Fetus* (1983), *Boxer's Omen* (1983) and *Seeding of a Ghost* (1983) were supplanted by lighter, more marketable fare. Hong Kong's horror-comedies emphasise the prosaic, unexceptional nature of the supernatural, making restless spirits and reanimated corpses an incongruously comic part of life's everyday business. Hong Kong's better horror-farces, such as *Spooky Encounters, The Dead and the Deadly* and *Mr. Vampire*, pay great attention to the common folklore, burial practices, and mortuary paraphernalia embedded in daily rituals. As Gildow says, even in the late twentieth century there were

> strewn across the countryside of both China and Taiwan . . . mummified corpses venerated as deities granting requests, sending dreams, enshrined, worshipped, often gilded, sometimes installed inside or below a religious statue or decorated to look indistinguishable or nearly so from a statue. (Gildow 2005: 1)

By advancing the paradox of a 'supernatural mundanity', the Hong Kong horror-comedy is fertile terrain for bisociation, as its narratives revolve around an inherently comic juxtaposition.

Admittedly, the weaving of supernatural belief into everyday life isn't particular to Chinese folkways; even postmodern cultures still integrate religious practice into ostensibly secular lifestyles. For instance, surveys show that between 70 and 80 per cent of Americans believe in the existence of angels,[1] and crucifixes and rosaries are as commonplace in the US as ancestral tablets are in China. Yet the Christian tradition (if we may overgeneralise) has done much to privatise and rarefy supernatural belief through Protestantism's esoteric 'personal relationships' with Jesus and Catholicism's secretive confessionals. Public manifestations of the Christian supernatural – say, the sighting of the Virgin in a tree – are singular miracles laden with an aura of sanctity. Likewise, Hollywood's supernatural horror films – in the manner of *The Exorcist* (1973) or *The Entity* (1982) – usually depict rare, individualised paranormal phenomena with an entirely straight face, even as they privilege supernatural explanations over scientific ones.

Hong Kong's horror-comedies of the late 1970s and 1980s, however, dispense with rarefied, individualised horror tropes and imagine a Chinese society in which premodern folk traditions are visibly ingrained in the practices of a more collectivistic society. Not coincidentally, many Hong Kong horror-comedies are set shortly after the 1911 revolution, as if to stress the incongruity between lingering superstition and ascendant modernity (an idea to which we will return). Furthermore, these films don't merely express the (comic) anachronism of religion in an age of science (as in *The Exorcist*), but gleefully lampoon Daoist superstition and ingrained folk beliefs – much unlike Hollywood's usual, self-serious

Christian horror films,[2] which affirm rather than subvert religious dogmas and symbolisms.

Liu Chia-liang's *The Shadow Boxing* (aka *Spiritual Boxer 2*, 1978) was among Hong Kong's first horror-comedies to normalise the presence of the supernatural. The film marks a departure from the director's prior *The Spiritual Boxer* (1975), a Mark Twain-like satire that emphasises not the omnipresence of real spirits but the gullibility of peasants fooled by a charlatan who claims to channel deities.[3] Putting aside this sceptical worldview, *The Shadow Boxing* begins with a voice-over that describes legendary 'corpse-herders', Daoist priests charged with escorting the reanimated bodies of the deceased to their hometowns for proper burial.[4] With *The Shadow Boxing*, the *jiangshi* – a rigid, reanimated corpse, though mistranslated as 'vampire' in most English-language film titles – becomes a central figure in Hong Kong's supernatural comedies. Resurrected through an ominous imbalance of yin and yang energies, the *jiangshi* is generally represented as a mummy dressed in Qing official garb, presumably because the deceased had died before the 1911 revolution. Impervious to the laws of gravity and stiffly hopping instead of walking (because rigor mortis has made the bending of joints impossible), the *jiangshi* can be subdued by the corpse-herder, who orchestrates the corpses' movements by affixing paper charms to their foreheads. It is unnecessary to review the storylines of most *jiangshi* comedies, as they usually recycle basic themes. Slapstick antics ensue when a corpse loses its controlling charms (because the Daoist's apprentice is incompetent); when a corpse becomes invested with demonic powers (because of inauspicious fortunes); or when humans pose as *jiangshi*, so intertwined are folk beliefs and everyday commerce. Exploiting the last of these themes, *The Shadow Boxing* concerns an outlaw (Gordon Liu) who, wrongly framed by corrupt officials, poses as a hopping corpse to escape capture, leading to the expected comedy of errors.[5] That the *jiangshi* is typically dressed in official Qing garb offers an easy opportunity for satire. At the film's end, hero Wang Yu captures a corrupt official and binds him to the back of a spinning *jiangshi*, suggesting that imperial officials – and bureaucracy as a whole – are hardly different from mindless, moribund bodies deserving of burial.[6]

Superficially, the herded *jiangshi*'s homeward journey is unsubtly provincial and nationalistic, for corpses not buried in native soil are (according to legend) susceptible to spiritual possession.[7] This nationalism is carried to self-parodic extremes in Billy Chan's *Crazy Safari* (1990), an improbable mix of *jiangshi* lore and Jamie Uys's *The Gods Must Be Crazy* (1984) that finds a clueless Chinese mummy lost in the wilds of South Africa, ridiculously far from its provincial instincts. Yet the nationalism of the corpses' blind odyssey home is only a pretext. Nearly every culture has mortuary rites that not only sanctify corpses but purify them, segregating unruly dead bodies and orderly living ones to maintain rational cultural categories, as anthropologist Mary Douglas had argued in *Purity and Danger*. *The Shadow Boxing* demonstrates the ever-present fear of supernatural contamination in its credit sequence, wherein apprentice corpse-herder Wang Yu warns townspeople to stay clear of the main road as he escorts a hopping procession of *jiangshi*. This theme of pollution had traditionally informed Chinese supernatural tales; ghost stories such as *The Enchanting Shadow* (1960) – and its oft-imitated update, *A Chinese Ghost Story* (1987) – routinely feature youthful scholars fatalistically entangled with pretty female ghosts. Of course, the tabooed relationship can never be consummated or affirmed, and as plot mechanics banish the mortal male and immortal female to their respective spheres, the need for order accrues a melancholy air of unrequited longing that embraces the impossible desire for an afterlife itself.

Some later films express more ambivalent views of folkloric dogma, pausing to question the ideological 'bigotry' of segregating the physical and metaphysical worlds – a bigotry always rationalised as 'fate'. In Sammo Hung's *Spooky Encounters 2* (1990), exorcist Lam Ching-ying (who made a veritable career from portraying Daoist masters) banishes a sympathetic female ghost to maintain heavenly orders, prompting Hung (playing the apprentice) to thrash Lam for his act of doctrinaire cruelty. In Confucian terms, it is unthinkable for an apprentice to attack his master – and yet later, when Lam asks the Heavens if he has behaved unjustly, an angry thunderclap suggests Hung's action was justified. Similarly, in *Mr. Vampire 3* (1987), bumbling exorcist Richard Ng must part with two sympathetic, domesticated ghosts when Lam Ching-ying (once again) arrives to dispel them. In a rare moment of satire, Ng explains to the older ghost that opposites cannot coexist, only for the spirit to ask, 'What about one country, two systems?' Yet the rules of religion – and of genre – remain fixed and unyielding, offering no room for sympathy or mutual understanding. The 'one country, two systems' joke amuses not because ghost–human tensions are analogous to those between the Mainland and Hong Kong, but because the Mainland's authoritarian policies are actually *less* dogmatic and more accommodating than those of an intransigent, undiplomatic fantasy world.

II: the *Jiangshi* as Comic Trope

Before examining how the *jiangshi* operates in metaphysical comedy (as opposed to physical comedy), we should first distinguish it from the Western vampire tradition, especially as the word 'vampire' commonly figured in film titles after the success of Ricky Lau's *Mr. Vampire* (1985). If the Western vampire topoi popularised by Bram Stoker propose an aristocratic anti-hero alternately monstrous and romantic, the *jiangshi* is quite the opposite, a hollow everyman preserved in stasis, not suffering a process of measured decay (distinguishing it from zombies as well). Not a desirous being, the *jiangshi* is a dehumanised automaton, an ossified body that refuses to splatter erotically when punctured. Even when it becomes spooked and lunges for a victim's neck with its fangs, the act is mechanical rather than inherently evil. At the same time, the *jiangshi*, though buffoonish, has little in common with the clowning tradition of American silent film. Whereas the clowns of Keaton and Chaplin generally lack self-consciousness and a sense of selfhood, the *jiangshi* properly has neither a self nor a consciousness to lack. Merely a vessel through which the spirit transiently passes, it has only a grave to which it must unthinkingly return. With a fated, singular destination, the *jiangshi* evokes neither the American allegories of upward striving embodied by Harold Lloyd nor the late capitalist satire popularised by *Dawn of the Dead*, in which the desirous zombie citizen is condemned to the corporatist pandemonium of the shopping mall.

If Western horror tropes frame the vampire as the undying residue of aristocracy in a rising age of science, *jiangshi* horror-comedies suggest their own historical allegory. It is no accident that most (though not all) take place shortly after 1911 revolution, when republican values and May Fourth modernity were replacing old Qing structures and bureaucracies. That *jiangshi* wear Qing officials' garb obviously can be read as a satire of antiquated values persisting – chaotically, manically – in the modern era, much as the *jiangshi*'s officious stiffness can be seen as a parody of Mainland communists, who have inherited the world's oldest, most rigid bureaucracy. Their nationalistic, backwards-looking attire notwithstanding, I cannot recall a scene in any *jiangshi* comedy in which the corpses arrive safely home and descend into their appointed graves. A standard postcolonial reading might emphasise the nomadic predicament of the *jiangshi*, searching for a homeland that is always absent or forestalled (through comic misadventure). On another level, however, the ambulating corpse, stuck between lively and lifeless worlds, mirrors the dualistic predicament of the bivalent spectator: much as the viewer of supernatural horror straddles worldly scepticism and wish-fulfilment, so does the monster simultaneously embody physical, comic action and metaphysical mandates. Yet the *jiangshi*, like the bivalent spectator unable to synthesise competing desires, remains betwixt and between, unable to realise either finality or the next stage of its existence.

Discussing general distinctions between comedy and tragedy, Walter Kerr suggests that while tragedy observes fatalistic ends, comedy is existentially endless, for 'only death will end the joke' (Kerr 1967: 171). Horror-comedies focusing on the undead apparently provide a notable exception, for they subvert death itself – effectively meaning that *even* death will not end the joke. Though often astray and pathetic, the *jiangshi* cannot be a tragicomic figure, however, for tragicomedy, like tragedy itself, entails a failed search for freedom. Clearly, the *jiangshi* seeks not freedom but a sense of grounded peace, yet fails even at that prearranged goal. In this sense, the *jiangshi*'s physical rigidity is only symptomatic of a larger existential trap, as it is forever stuck, like a broken clock, between this world and the next.

III: the Premodern Mechanics of the *Jiangshi*

Since at least the time of Plautus, the 'rigid' or unbending comic figure has represented obdurate conservatism and a failure to adapt to changing or unstable times. At odds with living, lively spirits, the rigid performer was doomed to failure or buffoonery. The naive optimism of the machine age began to change this view of rigidity, however, as did the machine-like clowns of silent cinema. In a fantastically, inorganically soundless universe, the stone-faced clowns of Keaton and Lloyd embodied a rigidity that was subtle, graceful and qualified by a comic sense of unexpected elasticity. Confronted with steamships (in *The Navigator*), locomotives (*The General*) and even the cinematic screen itself (*Sherlock, Jr.*), Keaton masters machines through a clownish mix of clockwork movements and sudden adaptability, overcoming challenges that would confound 'natural' men. Similarly, Lloyd nearly melds with the automobile in *Speedy*, performing superhuman feats through the medium of a machine. Chaplin's mechanisation is subtler and less aggressive: though machines can get the better of him (in *Modern Times*), he is governed by nervous, motoric energy, evincing the restless (and humorously misdirected) drive of a human wind-up toy. Exposing the foibles inherent in our interactions with the world of objects, the slapstick performer becomes himself an object acted upon by other worldly objects. The silent clowns of the machine age built upon this objectification by parodying the very idea of mechanisation, accruing heroic agency by becoming man-machine hybrids themselves.

The proto-cybernetic clown thus embodies Henri Bergson's famous theory of comic mechanisation, expounded in his 1900 essay *Laughter*. When 'something mechanical' becomes 'encrusted upon the living', Bergson theorises, the resulting 'mechanization of life' engenders a comedy of incongruity (Bergson 2009: 35). In literal terms, Bergson's description of comic mechanisation applies more to the unbending *jiangshi* than to the Keatonesque clown, who counterbalances his mechanisation with stealthy (if often unconscious) moments of ingenuity and adaptability. The oblivious clown may slip and fall, but he is funnier when he miraculously escapes calamity, defying our expectations. But the *jiangshi*, without will or cunning, always hops, crashes and falls in perfectly linear fashion, regardless of the objects within its trajectory. The *jiangshi*'s slapstick closely echoes Bergson's description of physical comedy: '. . . through lack of elasticity, through absentmindedness . . . and a kind of physical obstinacy . . . the muscles continue . . . to perform the same movement when the circumstances of the case call . . . for something else' (Ibid.: 20). Likely fearing the dehumanisation proposed by the machine age, Bergson believed an unthinking, mechanised life would become a 'binding force of habit' encrusted upon us. Later writers have questioned Bergson's implicit connection between mechanisation and modernity; after all, the body is itself machine-like, as Da Vinci knew, and Walter Kerr rightly points out that the Bergsonian 'crust is there from the beginning' (Ibid.: 246) – that is, our very organic and social natures inexorably 'bind' us with habits (if not neuroses) we cannot escape. Notably, the *jiangshi*'s paradoxical mechanism is at once inherent and encrusted, as its inelastic movements express both a fantastic organic state (living rigor) and the acculturation of collective folklore (the absurd mandate to bounce homeward).

Defying gravity, the *jiangshi* moves like a marionette, inheriting traditions of Punch and Judy puppetry and building upon the angularity and 'hard' falls of New Wave Hong Kong martial arts, as well as the slapstick falls advanced by Jackie Chan (in his Buster Keaton mode). For instance, in Sammo Hung's *Spooky Encounters* (1980), probably the first film to situate the *jiangshi* in a full-scale martial arts battle, Hung stumbles onto an especially malevolent corpse in a haunted house. With pantomimic movements and the occasional help of wirework, the costumed actor pivots on his toes, from which he radiates at straight angles. Like a spring-loaded jack-in-the-box, the monster pops up and down with each of Hung's hard blows. The finale of Hung's *Spooky Encounters 2* varies the usual *jiangshi* acrobatics when Hung fights cloth-wrapped mummies animated by an impious sorcerer. In genre fashion, however, the mummies behave like stiff-limbed, almost robotic *jiangshi*; when Hung chops them with his blade, they resound with a metallic echo, reinforcing the robotic association. Here, the monster embodies the comic action itself: whereas silent clowns – even semi-robotic ones – often exploit comedic props such as hoses, hammers, umbrellas, hats, and so forth, the objectified *jiangshi*, unable to wield tools, becomes a comic prop in itself.

Often *jiangshi* action sequences use literal, visible wires not only to accentuate the monster's grotesquely puppet-like movements but to expose or parody the 'metaphysical', aerial wirework of New Wave martial arts choreography. In Jeff Lau's *Mortuary Blues* (1990), for instance, members of a Peking opera troupe subdue a resurrected ghoul by ensnaring and twisting it within their swinging stage ropes, transfixing the creature within the artifice of the theatre. A more blatant example is provided by *Magic Cop* (1990), a rare contemporary story that sees a narcotics-trafficking Japanese sorceress utilising animated corpses as mindless drug mules. In a lengthy scene, the sorceress magically strings up one of her corpses by his hands and feet and literally pulls him like a marionette. Through sympathetic magic, the sorceress utilises the corpse like a life-size voodoo doll, transferring its puppet-like movements to the limbs of an investigating cop in a cleverly choreographed scene that sharply cross-cuts between the sorceress-controlled corpse and the (transitively) corpse-controlled cop. *New Mr. Vampire* (1987), mostly set in a post-revolutionary, art deco hotel, invokes the modern conflict that underpins the post-1911 *jiangshi* comedy. Here, an unusually resilient corpse, impervious to bullets, is finally strung up with a series of ropes and pulled in four different directions by four groups of soldiers. The soldiers' attempt to subdue the creature and turn it into an 'actual' puppet fail miserably, however, for the soldiers' human flexibility is no match for the *jiangshi*'s demonic stiffness. Ineffective as puppet masters, the soldiers finally wheel in a cannon and blow the *jiangshi* to pieces, symbolically (and perhaps anticlimactically) demolishing mouldy superstitions with revolutionary technology.

With its pointed toes and stiffened limbs, the combative *jiangshi* move in balletic ways that conventional – that is, human – martial artists do not. It has become a journalistic cliché to call almost any sort of martial arts choreography 'balletic', but the term is grossly misused, not merely overused. At least in its classical and romantic forms, ballet traditionally emphasises bodily stiffness and unnaturally straight lines, realising graceful forms within the limitations of a fragile body. Martial arts, on the other hand, generally seek to channel the fluidities of nature, not rigid artifice, and while martial arts obviously have their prescribed forms, these are not aesthetic ends unto themselves, as they are in ballet. In its gravity-defying perfor-mance, at once ungainly and agile, the *jiangshi* is graceful in the literal sense of the term – that is, touched by a spiritual presence, yet absent the mind-fulness of a martial artist. (Perhaps somewhere between martial artistry and the animated corpse lies the gracefully handled string-puppet that Kleist describes in his 1801 essay 'On the Marionette Theater'.[8]) Admittedly, the distinction is sometimes lost, especially as certain films blur it themselves. A running joke throughout *The Shadow Boxing*, for instance, has Wang Yu defeat villains by adopting jokey martial arts stances that mimic not deft animal postures but the *jiangshi*'s bouncing, mechanistic gestures – 'vampire greets the moon', 'vampire leaps over the hill', and so on. Though visually clever, these sequences are misleading, as martial artistry shouldn't mimic dead forms but nimbly draw upon vital organic energies.

Like madcap silent comedy, comic martial arts choreography depends upon disorienting speed. Just as a Harold Lloyd chase scene would fall flat without breakneck swiftness, a deliberately slow *jiangshi* martial arts sequence would rob the monster of the abrupt, automatic reflexes that are the sources of its comedy. The principle of speed is demonstrated in a mostly failed comic scene in Ricky Lau's *Mr. Vampire 2* (1986). A mod-ern-day story in which supernatural presences compete with scientific explanations, the film features a lengthy scene, set in an anthropologist's laboratory, in which two reanimated *jiangshi* – a male and female couple – besiege the unsuspecting heroes. The corpses defy gravity, glide across the floor (like a balletic bourrée), pivot on tiptoes (like ballerinas *en pointe*), and lunge at victims with bared fangs (like a Western vampire). When conventional martial arts fail, one hero hurls an explosive potion, labelled 'retardant', that slows down the action of anyone within its vapours. The ensuing slow-motion fracas – the actors pantomime slow-motion move-ments, while the film runs at normal speed – exposes the basic mechanics of martial arts choreography, but the ensuing action sorely lacks a sense of comic surprise, since viewers can foresee the result of each tediously protracted movement. As the early twentieth-century futurists observed, visceral excitement depends on the grinding mechanics of momentum and dialectical collision, and physical comedy is much the same. Without daredevil skill, the scene is useless – indeed, the value of martial arts choreography lies in its ability to demonstrate the outer limits of human ability with minimal special effects or intermediation (admitting the occa-sional use of wirework and camera 'undercranking').

Underlying the mechanics of the antic *jiangshi* is a Daoist, animis-tic worldview in which the spirit is not posited outside the body (as in

Descartes) but exists a priori and occupies multiple forms (human, corpse, ghost, and so on). The opportunistic profusion of *jiangshi* comedies in the late 1980s and early 1990s, however, mostly envisions one kind of animism: an unadapting stiffness that contrasts with the martial hero's suppleness. Yuen Woo-ping's *The Miracle Fighters* (1982) offers a more ingenious, less generic expression of this animism, highlighting the Daoist tendency to ignore distinctions between spirituality and materiality. Going beyond mere hopping corpses, the film envisions a phantasmagoric world in which nearly every object can be animated, reanimated or spiritually inhabited. Like most Hong Kong horror-farces, *The Miracle Fighters* focuses on the master–apprentice relationship, though here the young apprentice is torn between two rivalrous, cantankerous Daoist sorcerers. Much as cinema itself animates static frames, sorcery brings nearly everything to life, from one master's graven image above an altar, to a painting of a waterfall that spills forth real water, to an enchanted urn that sprouts the arms and legs of a pathetic child ghost imprisoned within. In the extraordinary climax, a sorcerer's competition staged in a psychedelic hell, humanoid mechanics are stripped to their bare essence when the young hero confronts a wooden, stick-figure guard, a fifteen-foot-tall tinker-toy brought to life with stop-motion animation. In this cleverly animated cum animistic sequence, Bergson's comic mechanisation is basically inverted. Rather than humanity being hindered by an acculturated, mechanical 'crust', a pure mechanism – constructed of primitive wooden blocks, no less – is rendered anthropomorphic.

While martial arts follow prescribed forms, they generally seek to shed society's mechanistic, Bergsonian crust and access a latent naturalness that grants practitioners untapped flexibility and adaptability. Indeed, many memorable comedic martial arts scenes emphasise heroes adapting and animating otherwise passive objects – consider Sammo Hung wielding a wooden stool in *Spooky Encounters*, Jet Li an umbrella in *Once Upon a Time in China* (1991), or Jackie Chan a ladder in *First Strike* (1994). *The Miracle Fighters* is atypical in this context because it suggests that 'mechanisms' are not necessarily encrusted or inhibiting. As the animistic wooden man adapts (and assembles) itself to human form from small wooden blocks that spring to life, the essence of martial arts is revealed as mechanical in content (it is made from automatic blocks) and human in its constructed form. Reflecting animism's overall rejection of categorical (or Cartesian) distinctions, this stop-motion sequence, envisioning a mechanics that is inherent rather than encrusted, reveals the mechanistic nature of biology itself – an idea Bergson largely ignores. Importantly, this idea, revealed through the scene's stop-motion animation, would be rendered invisible through the fraudulent fluidity of computer-generated imagery (CGI), which would not only dehumanise the action but also erase the distinction between the biological and the mechanical, reducing every action to a common denominator of digitised fantasy.

Indeed, when we judge how imaginary or 'ghostly' bodies perform on-screen, we return to our original theme of bivalence, or the dualistic perspective of spectators who balance competing, irreconcilable desires for screen realism and fantasy, for sympathetic embodiment and spiritual disembodiment. As we have said, even 'serious' ghost stories (like *The Shining*) automatically conjure a sort of comic bivalence, as spectators themselves become comically incongruous figures who absurdly attempt to balance their disbelief of supernatural plots and (momentary) acquiescence to wish-fulfilling fantasy. Much as the horror-comedy hybrid transfers the bivalent absurdity of supernatural horror to texts themselves, the acted performance of the *jiangshi* transfers the reality-fantasy conflict from the mind of the conflicted spectator to the screen itself. For a *jiangshi* performance to be affecting, the spectator must know a poor actor is beneath the costume, enduring the bruising, perilous falls alien to the fantastic role but endemic to the performing body.

Within the context of bivalent spectatorship, the use of CGI or 'posthuman' special effects is not merely a matter of taste or aesthetics, but a reminder of the need for pathos. We must be able to identify the actor in the *jiangshi* costume as both a human receiving pathetic blows and as a monster impervious to them. We might describe this pantomime as a 'rigorous rigidity', a term that suggests both rigor mortis and the dedication (rigor) of the stiff-limbed actor playing the hopping corpse. 'Jiangshi martial arts' are only really effective when performed by non-virtual actors who simultaneously embody the actor's own imperiled materiality and the role's spiritual otherness. A purely 'spectral', CGI rendering of a *jiangshi* would lack any pathetic materiality with which we could empathise. Put another way, emotionally engaging fantasy stems not from the total removal of limitations but on stretching recognisable (material) limitations to or past their breaking points, allowing us to see exactly when and where the body does or does not transcend its material boundaries. The duality of the *jiangshi* performance, simultaneously human and inhuman, thus opposes the monovalent aesthetics cum ideology of CGI, which reduces visuality to a single denominator of computerisation, in which even actors are digitised, plasticised, airbrushed and otherwise rendered immaterial to undisclosed degrees.

Conclusion: Politicising the Supernatural

Investigating the ways in which Hong Kong horror-comedies provoke and reflect the notion of bivalent spectatorship, we have (mostly) sidestepped the postcolonial and postmodern analyses that have become de rigueur in much Hong Kong film criticism. I have therefore not equated the *jiang-shi*'s quasi-nationalistic yet ever-incomplete journey towards the grave with the exilic condition of displaced Hong Kong citizens, who can never arrive at the earthly homeland they might desire. Nor have I insisted that the ambling corpse mirrors the nomadic postcolonial subject, wandering through a limbo of imagined but always forestalled futures. But even if we tire of invoking the tropes of postmodern dislocation, the exigencies of China's censorious policies force us from the realm of the spectator's subjectivity and into that of contentious – and symbolic – politics.

If tales of supernatural horror ironically reframe ancient superstitions as secular entertainments, China's official, post-1949 censorship policies more bluntly attempt to exorcise the ghosts of the past. Since 1949 China has stridently censored depictions of the supernatural in both foreign and domestic films, ostensibly to suppress vestiges of feudal superstition and promote a singular – or monovalent – modernity based (at least in theory) on socialist realism and dialectical materialism. (Unsurprisingly, the PRC's witless censorship policy presumes that supernaturally themed films must affirm – rather than mock – superstition.) As Laikwan Pang notes in his study of Mainland censorship, PRC censors are always on guard against the counter-revolutionary tendencies of ghost stores 'because, in their association with alternative realms, ghosts are politically fraught . . . a ghost can be highly allegorical, and its representations might be encoded and decoded in ways over which the state has no control' (Pang 2011: 461). Thus, as Hilary He Hongjin observes, Chinese authorities have secularised and ideologically sanitised certain high-profile films, reducing, for instance, Johnnie To's ninety-eight-minute *Running on Karma* (2003) to an '83-minute "non-superstitious" story' that, stripped of all references to karma, becomes 'motivated only by an inexplicit secular love between a man and a woman . . . leaving the Mainland audience baffled about the story . . .' (He Hongjin 2010: 10). Much as spiritually polluting *jiangshi* must be segregated from the populace at large, the mandates of socialist realism must keep supernaturalism at bay.[9] As we have suggested earlier, however, the ultimate joke is that humourless, bureaucratic post-Mao aesthetics draw lines far more rigid than the *jiangshi*'s robotic workings.

Pang's analysis emphasises Chinese authorities' fear of supernatural themes, which potentially induce interpretations beyond the purview of censors or even film-makers themselves. Here, allegorical *content* alone poses subversively bivalent possibilities. As I have suggested, however, bivalence is not merely a matter of interpretation but an element embedded in the very prospect of generic supernatural horror existing incongruously within a secular age. By forbidding supernatural genres outright, Chinese censors erase bivalent possibilities at their generic root, before allegorical contents even have the chance to occur. Aiming to establish uniform, centralised meanings as part of their system of domination, censors erase ghostly themes not because they offer film-makers a camouflage for political subversion, but because they make visible unsanctioned *valences* of meaning that oppose the official version of 'reality'. Furthermore, the bivalence conjured by supernatural themes – and by the comic incongruity they entail – threatens to co-opt the narrow dialectical materialism of communist dogma. Instead of advancing the objective, historicised dialecticism of orthodox communism, the bivalence inherent in comic horror proposes a *subjective* dialecticism, one that transpires in the private spaces of the spectator's conflicted desires.

Within the context of Chinese history, film censors' acts of suppression are part of a longer pattern of centralised state control that predates 1949. The *jiangshi*'s Qing costume signifies not a distant past but a lingering one: the PRC's current censorship policies are little different from those of the Qing Dynasty, which suppressed superstitious and rebellious cults because their alternate systems of authority and belief challenged dynastic power structures. Historically, Chinese officialdom had quashed superstition because it was linked to heterodox insurgencies, as was the case with the Taiping, White Lotus and Eight Trigram Rebellions. Today state authorities suppress Falun Gong and various deviant millenarian groups because they present possibilities for autonomous ways of being and perceiving that exist apart from state hegemony.[10] This suppressive tendency is hardly unique to totalitarian regimes, however. The US government, for instance, suppresses various apocalyptic anti-government groups (consider the incident in Waco, Texas) not because their religious beliefs are more irrational than most people's religious beliefs, but because their insurrectionary tendencies threaten state dominion.

It is therefore unsurprising that Mainland censors perceive ghost films not merely as symbols of a backwards past but as incitements to ways of seeing that threaten the dialecticism of their (pretended) Marxism. Orthodox dialectical materialism supposes a more or less linear progress of syntheses, eventually resulting in a promised utopian future. The comic bivalence we have discussed, however, proposes no futures; the very nature of comic experience demands that two incongruities clash without resolution, resulting not in progressive syntheses but an absurd stalemate. In our examples, the stalemate occurs in the mind of the spectator, who simultaneously desires realism and fantasy, logos and pathos, scientific knowledge and the promise of an afterlife. This comic stalemate (apparently) offers no chance for a different future, utopian or otherwise, nor does it seem to offer the 'trivalent' solution that Koestler suggests might or might not result from a comic clashing of two bivalently opposed ideas. And then there is the *jiangshi* itself, unable to adapt to anything, let alone foresee synthetic futures; for the comic monster, there is only a distant grave and an ultimate joke – it is not only blind to the future, but it can't even see its own, predetermined end.

Notes

1. 'Poll: Nearly 8 in 10 Americans believe in angels'. Available at <www.cbsnews.com/news/poll-nearly-8-in-10-americans-believe-in-angels/> (last accessed 8 September 2016).
2. Examples are probably unnecessary, but apart from the *Exorcist* trilogy (1973, 1976, 1990), consider *Stigmata* (1999), *End of Days* (1999), and so on, not to mention the US' recent phenomenon of 'Christian conservative' horror.
3. An atypical comedy, *The Spiritual Boxer* begins by demonstrating the 'reality' of supernatural martial arts but quickly changes modes, centring on a young apprentice (Wang Yu) who fools townspeople into believing he wields spiritual powers. Notably, the film's agnostic conclusion refuses a sentimental or revelatory moment in which Wang Yu realises spiritual verities. Instead, he fends off villains with cunning alone, and order is finally restored not by intervening gods but by gun-wielding police.
4. Though Daoist masters are usually treated reverently, they are occasionally subjected to light ridicule, especially when unscrupulous exorcists and fortune-tellers exploit folk beliefs for profit. In Ricky Lau's *Mr. Vampire* (1985), a rampaging corpse is unleashed after a crooked fortune-teller gives a family faulty burial instructions. In Lau's subsequent *Mr. Vampire 3* (1987), Richard Ng's bumbling Daoist conspires with two domesticated ghosts, releasing them to haunt unsuspecting 'customers' and then charging fees to exorcise the planted interlopers.
5. Similar is Ronny Yu's horror-comedy *The Trail* (1983), in which opium smugglers in the 1920s dress as *jiangshi* to pass by government checkpoints.
6. Attempts at social satire in *jiangshi* farces are rarely developed, however. For instance, Jeff Lau's *Haunted Cop Shop 2* (1988), with a screenplay by Wong Kar-wai, contains an early, amusing scene in which a police administrator besieged by vampires asks whether he can tax the undead to cover budget shortfalls. But the satire is soon dropped in favour of frantic slapstick.

7. Nationalism is not peculiar to Chinese horror; Western lore often claims that vampires must keep a plot of native earth nearby.
8. In his dialogic essay 'On the Marionette Theater' (1801), Kleist wonders if mechanical puppets could be more graceful than living bodies. Arguing with a friend, he concludes that 'grace appears most purely in that human form which either has no consciousness or an infinite consciousness . . . that is, in the puppet or in the god.' This is a particularly Western or Cartesian view, however; in the animistic world of Hong Kong horror, it is not the extreme forms that are graceful (puppet/god) but the intermediary form of the *jiang-shi*, which is simultaneously human and inhuman.
9. Chinese socialist realism was far stricter than that of the Soviets, who permitted fairy tales as long as they were rooted in nationalistic lore.
10. Philip Kuhn's 1990 study *Soulstealers: the Chinese Sorcery Scare of 1768* provides a now-classic account of how Chinese dynastic powers systematically quashed 'subversive' superstitions.

References

Bergson, Henri [1900] (2009), *Laughter*, Drew Burk (trans.), New York: Atropos Press.

Douglas, Mary (2002), *Purity and Danger: an Analysis of Concepts of Pollution and Taboo*, London: Routledge Classics.

Gildow, Douglas Matthew (2005), 'Flesh bodies, stiff corpses, and gathered gold: mummy worship, corpse processing, and mortuary ritual in contemporary Taiwan,' *Journal of Chinese Religions*, Boulder, CO: Society for the Study of Chinese Religions, 33, pp. 1–37.

He Hongjin, Hilary (2010), 'One movie, two versions: post-1997 Hong Kong cinema in the Mainland,' University of Western Sydney: David C. Lam Institute for East-West Studies, *Working Paper Series*, 103, September.

Kierkegaard, Søren (1962), *The Present Age*, Alexander Dru (trans.), New York: Harper and Row.

Kerr, Walter (1967), *Tragedy and Comedy*, New York: Simon and Schuster.

Kleist, Heinrich von [1801] (2016), 'On the Marionette Theater', Idris Parry (trans.), *Southern Cross Review*, 9, <www.southerncrossreview.org/9/kleist.htm> (last accessed 18 November 2016).

Koestler, Arthur (1964), *The Act of Creation*, London: Hutchinson & Co.

Kuhn, Philip A. (1990), *Soulstealers: the Chinese Sorcery Scare of 1768*, Cambridge, MA: Harvard University Press.

Pang, Laikwan (2011), 'The state against ghosts: a genealogy of China's film censorship policy', *Screen*, 52:4, pp. 461–76.

CHAPTER 6

Performing (Comic) Abjection in the Hong Kong Ghost Story

Felicia Chan

Horror cinema tends to offer a dual address: it is consumed as a popular genre, yet also frequently analysed as a psychic window into particular cultural practices at particular moments in time. Mark Gatiss's 2010 documentary survey of a history of horror cinema in Europe and the US notes how a certain comic self-reflexivity had begun to pervade the films once the genre had reached a stage of maturity in its cycle. Drawing on his own fascination for the genre in his youth, Gatiss notes in particular how the British Hammer horror films became increasingly camp in style and narrative as they moved into the 1970s. Indeed, Hammer Studios went as far as to collaborate with Hong Kong's Shaw Brothers on *The Legend of the 7 Golden Vampires* (1974) (Bettinson 2011). Gatiss also discusses American horror director Wes Craven's late career slasher revivals, *New Nightmare* (1994) and the successful *Scream* franchise (1996–2011), where the films employ meta-filmic strategies that both tapped into and commented on the viewer's prior knowledge of the genre's conventions (Church 2006), but to the extent that the 'heightened degree of intertextual referencing and self-reflexivity . . . ceases to function at the traditional level of tongue-in-cheek subtext, and emerges instead as the actual *text* of the films' (Wee 2005: 44).

Hong Kong cinema has been well noted for its extensive use of parody and pastiche (Aufderheide 1998). Likewise, while the 'horror' or 'ghost film' tradition in Hong Kong cinema is acknowledged to be drawn from Chinese literary roots and folklore traditions, the genre is also celebrated for its unabashed turn to comedy as a mode of cinematic presentation. In films such as *Mr. Vampire* (1985), ghosts, ghouls and monsters are frequently depicted comically, as hopping vampires, wandering spirits and underworld demons, mostly rendered in thick make-up, latex masks and movie slime. Yeh and Ng identify 'at least two narrative prototypes in Hong Kong horror': 'ghost erotica' and vampire or zombie '*jiangshi* (literally, stiff corpses)' (Yeh and Ng 2008: 2). Like the many popular genres in Hong Kong cinema, the horror or ghost film is seen to have had its best run during the industry's 'Second Wave' when the industry was at its most successful and creatively diverse, from around 1984 to the mid-1990s (Teo 1997: 184–203). Two of the best known 'ghost' films of this period – *A Chinese Ghost Story* (Ching Siu-tung/Tsui Hark, 1987) and *Rouge* (Stanley Kwan, 1988) – are today widely lauded as 'classics', and were both popularly received and critically acclaimed.

In this chapter, I offer a comparative reading of the horror film in Hong Kong cinema as a genre which appears to have eschewed terror in favour of a certain comic and self-reflexive address that may allow us to reflect on its differential relation to the realist, mimetic impulse of Western cinematic traditions.[1] In the tradition of Gothic literature, terror is experienced as fear in anticipation of an (horrific) event; in contrast, horror is experienced as a sense of revulsion after the event occurs. This distinction is first attributed to Ann Radcliffe, who wrote in 1826 that:

> Terror and horror are so far opposite, that the first expands the soul, and awakens the faculties to a high degree of life; the other contracts, freezes, and nearly annihilates them . . . and where lies the great difference between horror and terror, but in the uncertainty and obscurity, that accompany the first, respecting the dreaded evil?
> (Radcliffe 1826)

At the risk of some generalisation, Western horror films tend to slide between the two: terror is produced by the fear of the unknown (the monster, the ghost, the supernatural), and horror is produced when the unknown materialises as a physical body, usually in the form of the grotesque or the malformed. The canon is littered with examples: Nosferatu, Frankenstein's Creature, the Hunchback of Notre Dame and Freddy Kruger, among many others. In the late cycle of the genre, these depictions as noted by Gatiss, can enter the realm of self-conscious self-parody. By looking at the social, industrial and cultural contexts under which Hong Kong horror cinema operates, I contend that its self-reflexivity differs from the self-conscious, self-parodies of late cycle genre films in the British and American traditions. David Church, writing on the decline of American horror post-Wes Craven and post-*The Blair Witch Project* (1999), suggests that the success of American horror in previous decades had to an extent relied on the 'diegetic verisimilitude' of its assault on the physical or psychological bodies of the characters. In the post-reflexive, 'postmodern', and indeed, digital era of horror, after *The Blair Witch Project* instead located 'its horrors within the real, extra-diegetic world', and as 'CGI [computer-generated imagery] effects allow for greater simulated bodily destruction than ever before, the body has become a far less "real" site of violence in horror films'. Church concludes that following the 'contested authenticity of gore', the 'body as referent of the Real becomes lost in this new technology, violating the genre's traditional low-budget aesthetic' (Church 2006). Hong Kong cinema, and Hong Kong horror cinema in particular, has rarely invoked diegetic verisimilitude as a creative principle, drawing instead on mythological folklore, literary history and the performance traditions of Chinese stage opera. The two 'narrative prototypes' Yeh and Ng identify above, the ghost and the vampire-zombie, can be linked to these traditions. According to Stephen Teo, corporeal 'trans-substantiation', such as in the form of human to werewolf or vampire to bat, is 'unthinkable in Chinese culture since the rule of pragmatism requires that one's physical, human shape be kept intact for reincarnation and for the wheel of life to keep revolving' (Teo 1997: 219), although stories of the fox fairy often tell of its 'ability to transform itself, either into a horrible demon . . . or into a human being (preferably a beautiful woman who does mischief to mankind' (Bodde 1942: 348)). While malevolent spirits may take the form of human beings, the integrity of the corporeal form of the human body, even as buried remains, must remain intact. According to Teo, the 'reincarnation theme is the backbone of all ghost stories, and it is the ghost story which defines Hong Kong's horror genre' (Teo 1997: 221). Indeed, the narrative trajectories of both *Rouge* and *A Chinese Ghost Story* pivot on the obstructed reincarnations of the central ghostly figures in the form of Fleur (or Ruhua, played by Anita Mui) and Siu-sin (or Xiaoqian, played by Joey Wong) respectively.

Kwan's *Rouge* tells the story of the double suicide of a pair of lovers from 1930s Hong Kong. Mui's character, Fleur, returns to present-day Hong Kong (1980s) as a wandering ghost unable to pass on into the afterlife because of an unfulfilled wish to be reunited with her lover, known affectionately as the 'Twelfth Young Master', or Chan Chen-pang (played by Leslie Cheung). Most of the second half of the film tracks her search for the Twelfth Young Master in 1980s Hong Kong whose spatial geography by this point is totally unfamiliar to her. Dressed as a courtesan from the 1930s, with her form-fitting *cheongsam/qipao* and theatrical make-up, Fleur's archaic social mannerisms are presented in direct contrast to the modern, young couple (played by Alex Man and Emily Chu) whom she enlists to assist in her quest. By the end of the film, we learn that the Twelfth Young Master had not joined her in death but instead lived out the rest of his life in decadent self-indulgence and obscurity. When he is found, he is merely a shadow of his former young and virile self, a frail old man in his seventies, still trying to eke out a living as a Chinese opera stand-in, sleeping in the equally decrepit premises of the opera house.

Once Fleur discovers and accepts the truth of what had transpired, she passes successfully into the afterlife, ready to be reincarnated into a new being.

Although directing credits go to Ching Siu-tung, *A Chinese Ghost Story* is often creatively attributed to producer Tsui Hark (Morton 2001). The plot is based loosely on a short story within a classical collection of nearly 500 supernatural tales known as *Liaozhai Ziyi* (1740), usually translated into English as *Strange Stories from a Chinese Studio*, by Pu Songling. The film, set in a mythical historical past, follows the adventures of Ning Choi-san (Leslie Cheung), a hapless debt collector, who encounters a female ghost, Siu-sin. Siu-sin is unable to reincarnate into the human world because her remains are buried and held captive by an evil tree demon (Lau Siu-ming). Framed as an erotic-romantic-comedy-adventure, the film tracks the couple's attempts to free Siu-sin from the tree demon, assisted by a Daoist monk (Wu Ma). The fight sequences take on all the comic and visual excesses of Hong Kong costume dramas, replete with flailing sleeves, windblown hair, and improbable wirework stunts sending the actors flying through trees amidst a dark forest. The climactic, and memorable, fight sequence in the film involves the heroes battling the tree demon, whose signature weapon is her extra-long prosthetic tongue.

Second Wave Hong Kong films are said to focus on Hong Kong's contested identity in the run up to the 1997 handover from Britain to the People's Republic of China. The ghost film provides an allegorical device through which social and historical concerns can be articulated. As Stephen Teo puts it: '[Stanley] Kwan sees Hong Kong as homeland, a place where the heart is. His central character is literally a spirit of old Hong Kong who returns to haunt modern Hong Kong' (Teo 1997: 190). Bliss Cua Lim argues that ghost films 'make incongruous use of the vocabulary of the supernatural to articulate historical injustice', and offers the following reading of *Rouge*:

> Fleur is deeply coded by literary tradition as a profoundly eloquent figure for history. The spectral female courtesan's capacity to evoke the sense of an ending (though as a revenant she also evokes a sense of perpetuity) is exploited to intense effect in *Rouge*, grafting the phantom's literary antecedents to New Hong Kong Cinema's concerns over the impending return to Mainland China. Ghostly temporality, already heavy with references to more times than one, is thus powerfully combined with Chinese classical literature's affective structures for contemplating the passing of an age through the figure of a courtesan-specter. (Lim 2001: 316–17)

Fleur's return to 1980s Hong Kong alludes to a place and a time that are already lost. Indeed, she can barely maintain form, albeit still immaculately dressed, coiffed and made up, able to move through the streets of modern Hong Kong only at night, and weakened considerably by daylight. Rey Chow, in her 2001 essay, 'A Souvenir of Love', reads the semiotic representations of nostalgia in *Rouge* as simultaneously an attempt to recover the lost past of Hong Kong as well as an acknowledgement of the impossibility of its retrieval. In her analysis of the film, Rey Chow argues:

> Nostalgia is not simply a reaching towards a definite past from a definite present, but a subjective state that seeks to express itself in pictures imbued with particular memories of a certain pastness. *In film*, these subjectively pictorialized memories are there for everyone to see: nostalgia thus has a public life as much as a purely private one. The cinematic image, because of its visible nature, becomes a wonderfully appropriate embodiment of nostalgia's ambivalence between dream and reality, of nostalgia's insistence on seeing 'concrete' things in fantasy and memory. One could perhaps go as far as saying that Ruhua's recollections are not simply images of nostalgia; rather they contain a theory of the *filmic-image-as-nostalgia*. (Chow 2001: 215)

Here, Chow refers to the film's minute attention to recreating the material representation of 1930s Hong Kong: 'The social details from the past constitute a kind of ethnography, a culture-writing. In the process of conjuring up a different time, the details become native witnesses and aboriginal evidences that fascinate and persuade the contemporary viewer' (Chow 2001: 218–19). Indeed, the depiction of the 1930s in *Rouge* is sumptuous: within the pleasure houses of the courtesan, schooled in the arts of dance, song and polite conversation, colours are rich and saturated, fabrics are luxuriantly embroidered, furniture ornately carved. This is the world in which Fleur inhabits and one we are invited to look back on with rapture. This 'culture-writing' can be seen as a mode of writing the history of Hong Kong, which was already spectral. This vibrant world is presented in direct contrast to the blandness of the 1980s, with its washed out colours, grey concrete and prosaic substitution of sex for romance. The presence of the 1980s, far from inviting our spectatorial identification only draws attention to how far we may have come from the idealised image of the past. Yet, because there are barely any traces of the past left in fast-moving Hong Kong, films of a similar ilk are not, as Chow notes

> *nostalgic for the past* as it was; rather, they are, simply by their sensitivity to the movements of temporality, nostalgic in tendency. Their affect is interesting precisely because we cannot know its object for sure. Only the sense of loss it projects is finite. (Chow 2001: 225)

In other words, despite the hurtling towards an indeterminate future beyond 1997, the sense of the past is as spectral as the ghostly figure who has come to represent it.

Likewise, John Zou reads the pre-handover political concerns of Hong Kong in *A Chinese Ghost Story*. He writes:

> Although the film seems to haphazardly combine romance, martial arts and period drama, its programmatic imprudence, excessive self-mockery and dizziness result-ing from hasty production all contribute to a uniquely potent configuration of sexu-ality, history and contemporary Hong Kong politics. (Zou 2008: 56–7)

However, his reading focuses not on the spectral figure of the female ghost but on the body of whom he calls 'the Final Boy', Ning Choi-san, played by the iconic Leslie Cheung:

> I argue that in the Final Boy – rather than the Final Girl – embodied in the charis-matic Leslie Cheung, Hong Kong sets up a lucky, innocent but helplessly gullible, imperialist figure, to be eternally staged, tantalised and seduced by a feminised Hong Kong undergoing repeated colonising ravishment. The presumed straight male gaze of the cinematic subject undergoes a similar process of masochistic self-articulation, not through identification with a female final survivor, but by projecting a feminised passion by which the want for men is satisfied through a seemingly passive but indeed predatory entrapment. (Zou 2008: 59)

Zou goes as far as to add that:

> when the cinematic gaze is focused upon Leslie Cheung, a gay man playing the heterosexual lead, the masochist identification with his threatened body by a 'straight' audience is inevitably correlated with a male homosexual projection of desire, for which the Final Boy constitutes the object of passion rather than the designation of the self. (Zou 2008: 59)

As Cheung is said to have come out publicly as gay only after his role in Wong Kar-wai's *Happy Together* (1997) (Bergan 2003), it is uncertain if audiences in the late 1980s would have read this sexual coding, though Cheung's sexual orientation had been a subject for tabloid speculation for a number of years. Nonetheless, Zou's alternative reading of the cinematic gaze here provides fertile ground for a broader political reading of the anxieties produced by the colonial gaze within the Hong Kong ghost story:

> The Hong Kong horror genre in the last two decades of the twentieth century . . . specifically addresses subject formation under the shadow of agonising and riveting anticipation of radical socio-political change – Hong Kong's 'post'-colonial repatria-tion. Here, the source of anxiety is not so much the reconfiguration of pre-existing structures as the advent of the absolutely new. (Zou 2008: 59)

The ghostly and the spectral in these films therefore stand in for a kind of indeterminacy of the past, the present, as well as the future. It remains there on-screen as a presence but is yet ungraspable, and it should be noted that both Fleur and Siu-sin effectively fail in their quests. In meeting the forlorn figure of her past lover as an old man, now addicted to opium, Fleur's reunification with him is thwarted. Siu-sin and her compatriots lose the initial battle with the demon and they fail to save her soul, condemning her to the underworld, to which the heroes then have to descend to rescue her. Though there remains a glimmer of hope at the end when her remains are reburied, it is only in the animated version of the film (also subtitled 'The Tsui Hark Animation', 2011) that Siu-sin's reincarnation is directly referenced and the lovers are reunited. Significantly, this ending transmutes itself into the form of a traditional Chinese painting before the credits roll. Accordingly, Bliss Cua Lim notes that

> the ghost narrative opens the possibility of a radicalized concept of noncontemporaneity; haunting as ghostly return precisely refuses the idea that things are just left behind', that the past is inert and the present uniform. Put simply, the ghost forces the point of nonsynchronism. It is this challenge to received ideas of time that makes the specter a particularly provocative figure for the claims of history. (Lim 2001: 288)

In reflecting on the historical and political allegories of these films, I now turn to the textual qualities of the films themselves, and draw on Wee's remark on the *Scream* trilogy noted at the beginning of this chapter, where she notes that the self-reflexivity of the films emerge 'as the actual *text* of the films' themselves (Wee 2005: 44). Here I argue that comic reflexivity of performance in *Rouge* and *A Chinese Ghost Story* draws on Chinese performance traditions on stage and screen, which have differential negotiations with cinema as a photo-realist medium, and may allow us to rethink Hong Kong (horror) cinema's relation to the 'abject' as originally articulated by Julia Kristeva and widely applied to Western horror films (Magistrale 2005). In *Powers of Horror: an Essay on Abjection* (1980), Kristeva argues that the catharsis of horror allows for a kind of 'purification' of the abject, 'the jettisoned object', which occupies 'the place where meaning collapses' (Kristeva 1982: 2). Magistrale cites examples of the abject

> found in the excessive blood imagery that is associated with Carrie's menstruation and symbolic prom-queen sacrificing; it is located in the open maw of the Alien creature that continually secretes a toxic saliva; and it is likewise in the various horrific wombs of horror cinema that give birth to nonhuman offspring . . . as well as in the ghostly visitations contained and vented inside physical dwellings (Magistrale 2005: 7)

Abjection in Western horror cinema is also widely associated with the depiction of the 'monstrous feminine' (Creed 1986). In *Rouge* and *A*

Chinese Ghost Story, however, there is little that actually repels us. No doubt Fleur's initial appearance and discovery induces fear in the modern couple she meets, but our identification is not with them but with her. As Rey Chow notes, in *Rouge* we are drawn to Fleur because the 'degree of our "historical" interest in the world of the 1930s is in many ways in direct proportion to the degree of our "irrational" mesmerisation by a passion we feel is foreign to our time' (Chow 2001: 220). Seen through the frame of Fleur's time, the modern couple are relatively colourless, lacking both passion and grace. In *A Chinese Ghost Story*, the monstrous tongue of the tree demon, dripping with slime and saliva as it may be, is so excessive and artificial that unlike Ripley in *Alien* (Ridley Scott, 1979), if we are repulsed by it, we are also prone to laugh. Diegetic verisimilitude is dependent on a suspension of disbelief that is frequently punctured in Hong Kong cinema.

When André Bazin celebrated the power of cinema to capture what he saw as unmediated reality, he also attributed to it the capacity to collapse the split he saw in the debates on realism within Western aesthetics. Bazin writes in his 1960 essay, 'The Ontology of the Photographic Image':

> The quarrel over realism in art stems from a misunderstanding, from a confusion between the aesthetic and the psychological; between true realism, the need that is to give significant expression to the world both concretely and its essence, and the pseudorealism of a deception aimed at fooling the eye (or for that matter the mind); a pseudorealism content in other words with illusory appearance. (Bazin 1960: 7)

'The objective nature of photography', he argued,

> confers upon it a quality of credibility absent from all other picturemaking. In spite of any objections our critical spirit may offer, we are forced to accept as real the existence of the object reproduced, actually re-presented, set before us, that is to say, in time and space. (Bazin 1960: 7–8)

This philosophical position tends to underpin the representation of diegetic verisimilitude in Western cinema, even (or especially?) in films with fantastical narratives or settings. In mainstream Hollywood cinema, Superman's ability to fly must look believable within the diegesis (even though what looks believable is conditioned by the technological capabilities of the time), inasmuch as the Alien's assault on Ripley must look and feel believable to the audience, who has been conditioned by the logic of the genre and the diegesis to suspend its disbelief of any 'real' examples of flying humanoids or alien creatures. For this reason, the development of computer-generated imagery in contemporary Hollywood cinema is largely geared towards making fantastical spectacles more and more 'real-istic', or what Jean-Louis Comolli already termed in 1980, 'reality effects' (Comolli 1980: 131). I argue that the imperative for visual and diegetic verisimilitude is less prevalent in Hong Kong cinema, which has histori-cally drawn its aesthetics from the more dramatic arts of theatre and the stage (see Pang 2006).

In her analysis of *Rouge*, Lim draws attention to a particular scene where a reference to Cantonese stage opera is made:

> In *Rouge*, the ghost of a courtesan who seeks her lost lover among the living weeps at the drab sight of Hong Kong's former red-light district, Shitangzui, in 1987. In one of the film's most telling images, the revenant walks past a shop window, and we see reflected on it, as if on a screen, the shadowy performance of an old Cantonese opera at the theater that the storefront has replaced. In a visual palimpsest, this film sequence depicts one space as splintered yet whole: an antiseptic shopping mall in the late 1980s, in whose dark glass we glimpse the warm glamour of the demolished Tai Ping Theater. (Lim 2001: 290–1)

This moment is, Lim adds, 'arresting in [its] nostalgic inscription of postcolonial histories within the context of the ghost narrative' (Lim 2001: 291). The reference to Cantonese opera as a shadowy palimpsest is echoed in the final denouement and discovery of the aged Twelfth Young Master's sorry fate. The decline in his prospects is aligned with the fate of traditional Chinese opera in the face of modern Chinese film-making, which in the closing scenes in *Rouge* is represented by the historical mar-tial arts film Hong Kong cinema was once known for. In the sequence we are presented with a brief instance of a film being made on the set with an actor in historical costume being drawn across the screen with wires and special effects. The ghostly spectre alluded to here is not just the spectre of history but also the spectre of (and the nostalgia for) the history of the form, the genre and the industry which gave rise to it. By the late 1980s the historical sword-fighting fantasies (*wuxia*) rooted in the balletic forms of Chinese opera and popularised by the Shaw Brothers studio had given way to the more contemporary fist-fighting (*kungfu*) features of the new Golden Harvest studio (Teo 1997: 80). In both *Rouge* and *A Chinese Ghost Story*, the comic and self-reflexive presentation (rather than 'represen-tation' in the mimetic sense) of such abject subjects, where the know-ing exposure of the cinematic machinery of costume and special effects, appears to put it at odds with the spectral affectivity described by Ackbar Abbas as Hong Kong's culture of 'disappearance' (Abbas 1994).

Historically, another reason why Hong Kong horror films have eschewed diegetic verisimilitude may be due to censorship laws and practices exercised by the People's Republic of China (PRC), whose predisposition for social realism mandates a ban on the depiction of the supernatural in films. Although Hong Kong did not come under the jurisdiction of the PRC until 1997, its films certainly circulated there. Laikwan Pang surveys the implications of such a policy, and explains how ghost stories can be seen to undermine state power. 'A ghost', she argues, and as we have seen, 'can be highly allegorical, and its representations might be encoded and decoded in ways over which the state has no control' (Pang 2011: 461). She further adds that '[e]nriched by Buddhist, Daoist and Confucian ideas, ghosts become instruments of political satire, vehicles for wild imaginations, channels for escapism, allegories of sexual freedom or simply exalted literary or artistic expressions in their own right' (Ibid.: 474). Despite these restrictions, film-makers have nonetheless worked creatively around them, by, for example, depicting 'the main characters . . . as psychopaths, or else there is a story within a story and all the horrific elements are shown to be either delusions or fictitious' (Ibid.: 472). Supernatural films remain popular within Chinese markets, especially given the rise of horror cinema from Japan and Korea in the 2000s, and indeed the history of such Chinese storytelling predates the cinema. As Andrew Ng notes of the 'Asian gothic', 'Asian literature is rich with narratives of haunting, the uncanny, and the monstrous' (Ng 2008: 2), and argues that the gothic has played a central role in the development of modern Chinese literature:

> After the Cultural Revolution and the fall of the Gang of Four . . . an innovative mode of fictive expression known as New Wave Fiction, practitioners of which include writers such as Mo Yan, Su Tong, Can Xue and Jia Pinghwa, came to dominate the literal scene of China. Much of this fiction can be defined as Gothic because of its unabashed representation of excess, horror, terror and violence. Characters who inhabit the world of New Wave writings are often extravagantly grotesque configurations; generically, many such narratives resemble postmodern bricolages that cover realism, the fantastic and the horrific. Whether they be tales of the supernatural, the fantastic or the grotesque, one important feature in New Wave fiction is its utilisation of the body as a metaphor of resistance. (Ng 2008: 9)

The rise of the pan-Asian horror trend in the 2000s seems to have set the Hong Kong horror film back somewhat, as the Hong Kong film industry which was, according to Pang, 'once famous for churning out hundreds of formulaic horror films has almost completely died out – precisely because of the industry's fraught efforts to adapt to the Chinese market and its policy environment' (Pang 2011: 474). In fact, Bliss Cua Lim is sceptical of the 'Asian horror' label invoked by Hollywood agencies, and argues that such a label points not only to

a film cycle but also [to] a complex generative act of naming, a discursive formation, regionalist and globalist in character, that allows an array of movies to become
coherent and marketable in particular ways . . . [establishing] a horizon of reception
for Asian horror across the board for Hollywood studios, producers, distributors,
exhibitors, critics and audiences. (Lim 2007: 117)

Local specificities are effaced. A cast of the eye towards more recent Hong
Kong horror cinema suggests the reality is otherwise. Although production has declined in numbers, recent Hong Kong horror films such as
Visible Secret (Ann Hui, 2001), *My Left Eye Sees Ghosts* (Johnnie To,
2002) and *Rigor Mortis* (Juno Mak, 2013), while apparently appearing to
capitulate to the broader trend of pan-Asian horror cinema nonetheless
retain much of their local 'Hong Kong' flavour. Unlike the truly terrifying supernatural horror films that emerged from Japan in the late 1990s,
like *The Ring / Ringu* (Hideo Nakata, 1998), these Hong Kong incarnations retain their comedic cores. Computer-generated imagery may have
replaced animatronic mechanisms in the creation of their ghostly encounters, but even these remain resolutely theatrical. A scene in Hui's *Visible
Secret* places a female ghost on the subway train, who like Fleur in *Rouge*
is dressed in traditional dress and exaggerated white facial make-up, allud-
ing not only to Kwan's film but also to the Chinese operatic tradition of
masked ghosts. To's *My Left Eye Sees Ghosts* unabashedly rips off the
CGI excesses of Jim Carrey's cartoon-like character in *The Mask* (Charles
Russell, 1994), where an animated mask of a skull with bulging bloodshot
eyes and extended, snake-like tongue is suddenly superimposed on Lau
Ching-wan's face. The female protagonist, May Ho, whose eponymous
left eye bears the ability to see ghosts, is played by Sammi Cheng, one of
Hong Kong's most prolific comic actresses. Mak's *Rigor Mortis* returns to
the hopping vampire / zombie trope, albeit with higher production values
than its 1980s and 1990s counterparts. The comedy is less slapstick and
lies more in subtle references to the genre films of the past, such as the
presence of a virgin boy whose urine (as audiences familiar with the genre
will know) is said to deter zombies. That the ruse does not work suggests
that the film is less concerned with reviving the genre than paying homage
to it. It is this emphasis on theatricality and performance that sustains the
culture of invention, repetition and reinvention in Hong Kong cinema. As
Lim remarks on the 'repetitive cannibalism of genre': 'Repetition draws us
inexorably into the local specific character of Hong Kong cinema as well
as to transnational generic exchange in regionalist and globalist perspectives' (Lim 2007: 109). And it is by allowing us to laugh at the abject, by
continually extending the comic possibilities of the form and the genre,
whether at the height of film production in the 1980s, or in more recent

post-1997 incarnations, that the Hong Kong ghost story is able to fully inhabit the spectrality thrust upon it by the unrelenting forces of history.

Note

1. My thanks to Robin Loon for pointing out that in Mandarin Chinese, the word 邪 xie in 邪恶 xie-e (evil) sounds the same as the 谐 xie in 诙谐 hui-xie (comedic).

References

Abbas, Ackbar (1994), 'The new Hong Kong cinema and the "déjà disparu"', *Discourse*, 16:3, pp. 65–77.

Aufderheide, Patricia (1998), 'Made in Hong Kong: translation and transmutation', in Andrew Horton and Stuart Y. McDougal (eds), *Play it Again, Sam: Retakes on Remakes*, Berkeley: University of California Press, pp. 191–9.

Bazin, André (1960), 'The ontology of the photographic image', *Film Quarterly*, 13:4, pp. 4–9.

Bergan, Ronald (2003), 'Leslie Cheung', obituary, *The Guardian*, 5 April, <https://www.theguardian.com/news/2003/apr/05/guardianobituaries> (last accessed 30 August 2016).

Bettinson, Gary (2011), 'The Shaw Brothers meet Hammer: coproduction, coherence, and cult film criteria', *Asian Cinema*, 22:1, pp. 122–37.

Bodde, Derk (1942), 'Some Chinese tales of the supernatural', *Harvard Journal of Asiatic Studies*, 6:3/4, pp. 338–57.

Chow, Rey (2001), 'A souvenir of love', in Esther C. M. Yau (ed.), *At Full Speed: Hong Kong Cinema in a Borderless World*, Minneapolis: University of Minnesota Press, pp. 209–29.

Church, David (2006), 'Return of the return of the repressed: notes on the American horror film (1991–2006)', *Off Screen*, 10:10, http://offscreen.com/view/return_of_the_repressed> (last accessed 30 August 2016).

Comolli, Jean-Louis (1980), 'Machines of the visible', in Teresa de Lauretis and Stephen Heath (eds), *The Cinematic Apparatus*, London: Macmillan, pp. 121–42.

Creed, Barbara (1986), 'Horror and the monstrous feminine: an imaginary abjection', *Screen*, 27:1, pp. 44–71.

Gatiss, Mark (2010), *A History of Horror*, John Das and Rachel Jardine (dirs), originally aired 11–25 October, BBC Four.

Kristeva, Julia [1980] (1982), *Powers of Horror: an Essay on Abjection*, Leon S. Roudiez (trans.), New York: Columbia University Press.

Lim, Bliss Cua (2001), 'Spectral times: the ghost film as historical allegory', *Positions: East Asia Cultures Critique*, 9:2, pp. 287–329.

Lim, Bliss Cua (2007), 'Generic ghosts: remaking the new "Asian horror film"', in Gina Marchetti and Tan See Kam (eds), *Hong Kong Film, Hollywood and the New Global Cinema: No Film is an Island*, London: Routledge, pp. 109–25.

Magistrale, Tony (2005), *Abject Terrors: Surveying the Modern and Postmodern Horror Film*, New York: Peter Lang.

Morton, Lisa (2001), *The Cinema of Tsui Hark*, Jefferson: McFarland.

Ng, Andrew Hock Soon (2008), 'Introduction: the Gothic visage of Asian narratives', in Andrew Hock Soon Ng (ed.), *Asian Gothic: Essays on Literature, Film and Anime*, Jefferson: McFarland, pp. 1–15.

Pang, Laikwan (2006), 'Walking into and out of the spectacle: China's earliest film scene', *Screen*, 47:1, pp. 66–80.

Pang, Laikwan (2011), 'The state against ghosts: a genealogy of China's film censorship policy', *Screen*, 52:4, pp. 461–76.

Radcliffe, Ann (1826), 'On the supernatural in poetry', *New Monthly Magazine* 16:1, pp. 145–52, <https://www.saylor.org/site/wp-content/uploads/2011/01/On-the-Supernatural-in-Poetry.pdf> (last accessed 27 December 2016).

Teo, Stephen (1997), *Hong Kong Cinema: the Extra Dimensions*, London: British Film Institute.

Wee, Valerie (2005), 'The *Scream* trilogy, "hyperpostmodernism", and the late-nineties teen slasher film', *Journal of Film and Video*, 57:3, pp. 44–61.

Yeh, Emilie Yueh-yu and Ng, Neda Hei-tung (2008), 'Magic, medicine, cannibalism: the China demon in Hong Kong horror', *LEWI Working Paper Series*, 74, Hong Kong: David C. Lam Institute for East-West Studies, April.

Zou, John (2008), '*A Chinese Ghost Story*: ghostly counsel and innocent man', in Chris Berry (ed.), *Chinese Films in Focus II*, London: British Film Institute, pp. 56–63.

CHAPTER 7

Hands, Fingers and Fists: 'Grasping' Hong Kong Horror Films

David Scott Diffrient

In an essay concerning the 1970s kung fu craze, film scholar David Desser draws attention to a curious cultural phenomenon, pinpointing an unprecedented moment in motion picture history when three foreign releases topped the US box-office charts (2000). Those three films – *Fists of Fury* (aka *The Big Boss*, 1971), *Deep Thrust: the Hand of Death* (aka *Lady Whirlwind*, 1972) and *Five Fingers of Death* (aka *King Boxer*, 1972) – ranked first, second and third among all North American theatrical releases during the week of 16 May 1973, and that initial success paved the way for what Desser refers to as the 'high point' of martial arts cinema's commercial dominance the following month (Desser 2000: 23). Indeed, during the week of 20 June 1973, the above trio of releases was joined by several other Hong Kong productions, including *Duel of the Iron Fist* (aka *The Duel*, 1971), *Kung Fu: The Invisible Fist* (1972) and *Thunderbolt Fist* (1972), which not only contributed to Stateside audiences' growing interest in Chinese martial arts but also similarly foregrounded – through their English-language titles – the centrality of hand-to-hand combat in the iconographic constitution of the genre. Subsequent productions such as the Shaw Brothers' *Shaolin Hand Lock* (1978) further solidified the cultural imaginary of kung fu cinema, which has since been codified as a physically balletic and graceful, if also violently bloody and brutal, genre defined in part by the persistent presence of deadly thrusting hands.

Of course, hands are also central to another type of cultural production, one that, within China, has often incorporated kung fu action and martial arts iconography. Although the genre can be traced back to the earliest years of Cantonese- and Mandarin-language sound film production (1930s), Hong Kong's horror cinema began to gain international prominence in the 1970s and 1980s, thanks to the circulation of works that were at least partially inspired by *jiangshi* fiction – literary texts featuring sundry forms of reanimated (or 'hopping') corpses and (un)healthy doses of scatological humor. With examples ranging from Yiu Hua Hsi-men's

Demon Strike (1979) and Sammo Hung's *Spooky Encounters* (1980) to Hwa I Hung's *Kung Fu Zombie* (1982) and Sun Chung's *Human Lanterns* (1982), horror films from that period played upon local and global audiences' familiarity with genre conventions, including the tendency to showcase human and non-human hands as both embodied and disembodied manifestations of physical danger or psychological dread. Although much has already been written about the prevalence of 'clutching hands' in US and European motion pictures, particularly with regard to the converging strains of Gothic thrillers and monster movies that followed the release of Paul Leni's Universal Pictures production *The Cat and the Canary* (1927) (Koszarski 1994: 186), little has been made of the equally prominent place such imagery occupies in Hong Kong cinema. This chapter attempts to fill that gap by assessing a broad range of motion pictures that showcase hands in thematically complex and symptomatically relevant ways, be they the severed anatomical remnants of long-departed souls sprung back to life in *Witch from Nepal* (1986) or the skeletal appendages that comically grab the protagonist's crotch in the aforementioned *Spooky Encounters*.

That latter film, a spectacularly choreographed classic of the genre starring Sammo Hung as the tellingly named 'Bold' Cheung, will serve as a key case study in the final third of this chapter; not only because it includes a humorous scene involving a possessed hand (anticipating a similar moment in Sam Raimi's low-budget *Evil Dead II*, 1987) but also for its demonstration of the mind–body division that structures *all* horror films (regardless of their national origins). 'Bold' indeed boldly goes into an abandoned house where he encounters one frightful yet funny sight after another (including a terrorising vampire), yet it is his own grasping hand (which he no longer controls thanks to black magic) that proves to be his worst nemesis. In attempting to get a handle on that hand (literally and figuratively), he and we strive to pin down the powerful forces that lay dormant within the genre, including its tendency to dredge up and display moments of excessive, other-wordly violence for which there is seemingly no rational explanation. The ethical dimensions of the genre are thus crystalised in that divide between the *hand* as a means of enacting such violence and the *mind* that might try to make sense of it. We should therefore consider the two distinct notions of the word 'grasping' that underscore classic and contemporary horror films, such as *Spooky Encounters* and more recent productions like *Forest of Death* (2007) and *The Child's Eye* (2010), which demonstrate how physical and mental operations – the corporeal *clutching* as well as the cognitive *understanding* specific to the genre – can be bridged, if only momentarily, through hand imagery.

A Farewell to Arms: (Dis)Embodied Horror

'I didn't see anyone. Just a hand.'
– Rainie, a traumatised young woman recounting the most terrifying part of her latest dream to her friends, in the 2002 Hong Kong horror film *The Child's Eye*

Prior to the advent of motion pictures as a medium of technological wonder, visual spectacle, and narrative storytelling at the turn of the twentieth century, Western literary texts in the Gothic tradition of the 1800s had foregrounded hand imagery as operative means of exploring the divide between sanity and madness, the conscious and unconscious minds. Such themes, according to Barry Langford, are also central to the horror film, which distinguishes itself from other genres partly by demonstrating how the 'transgression of limits' is made experientially palpable or 'graspable' (at the cognitive and corporeal levels) through images of bodily fragmentation and destruction (Langford 2005: 158). Cinema, it has been argued, has at least one advantage over literature: namely the visual register that forms its ontological base and, in the words of Barbara Antonucci, 'gives thickness to words' (Antonucci 2007: 166). Covering a 'wider range of direct sensory experience' than other types of cultural production, film literalises or 'fleshes out' what would otherwise be metaphorical ideas on the printed page, lending those concepts an 'affective charge' (Langford 2005: 158; Costanzo 2004: 4–5). Still, a brief consideration of literary horror's fixation on hands will be useful as a preamble to the discussion of Hong Kong cinema that follows, for it situates the latter in a cross-cultural, cross-media lineage of international publications and productions that are similarly drawn to the body as a site of rational and irrational fears.

An exemplary English-language text in this light is Sheridan Le Fanu's 'Narrative of the Ghost of a Hand', a much-anthologised short story that the Irish writer originally interpolated as an embedded tale within his 1863 mystery novel *The House by the Churchyard*. As denoted by its title, phalangeal fears are the root of this supernatural story, which anticipated the same author's more famous 'sensation novel' *Wylder's Hand* (1864) by one year. 'Narrative of the Ghost of a Hand' concerns a husband and wife – the wealthy Prosser family – who grow increasingly distressed by the sight and sound of a seemingly dismembered hand intruding upon their otherwise peaceful life in Dublin. The doors and windows of the couple's cottage do little to shield their insulated existence from this supernatural, unknowable threat, and as thresholds to the outside world these architectural features suggest a movie screen. Tellingly, the hand's first manifestation occurs one August evening when Mrs Prosser, sitting alone in her parlour, catches sight of the weirdly moving object outside her window, which looks out onto the estate's beautiful orchard. Placed upon the stone windowsill, the 'handsomely formed' hand, which is described as being 'white and plump' with clenched knuckles, suddenly withdraws at the sound of the woman's loud scream (Le Fanu 1964: 402). Her 'ejaculation of terror' in this scene hints at the correlation between sexual fulfilment and fear of the unknown – two recurring themes in horror film, which treats the screen as both a fleshy skin to be penetrated and as a 'window onto the world' that grants temporary access to its many mysteries or 'secrets'. Like those perennial motifs, the severed hand does not depart for good in this Victorian-era story, but keeps coming back over several pages, inserting its ghostly yet physical presence into the lives of the cleaning and cooking staff in addition to the Prossers' bedridden son, a toddler whose 'strange sickness' is attributed to it (Ibid.: 406).

Lacking a properly conclusive conclusion, the tale culminates ambig-uously with the narrator musing that 'the person to whom that hand belonged never once appeared; nor was it a hand separated from a body, but only a hand so manifested and introduced that its owner was always, by some crafty accident, hidden from view' (Ibid.: 407). Thus, the titular thing that cannot be caught or expelled from the house is paradoxically corporeal and discarnate, there but not there – the synecdochal stand-in for a larger threat that simply cannot be seen or 'grasped' in its entirety. Meta-textually, the hand, shorn from its ghostly owner's body, can be said to represent the story itself. That is, in being separately anthologised, this 'dismembered' tale has been removed from its original container (the aforementioned novel *The House by the Churchyard*) and now exerts autonomy as a recontextualised narrative, as part of a larger whole that has been granted its own wholeness.

Le Fanu's 'Narrative of the Ghost of a Hand' is certainly not the only example of Gothic literature to locate social anxieties and psychological traumas at the site of a body part that is unique – uniquely contradictory – in its power to either create something of value or rob a person of life (through choking/strangulation or the wielding of a weapon), sometimes seemingly on its own accord. For example, several anonymously written detective stories published its wake, including 'The Mystery of the Bloody Hand' (1865), 'The Maimed Hand' (1875) and 'The Black Dogs and the Thumbless Hand' (1896), hinge on a shared narrative premise: that of a criminal or victim being identified by his or her wounded hand, which represents the violence committed by or inflicted upon a person who is 'reduced' to that titular body part (Briefel 2015: 14). As explained by Aviva Briefel, the culprit in many of these and other stories is typically 'recognized through a manual injury acquired while committing the crime'; in other cases, 'a dead victim's detached hand offers proof of the sort of violence done to its owner' (Ibid.). Moreover, Briefel argues that the otherworldly 'racialized hands' of Egyptian mummies in several *fin-de-siècle* fantastical fictions (for example, Edgar Allan Poe's 'Some Words with a Mummy' (1845), Sir Arthur Conan Doyle's 'Lot No. 249' (1892), and so on) occupy 'a tenuous position between body parts and material artifacts.' She states, 'While they are remnants of the dead and evoke the productive hands of long-deceased artists, they also "survive" as concrete remains from the past, material evidence of enduring manual productions' (Ibid.: 24). As a detached part of the missing whole (that is, the embalmed/mummified figure, which is both 'a person and a thing'), the synecdochal hand in this context presents the reader with an 'uncanny duality' (Ibid.: 80). Much like M. C. Escher's iconic lithograph *Drawing Hands* (1948), which 'breaks down the distinction between creator and created' by showing each feeding into the other, the mummy's hand brings together human labour and the inhuman products of that labour. Paradoxes mount as one recognises that the Victorian-era mummy's hand is both a gruesome signifier of irreducible otherness – something to be avoided at all costs – and a talismanic fetish object to be treasured by collector–consumers of the 'mysterious' Orient.

Other works of the nineteenth century likewise tapped into the allegorical and sexual suggestiveness of hands, most notably Robert Louis Stevenson's 1886 novella *Strange Case of Dr. Jekyll and Mr. Hyde*. This classic tale of man's inherent dualities (civilisation vs barbarism, rational restraint vs irrational desire) makes the hand a conspicuous part of its diegetic universe. As discussed by Elaine Showalter, the fractured protagonist's hands 'seem almost to have a life of their own', with the right hand being indicative of 'patriarchal respectability and constraint' (which Jekyll seems to have inherited from his father) and the left hand being suggestive of immorality and rebelliousness (soon to manifest in Hyde's sinister dealings with unsuspecting victims) (Showalter 2000: 197). When Jekyll discovers that his metamorphosis is beyond his control, 'he wakes up to find that his own hand, the hand of his father, the "large, firm, white and comely" hand of the successful professional, has turned into the "lean, corded, knuckly" and hairy hand of Hyde' (Ibid.). In the words of Showalter, 'the implied phallic image here also suggests the difference between the properly socialized sexual desires of the dominant society and the twisted, sadistic, and animal desires of the other side' (Ibid.). And yet, as Slavoj Žižek reminds us, the hand, even when clenched into a fist, is 'the organ par excellence not of spontaneous pleasure but of instrumental activity, of work and exploration' (Žižek 1997: 16).

Tellingly, the first moment of Rouben Mamoulian's big-screen adaptation *Dr. Jekyll and Mr. Hyde* (1931) is a point of view shot from the title character's position as he sits at a pipe organ inside his posh London residence, his arms outstretched before the instrument. His fingers explore the keys of the three-tiered organ in a way that anticipates his later interaction with bar singer Ivy Pearson, whose leg garter he impishly caresses before she halts the movement of his roving hand. As 'organs' atop the organ, the English doctor's hands are initially presented to the audience as *producers* of (musical) pleasure, but are eventually revealed to be *partakers* of (libidinal) pleasure. Later, once smooth skin gives way to hirsute knuckles, the ape-like Hyde becomes, in the words of Monica Germanà, the 'savage other' – a creature whose 'protruding teeth, unkempt eyebrows, and [large] nose' lend credence to Barry Keith Grant's notion that 'the experience of horror in the cinema is almost always grounded in the visual representation of bodily difference' (Grant 1996/2015: 6). Indeed, the 'dread of difference' (to borrow the title of Grant's 1996 book) that permeates the genre is exacerbated by the fact that, in many films, the monstrous other is often only an arm's length away; literally 'armed' with elongated hands that, Hyde-like, grasp at us (or, rather, our onscreen surrogates) just as *we* figuratively try to grasp at – to make sense of – it. What makes the opening scene of *Dr. Jekyll and Mr. Hyde* so disconcerting is the presence of arms and hands untethered to a body, which in its momentary absence has been replaced by the cinematic apparatus – the camera that adopts the title character's point of view (seated before the musical instrument). Even at this early stage of the narrative, Jekyll's internal struggle is externally divulged in the way that he keeps each hand on a different level of the tiered organ keys, as if these two 'instruments' of creation and destruction can play the musical tune in unison only by being physically separated, one from the other.

Another studio-era horror film based on a nineteenth-century literary classic, director James Whale's Universal production *Frankenstein* (1931), foregrounds the monster's hands even earlier, during its opening credits. Following a brief curtain-parting prologue in which character actor Edward Van Sloan stands on a stage and warns the audience of the shocks and thrills that await them, the film's title card combines an image of savagely clawing hands with large staring eyes, two of the most frequently repeated visual motifs across the genre's history (Prawer 1980: 24). Although Henry Frankenstein's hideous progeny is a mishmash of cobbled-together body parts (excavated from newly dug-up graves), its hands are given pride of place among that unholy assemblage. Indeed, the audience's first glimpse of the monster as a living creature is delivered as a close-up shot of its right hand moving – visible evidence that the mad scientist has succeeded in bringing his creation to life. Set in Henry's laboratory, this scene puts so much visual emphasis on the monster's hand that it seems detached from the larger body strapped onto the operating table. This close-up is immediately followed by a medium shot of the scientist looking at the hand in awe, acknowledging its movement before delivering the film's most famous line: 'It's alive! It's alive!'[1] Although the subject of Henry's exclamation is the entire creature to whom the hand belongs, his eyes are initially fixated on the latter, as if that individual body part's animation is what matters most to the man whose own hands worked to shape and create the thing. In that sense, the character's euphoria at seeing the monster move is a meta-textual response to movement itself (a distinctive characteristic of the motion picture medium) as well as an acknowledgement that his godlike power derives from being able *to produce the ability to produce*. With his own hands *he has made hands* that have the power to either create or destroy.

By the time that Whale's *Frankenstein* was theatrically released, several English-language horror films and mystery thrillers had already made the hand an entrenched part of the motion picture medium's now-standardised '*mise-en-scène* of fear'.[2] So entrenched was it that, for many critics, the image of 'a hand gliding along a banister' had become as central and formulaic a scare-generating device as the presence of 'Gothic manors lit by lightning' and 'shadows glimpsed under doors' (White 1971). As one critic states, 'clutching hands' became a cornerstone of the genre following the 1927 release of *The Cat and the Canary*, a prototypical 'Old Dark House' film that also features such atmospheric elements as 'sliding panels, thunderstorms, [and] billowing curtains in darkened hallways' (Hallenbeck 2003: 13). Beginning in the 1930s, numerous other films around the world would refine and expand the horror genre's repertoire of stock images, including US and UK studio productions such as director Karl Freund's *Mad Love* (1935), Robert Florey's *The Beast with Five Fingers* (1946) and Freddie Francis's *Dr. Terror's House of Horrors* (1964), three of the many motion pictures that deploy disembodied hands as metaphors of the 'anxieties about bodily control and integrity' (Hutchings 2008: 99).[3] Regardless of whether these severed body parts are simply figments of characters' imaginations or the actual physical remainder of wronged individuals who seek revenge from beyond the grave, hands have been operationally encoded as signs of characters' 'tortured consciousness' (be it that of the victim or the villain) – a fixture of the genre that Peter Hutchings alludes to in his discussion of Oliver Stone's 1981 psychological horror film *The Hand* (Ibid.). Not surprisingly, the promotional material (posters, lobby cards, and so on) surrounding this and other films (*The Hands of Orlac* (1960), *Hands of a Stranger* (1962), *The Crawling Hand* (1963), and so on) foreground the titular body part, free-floating in space as a weirdly static yet animated limb that appears to have a 'mind of its own'.[4] And yet, as I will explain in my discussion of Hong Kong horror films that follows, attributing cognition or even consciousness to the fleshy appendage conflates manual and mental operations, making it difficult to pull apart action and intention in stories that hinge on unimaginably gruesome acts (usually performed by, and sometimes on, hands).

The expression 'at the hands of', which means 'because of someone's actions' (rooted etymologically in the German word *hand-lung*, meaning 'act' or 'deed') (Rickels 2016: 85), is commonly used by cultural critics and genre specialists when describing the graphic, grisly violence that plays out both on-screen and off-screen – across the bodies of characters and spectators – in horror cinema. One example of this can be found in Angela Ndalianis's book *The Horror Sensorium: Media and the Senses*, where she states that heroes and bystanders alike suffer such violence 'at the hands of the monsters [. . .] hands that tear open an abdomen to reveal the slippery internal organs, the same hands that rip limbs from pulsating bodies' (Ndalianis 2012: 5–6). But, in ascribing that abdomen-tearing and limb-ripping activity to hands, we ironically take the monster as a whole out of the equation, reducing its uncanny (irreducible) presence in the text to individual instances of irrational action. All of the clawing, clutching, grasping, ripping, stabbing, strangling and tearing that goes on in horror films is one sign that irrational impulses prevail in this genre, which, in the words of Isabel Cristina Pinedo, exposes in its transgressions 'the limits of rationality' (Pinedo 2004: 113). Rhetorically framed in this way, it is as if the 'head' – the monster's or villain's mental faculties – has nothing to do with such 'mindless' actions, which are presented as automatic motor responses originating in the hand. However, media theorist Laurence Rickels offers a way forward (past mere transference) by reminding us that the hand, like an 'externalized brain', translates thought into action. Quoting the German philosopher Ernst Kapp, Rickels emphasises that this organ, which 'grasps and concerns itself with bodily things', is also 'the organ that essentially supports the release of *ideas* and *their mental grasp*' (italics added) (Rickels 2016: 85).

Not insignificantly, reviewers and general audiences who bemoan the privileging of graphic violence and visual spectacle over character development and dramatically compelling storytelling in both horror films and martial arts cinema sometimes resort to using the expression 'mindless action' when describing scenes in which hands grasp at unsuspecting victims and fists fly with delirious abandon.[5] However, rather than being mind-numbing 'gore-fests', the many expertly timed, show-stopping scenes in Hong Kong action films and monster movies have also been referred to by Stefan Hammond and Mike Wilkins (authors of *Sex and Zen & A Bullet in the Head: the Essential Guide to Hong Kong's Mind-bending Films*) as 'poignant moments . . . packed full of rapid-fire mood swings' (Hammond and Wilkins 1996). Although Hammond and Wilkins are speaking specifically about action scenes in the 'heroic bloodshed' crime thrillers directed by John Woo (such as *A Better Tomorrow* and *Hard Boiled* (1992)), which showcase ballistic gunplay rather than elaborate kung fu acrobatics, their comments can be applied to Hong Kong horror films and martial arts cinema generally, given the many tonal shifts (for example, between fright and laughter, dread and humour, and so on) that occur within those genres. Horror films in particular, with their fusion of broad physical comedy and terrifying bodily destruction, demonstrate Hong Kong cinema's aforementioned 'mood swings' while illustrating how the hand is anything *but* 'mindless' in its capacity to translate thought into action. Sure, silliness abounds in such productions as director Chu Yen-ping's *Fantasy Mission Force* (1983) and Ngai Choi Lam's *The Ghost Snatchers* (1986). But the hands that spring to life and terrorise the ill-fated characters in these seemingly mindless, horror-infused action films deserve serious consideration as instruments of patriarchal control, military authority and religious doctrine that are made more disturbing by virtue of their apparent autonomy.

One Body, Two Systems: Being 'Mindful' of Hands in Hong Kong Cinema

The above overview of Western literary and cinematic texts' adoption of hand imagery, though abbreviated, suggests the extent to which the iconography of horror was established early on and revised often over the course of its transmedia life as a type of cultural production that continues to cross national boundaries and corporeal thresholds. My reason for including this geographically uprooted prelude to the discussion of Hong Kong horror films that follows is twofold: first, it establishes some of the images and themes that will take on slightly different permutations in an East Asian context where issues of racial alterity, sexuality, transgression and male power (or patriarchal authority) require additional or alternative interpretative frameworks than those adopted in North American and European contexts. Second, Hong Kong, a former British colony that is now officially recognised as a Special Administrative Region of the People's Republic of China (following the 1997 'handover'), has itself been mired in the rhetoric of national boundaries and corporeal thresholds for decades. An autonomous territory that is nevertheless part of the larger 'body' of China proper, Hong Kong can be characterised as a culturally hybrid and spatially severed zone, and Great Britain's 'handing over' of it does not erase the century-and-a-half history of colonial rule that continues to soak through into its popular culture even after the transfer of sovereignty. Horror film expert Ken Gelder, describing Hong Kong as a 'postmodern, global city that is also colonial', alludes to this paradoxical positionality, and for him and others its 'movement forwards' (towards China) is also 'a kind of belated return' (Gelder 2000: 351). In the words of Brian Chan Hok-shing, '[I]t is both Chinese and Western and yet neither (completely) Chinese nor (completely) Western' (Chan 2007: 189). Although 'geographically peripheral to the Chinese borders and politically separated from the motherland' (Ibid.), Hong Kong has been 'imagined, fantasized, and claimed as 'authentically' Chinese' (Chu 2003: 63). This is thanks in part to the many Mandarin-language film productions shot at Shaw Brothers Studios and Cathay Studios beginning in the 1960s – *wuxia* films, period dramas and horror films that, according to Mirana May Szeto and Yun-chung Chen, draw creative inspiration from the long tradition of 'Chinese folk tales and literature on martial arts, romance, and ghost genres that have survived in Hong Kong film and print media while being censored in China and Taiwan during the Cold War' (Szeto and Chen 2015: 91).

Thus, several films from that era, ranging from director Li Han Hsiang's costume fantasy *Enchanting Shadow* (1960) to *The Legend of the 7 Golden Vampires* (1974), a Shaw Brothers–Hammer Studios co-production bringing together martial arts legends like David Chiang and Szu Shih and British star Peter Cushing, collectively attest to 'the duality of Hong Kong's geopolitical identity' (Chu 2003: 63). As Kevin Heffernan points out, that duality is apparent in two horror films released within months of one another in 1975, director Ho Meng Hua's *Black Magic* and Kuei Chih-Hung's *Killer Snakes*, which are 'localized variations' on earlier Hollywood hits: *The Exorcist* (1973) and *Willard* (1971), respectively (Heffernan 2009: 60). Of these two Shaw Brothers productions, *Black Magic* is more representative as a text steeped in the themes and iconography of supernatural ghost stories involving sorcery, possession, resurrection and reanimation. Flayed skin, rotting flesh, crawling worms and copious amounts of spilled blood flood the screen over the course of this film's rollicking narrative, which revolves around two forest-dwelling witch doctors – one good, the other evil – who lend their spell-casting services to men and women seeking romantic and sexual fulfilment. Although that latter element is a marked departure from the main storyline of director William Friedkin's *The Exorcist*, much of *Black Magic*'s thematic and visual material can be found in examples of cinematic (and literary) horror produced in other national and cultural contexts. And its various scare tactics, including the jolt-inducing intrusion of an old hag's dirty hand as it grabs the male protagonist's shoulder (sending him and the audience into a momentary state of shock), are not uncommon within Western texts.[6] However, other elements, including the presence of four female 'hopping spirits' who haunt a young woman's dreams in the moments leading up to the film's final showdown between the dueling necromancers (set, incongruously, at a construction site in the modern metropolis), hint at *Black Magic*'s cultural ties to China – specifically, to the history of *jiangshi*-based storytelling that has been Hong Kong horror cinema's major source of inspiration for decades (going back to the 1930s, when such films as *Midnight Vampire* (1936), *Vampire of the Haunted Mansion* (1939), and *Three-Thousand-Year-Old Vampire* (1939) were theatrically released) (Bai 2013: 110).

Fittingly, the literary and folkloric genre of *jiangshi* fiction takes its name from the appropriately hybrid, frequently hopping creature that exists liminally between the world of the living and the world of the dead; a being that is neither wholly a zombie nor wholly a vampire, but a mixture of both. The *jiangshi*, typically adorned in Qing-era robes but also strangely redolent of the supernatural monsters that populate Western cinemas (particularly 'ugly, strong, hairy creatures with long fingernails' who, like Mr Hyde, delight in frightening young women with their 'otherness'), is a sign of the aforementioned duality that characterises Hong Kong's cultural identity, situated between two worlds (Ibid.: 109). The creature's name, rooted in the Chinese character for *jiang* (meaning hard or stiff), indicates its paradoxical status as an animated corpse in a frozen state of decay, with rigor mortis being the reason for its Frankensteinian flinging up of arms toward frightened victims. As one cultural historian explains, because of its inability to bend its limbs and body in a way that most humans can, the *jiangshi* moves around by jumping like a kangaroo 'while keeping its arms outstretched for mobility' (Pettigrove 2005: 98). It feeds off the breath or 'essence' (*qi*) of living humans, yet is unable to communicate verbally with them, having 'lost the rational part of its mind with only the animal's desire remaining' (Bai 2013: 108). And, in general, the only person capable of dispatching or exorcising this unholy threat is a Taoist priest, hence the preponderance of traditional religious iconography (clothing, amulets, scriptures, paintings, architecture, and so on) not just in period pieces such as Ricky Lau's *Mr. Vampire* (1985) and

Ching Siu-tung's *A Chinese Ghost Story* (1987) but also in urban horror films set in modern-day Hong Kong, such as Stephen Tung's *Magic Cop* (1990) and Juno Mak's *Rigor Mortis* (2013). As viewers of *Magic Cop* and *Rigor Mortis* are aware, it is often through Taoist priests' elaborate hand signs (*shoujue*), which bear the influence of earlier Buddhist *mudras* or 'hand seals', (Mitamura 2002: 235) that the *jiangshi* threat is eventually eliminated in these and other horror films, reminding us of the intrinsic way in which *Chinese* cultural references saturate tales that also bear passing similarities to Western horror films.

Tellingly, the original title of *Rigor Mortis* – *Jiangshi* (in Mandarin) and *Goeng-si* (in Cantonese, the language in which the film was shot) – attests to the perennial status and centrality of this uncanny, liminal figure, which can additionally be situated between 'masculine' and 'feminine' identities, a gender binary that is both deconstructed and strengthened in many Hong Kong horror films. Indeed, the creature is often distinguished by its long, claw-like fingernails, which can shoot out like phallic knives and pierce a person's flesh like butter, as witnessed in everything from *Spooky Encounters* to *A Chinese Ghost Story III* (1991). In the latter film, the evil spirit from 'beyond' is given the name Butterfly and visually coded as female, with stereotypically feminine features like long flowing hair, jewellery, and make-up only partially masked by prosthetics. But in *Rigor Mortis*, the *jiangshi* – the reanimated corpse of a character named Uncle Tung – is coded as male, albeit one whose fingernails elongate and appear like those of a woman. The undead version of Uncle Tung can also be thought of as a 'castrating' figure, who literally twists the arm off of a retired demon hunter named Yau in the film's penultimate scene.[7] The image of Yau's unattached member is one of several instances in *Rigor Mortis* when hands and arms are shown to be on the receiving end of both physical and psychical attempts at annihilation. One example is an earlier scene – the hallucination of a suicidal man, Chin, right before he tries to hang himself – depicting a middle-class family of three (Chin, his wife and their young son) sitting down to eat at an all-white breakfast table that is suddenly stained by the red blood that pours from their hands and wrists. An even more disquieting moment occurs when a man rapes two women (a pair of twins), plunging a knife into one of their hands to keep her in place throughout the gruelling ordeal (which ends when the other twin stabs the rapist with a pair of scissors). Significantly, director Juno Mak frequently cuts to close-ups of hands in order to show whether or not a character has died as a result of such violence (in the case of Chin, his suicide attempt fails, as denoted by a shot of his still-moving fingers). Moreover, at various points in *Rigor Mortis*, sacred hand gestures 'activate protective or exorcistic powers' on the part of those for whom 'fingers have [a] cosmological significance' (Mitamura 2002: 246). As explained by Keiko Mitamura, besides being used 'for exorcism of evil forces, control over spirits, [and the] healing of diseases', the hand helps to enhance a 'transformation of the body into a locus of contact with, and merging into, the otherworldly realm of the Dao' (Ibid.: 237).

While *Rigor Mortis* and several other Hong Kong films foreground the perennial hopping corpse more frequently than *Black Magic*, Ho Meng Hua's 1975 production puts tremendous emphasis on Taoist rituals and continues to be singled out by genre enthusiasts as a foundational text, setting the template for several of the 'sleazy', 'schlocky', and 'exploitative' motion pictures that followed in its wake. This includes the 1983 Shaw Brothers production *Seeding of a Ghost*, one of a series of so-called 'fiendish foetus' films that combines soft-core titillation and gratuitous female nudity with Corman-meets-Cronenberg 'body horror' and gross-out effects (Tombs 1998: 40).[8] Although the film's most notorious scene shows a demonic placenta – or, rather, a 'throbbing lump of pus and gristle' (Ibid.) – exploding from an expectant mother's belly (recalling a similar moment in Ridley Scott's *Alien*, 1979), there are several instances when the hands of the male protagonist – a lowly cab driver whose wife has been raped and killed by a pair of horny hooligans – are singled out as small yet significant parts of a larger body that gradually succumbs to disease. At the narrative's midpoint, the husband, assisted by an ageing witch doctor (whose services he has enlisted as part of his vengeance plot), begins to notice crusty scabs on his hands. When the young man asks about this sudden development, the sorcerer informs him that this new deformity 'is the price [one pays when] using black magic'. 'It will get more serious in the next couple of days,' the old man says, and indeed the brown epidermal blisters spread from the protagonist's hands to his arms, shoulders and upper torso. Eventually, he pokes a needle into his arm, drawing the blood out and feeding it to the animated corpse of his dead wife, who is referred to as a *plazawa*. As his diseased limb palpitates, the audience is invited to consider the suggestiveness of this image; the idea that both corruption and salvation originate not in the brain but in the hand, which has the power to either destroy lives or restore hope – heady themes for so 'mindless' and 'sleazy' a motion picture.

For all of the weight given to gory images of blood-drinking, brain-eating and worm-vomiting in *Seeding of a Ghost*, the film's most disturbing scene involves the rape of the main character's wife, an unfaithful woman who is forced to 'pay the price' for her philandering in the most brutal way imaginable. This, lamentably, is a recurring feature of Hong

Kong horror films produced in the 1970s and 1980s, but can also be found in martial arts films lacking the semantic and syntactical elements of the horror genre. For instance, director–star Sammo Hung's kung fu classic *The Iron-Fisted Monk* (1977) features numerous shots of women being sexually violated by a high-ranking Manchu officer and voyeuristically framed by the camera as objects of a lascivious male gaze. No less problematic, the previously mentioned Shaw Brothers production *The Killer Snakes* begins with the off-screen sound of a woman being slapped by her sexual partner, grafted onto the black-and-white image of a young boy seated at a desk doing schoolwork and hearing the moans of his climaxing mother in the adjacent room. A brief insert shot – an extreme close-up of the woman's perspiration-dotted lips parting in preparation for a scream – suggests that all the slapping (dealt out by the hand of the unseen man) brings an equal measure of pleasure and pain to audiences of both martial arts films and horror films, which are littered with such scenes.

For instance, director Kuei Chih-Hung's *Hex* (1980), a cross-cultural remake of Henri-Georges Clouzot's *Les Diaboliques* (1955), pivots on the impromptu decision of a deathly ill woman (who is wracked with consumption) and her conspiring nursemaid to murder her husband, a belligerent troll who doles out verbal and physical abuse whenever he is not busy drinking or gambling.[9] Because of feudal China's marriage laws, divorce is not an option for Madam Chan. Before she and her female servant Yi Wah drown the man and dispose of his body in a nearby pond, he is shown beating and slapping the two women, to the point where the younger woman points her own finger at him and declares that he is 'not a man'. This is the first of several moments when hands emerge as accusatory or retaliatory instruments used by victims and villains alike, an image of finger-pointing that anticipates similar shots in the Pang Brothers' more recent horror films *The Eye* (2002) and *Re-Cycle* (2006). Tellingly, as the seemingly lifeless body of this hideous man, this monstrous form of masculinity, disappears into the swampy water, his right hand is the last thing to go under, submerging momentarily only to come back – albeit in spectral form – in a subsequent dream sequence. The widow, beset by guilt, wakes from a nightmare in which she is harassed by the dead man's grasping hands, which clamp down on the woman's throat and nearly kill her in her sleep. Eventually, Madam Chan does die, not from consumption but from fright, and in the aftermath of her funeral we learn that her husband, who actually faked his death (holding his breath under the water), had been conspiring with Yi Wah, the double-crossing handmaiden, all along. But, in a manner that recalls the long-haired female spirits found in Japanese and South Korean horror films (for example,

Ring (1998), *Ju-on: The Grudge* (2002), *Acacia* (2003), *Bunsinsaba* (2004), *Arang* (2006), and so on), the wronged woman gets her revenge in the end, emerging from her coffin and using her own severed hand – a crawling appendage that looks suspiciously like a white plaster cast – to go after the priest who is performing the last rites.[10]

The image of a crawling hand acting independently on its own, a throwback to earlier American, British and French productions (ranging from Maurice Renard's 1920 horror novel *Les mains d'Orlac* to the US television series *The Addams Family* (1964–66) to a segment of the 1972 Amicus anthology film *Asylum*), can be found in other Hong Kong horror films theatrically released in 1980 (the same year that *Hex* created a stir among local audiences). Indeed, two films – director Tsui Hark's *We're Going to Eat You* and Sammo Hung's *Spooky Encounters* – employ severed and possessed hands as a means of demonstrating the relationship between victims and perpetrators of violence, but with more than a modicum of silliness to help offset (or distract from) the otherwise disturbing gender politics at the heart of these and other Hong Kong horror films. For example, *We're Going to Eat You* incorporates a humorous gag in which the male hero, an agent of the Central Surveillance Agency who has tracked the movements of a notorious thief to an isolated village, mistakes a severed hand for his own (a shock moment, contained within the protagonist's dream, which wakes him from sleep) (O'Brien 2003: 17). It also depicts a Taoist priest as the most 'bumbling, ineffectual' member of the village, a portrayal that, with a few exceptions, runs counter to other *jiangshi*-laden horror films and which critic Daniel O'Brien sees as a sign of Tsui Hark's satirical approach to his subject (Ibid.). Not surprisingly (given its title), this film revolves around gruesome acts of consumption/cannibalism, but the repulsiveness of that subject is offset by dollops of slapstick action and comic pratfalls involving the emaciated, mask-wearing villagers, who are given 'handouts' of human steak – the fleshy remains of unlucky passersby – as if living in a commune. Several critics have pointed out this film's blatant anti-communist message, not-so-subtly telegraphed in scenes showing the military uniformed village chief's 'inequitable distribution of the "meat" to his starving masses' (Morton 2001: 38). This, according to Lisa Morton, is one reason why the film has been interpreted as political satire, as an early warning of what might transpire once Hong Kong is handed over to China. But that allegorical reference perhaps gets lost amidst the copious, conspicuous nods to European mondo movies, spaghetti westerns and other horror films of the 1960s and 1970s (everything from *The Texas Chainsaw Massacre* (1974) to the contemporaneous *Cannibal Holocaust* (1980)), which form the densely intertextual foundation for the appropriately titled *We're Going to Eat You*, a cannibal film about the literal and figurative ingestion of other 'bodies' (Ibid.).

Dueling Hands: Fighting Authority and Re-inscribing Patriarchy in *Spooky Encounters*

Few horror films of the 1980s have stood the test of time quite so well as *Spooky Encounters*, thanks mainly to Sammo Hung's inspired direction and fight choreography as well as his vigorous performance as the pedicab driver 'Bold' Cheung, a commoner who is placed into extraordinary circumstances in a turn-of-the-century rural setting. Like other productions of that era, this film brings a number of traditional Chinese signifiers to bear on a scenario that is rooted in superstitions but also weirdly contemporary and even prescient in its hybridised mix of cultural elements and its satirical critique of corrupt, authoritarian public figures. Recalling the narrative premise of the aforementioned *Black Magic*, *Spooky Encounters* revolves around two dueling mystics – one good, the other evil – who each get entangled in the romantic troubles of local villagers. Chin Hoi, a Taoist mercenary priest, works for Cheung's tyrannical boss, Master Tam, a town official who wishes to assassinate the dim-witted hero so as to keep his adulterous affair with Cheung's wife from being discovered. Cheung, initially oblivious of his wife and the would-be mayor's relationship, is counselled by another, more virtuous *sifu* (master), Tsui. As the brother of Chin Hoi, Tsui lends support to the hero when the latter is forced to fend off a hopping corpse in a haunted temple over the course of two consecutive nights. Those midnight romps are some of *Spooky Encounters'* most memorable and hilarious scenes, a showcase for Sammo Hung's skills as a plus-sized performer as well as a demonstration of the way in which hands can be instrumentally employed as corporeal metaphors of an 'unthinking' or 'irrational' violence that will assume considerably less funny, truly horrific connotations by the end of the film.

After being tricked into spending his first night in the dilapidated temple, Cheung climbs the rafters in fear, watching the coffins below with nervous anticipation. And, indeed, a reanimated corpse makes an appearance in this scene, thanks to the evil necromancer Chin Hoi, who controls the creature from afar through voodoo-like dark magic. When the top of the coffin slides open and the hideous looking corpse inside becomes visible, its hands appear first. Long, sharp fingernails point towards the ceiling, and the arms of the traditionally robed *jiangshi* stretch out to probe the room, like the dials of a compass or sensors in search of its prey. Each thud of the corpse's hop sends another spray of sweat from Cheung's brow. His fear begins to abate once the thing hops back into its coffin. The priest does not relent, however, and uses elaborate hand movements to whip the *jiangshi* back to its feet, leading to the first of many kung fu fights in the film (not counting the opening title sequence, a confrontation with skeletons and flesh-eating monsters that is revealed to be a dream). Notably, the chopping movements of the *jiangshi*, performed in robotic-staccato fashion (in contrast to the fluid acrobatics of the chubbier Cheung), put additional emphasis on its hands, which appear to independently lead the creature toward its moving target, at least until the rising sun outside the temple sends it back to its coffin.

Against his will, Cheung's own hand takes the lead in a later scene, set in a village market, after he has escaped from prison (where he was held captive on suspicions of killing his wife, who is in fact alive). He and his famished protector, Tsui, sit down for bowls of rice. Meanwhile, Chin Hoi, who is in a nearby forest grove, unleashes yet another *fashu* (incantation) – a puppetmaster curse that takes control of the hero's right hand at the moment when he lifts his spoon to his mouth. Soon, a clearly mystified Cheung finds himself in a battle with himself and others, throwing punches at his fellow patrons and trying to control a part of his body that is no longer connected to his mind.[11] That is, his hand seems to have a 'mind of its own', and can only be brought back to the corporeal/mental fold once Tsui rushes to his aid, defeating Chin Hoi, who, before scampering away, promises that he will return. And return he does, in an epic battle that pits the two sorcerers against each other one final time outside Master Tam's residence. Tellingly, Chin Hoi is ultimately defeated by a long blast of fire shot by Tsui from his fingertips, although the latter also dies from exhaustion. Having killed Master Tam by thrusting a sword through his chest, Cheung would appear to be the only person left alive in this final scene. However, his long-missing wife emerges from the wings, crying crocodile tears and lying that his boss tried to rape her. No longer the rube he was at the beginning of the film, our hero suddenly pushes her away and lands seven punches to her stomach. 'I knew you were having an affair,' he screams at her, before viciously thrusting his hand into her abdomen one final time and launching the woman into the air with a degree of rage not yet seen in the film. Superimposed atop this last image of the film are the words 'The End', rendered as a freeze frame that suspends time and leaves the audience with a bitter taste that is at odds with the generally sweet nature of the likeable main character. Culminating with this frankly shocking image of male violence directed at a woman, *Spooky Encounters* – despite its distinctiveness as an artfully choreographed and formally inventive horror-comedy – reveals itself to be just as misogynistic as the many other Hong Kong films from the 1970s and 1980s that treat the topics of rape and domestic abuse in an exploitative manner.

What makes this conclusion even more troubling, though, is the frequency with which hands had been foregrounded throughout the film as signs of an irrational, unthinking violence that gradually becomes understandable or 'graspable' to an audience that yearns for the woman's comeuppance by the end. As early as its opening credits, *Spooky Encounters* has brought forth images of supernatural monsters clutching and grasping at the hapless hero, from the skeletal phalanges that comically pinch his bottom to a decomposing female ghost who, from the other side of a mirror, pokes her long red fingernails through the reflective surface in search of her male prey. It is noteworthy that Cheung is able to fend off this spectral mirror-woman by cutting off her hand, which he then stabs with a knife – a precursor to the more ferocious, curiously spur-of-the-moment yet premeditated attack that he launches against his wife in the film's final shot. Here, once again, we are invited to speculate on the ethical dimensions of a genre that is often reductively conceived of as grossly misogynistic, but which also highlights a gap between the hand as an instrument of violence and the mind that creates the conditions for violence to emerge in the first place – conditions that are not always (or simply) a result of sexism but which are likely rooted in larger social divisions, including the separation of those wielding institutional power (for whom Master Tam is a representative) and those lacking that power (for whom Cheung is a representative).

Conclusion

'Precisely because of its innocence it has become particularly dangerous.'
– Elias Canetti, discussing the hand, in *Crowds and Power* (1960)

As stated above, Hong Kong cinema has long been described by cultural critics as having an 'East–West identity', owing to the fact that, for years, film-makers working in the mainstream industry have mixed 'indigenous sources from legends, folklore and the supernatural [. . .] with different Western devices of narrativity' (Yue 2000: 365). This is especially true in the context of horror films, which 'produce an ambivalent milieu where ghosts are modernized in a modernity that nevertheless longs for traditionalism' (Ibid.). But in the presence of so much discourse surrounding Hong Kong's liminal state, which is visually encoded in the *jiangshi*-based iconography of horror films featuring 'Manchu-costumed vampires, Daoist priests, and the blood-sucking contagious qualities of the

Western Dracula' (Ibid.) the relative absence of critical literature dealing with that most important yet understudied body part in the genre is made all the more stark.

As I have endeavored to illustrate through examples drawn from various corners of the world, the hand is an especially significant organ in the horror genre, presented as an independent agent of destruction, regardless of whether or not it is attached to a person's or monster's body. 'Grasping' it, then, is of utmost importance if we are to make sense of the seemingly senseless violence and mindless action that has long characterised horror films.

More specifically, with the 'reattachment' of Hong Kong to the larger body of China following the transfer of postcolonial sovereignty in 1997, the horror genre's corporeal tropes and predilection for what Barry Langford has called the 'transgression of limits' become all the more noteworthy. Taking a cue from recent films like *Rigor Mortis*, which, according to one critic, is 'a horrifying statement about the older generation devouring the young and the specters of China crowding out the space of quotidian Hong Kong' (Szeto and Chen 2015: 96), we might speculate on the growing cultural 'worth' or value of future horror films, which – even at their cheesiest – confront viewers with their worst fears but also provide purgative social and libidinal release at times when free expression comes under attack. Of course, not knowing what will happen in the future of Hong Kong–China relations is what lends additional frisson to motion pictures in which the spread of dread cannot be stopped. Tellingly, the pro-democracy demonstrations that swept through the streets of this 'Special Administrative Region' in September of 2014 were made up of young protestors who, inspired by the people of Ferguson, Missouri, raised their arms in unison and yelled 'Hands up, don't shoot.' This peaceful, non-violent reaction to the Chinese government's decision to renege on its promise to grant its citizens full democracy, while worlds away from the period setting and kooky antics of *Spooky Encounters*, presents a more chilling backdrop against which the hand has begun to assume allegorical significance as part of a larger effort to unite, rather than divide, thought and action. Here I am reminded of the words of Thomas M. Sipos, who, in his discussion of horror as an 'emotive genre', states, 'Horror audiences stick their hands into a black box, knowing something will bite, only uncertain as to how and when' (Sipos 2010: 5). Just how deep that 'black box' is, in terms of Hong Kong's cinema's capacity for generating both hope and fear in the midst of tremendous social and political change, is a question that horror films are perhaps best armed to explore.

Notes

1. Tony Williams argues that close-up shots of hands in James Whale's *Frankenstein* are what most decisively connect Henry and his creature. Not only is the hand 'the first object moving on the operating table', but an image of Henry's hand 'stroking the coffin' during the film's earlier disinterment sequence further links the two, suggesting that production and destruction, life and death, are dialectically aligned. This corporealised theme is picked up again in the film's 1935 sequel, *Bride of Frankenstein*. As Williams points out, the film begins with a tête-à-tête between *Frankenstein* author Mary Shelley and poet Lord Byron, the latter admiring the former's creative process and remarking, 'It was these fragile, white fingers that wrote the nightmare.' When she accidentally pricks her finger with an embroidery needle, 'the flow of blood causes Mary consternation'. 'This action', according to Williams, 'anticipates the creatures attempt to stroke his bride's hands toward the end of the film, an action that leads to rejection' (Williams 1996: 39–40).

2. For example, director Roland West's horror-comedy *The Monster* (1925), one of many 'Old Dark House' films made during the silent era, features a scene in which a hand reaches out from behind a curtain, about to grab the milquetoast hero, followed by a cutaway shot of the film's heroine, on a slab, being brought down by a pair of arms perched above her heaving chest.

3. In addition to the motion pictures mentioned in the body of this chapter, other US horror films showing severed hands include *The Beast Within* (1982), in which a dog carries a human hand in its mouth, and *Psycho III* (1986), which culminates with a shot of Norman Bates in the back of a squad car, caressing the disembodied hand of his 'mother' as he is being driven to the mental institution.

4. In the case of Sam Raimi's *Evil Dead II*, the flapping hand, which pulls at Ash's hair and smashes dishes on his head, is given a mind of its own and is even endowed with both vocal and sight abilities (despite its lack of mouth and eyes).

5. See, for example, Ed Nguyen's review of *Iron Monkey* for *DVD Movie Central* (2002) and Roger Ebert's 2001 Review of *Time and Tide*.

6. Robert Baird (2000) points out that several popular US horror films, including *The Exorcist* (1973), *Jaws* (1975), *Halloween* (1978) and *Aliens* (1986) employ 'the old tap-on-the-shoulder routine', a false startle effect that likewise occurs with frequency across the history of Hong Kong horror.

7. This arm-ripping scene in *Rigor Mortis* reminds me of the final showdown between the Chinese hero and his Japanese adversary in the Shaw Brothers' 1972 martial arts film *Thunderbolt Fist*. As the culmination to a story about Japan's incursions into north-eastern China, the film pits the protagonist Tie Wa (whose hand had been maimed by thugs when he refused to divulge the location of the resistance movement's hideout) against an opponent whose

arm is torn off, resulting in an arterial spray and a final shot of the bloody body part lying next to the fallen man in the boxing ring.

8. Other examples of 'fiendish foetus' films include *Ghost Nursing* (1982) and *Devil Fetus* (1983).

9. By the time of *Hex*'s theatrical release, so commonplace was the image of a man slapping a woman in Hong Kong horror and martial arts films that Lau Kar Leung, the director of *Heroes of the East* (1978), felt a need to include a scene in which an ageing father tells his abusive son (who has just married a Japanese woman), 'a couple should love and respect each other.' The 'most despicable' thing a husband can do, according to the old man, is to 'bully his wife'.

10. Or, at least, that is what the audience is led to believe until the film's denouement reveals the truth behind Madam Chan's death and revenge, exacted on her behalf by her long-lost twin sister.

11. Another example of a character losing control of his arm and hand occurs in the Hong Kong–Malaysian co-production *Hungry Ghost Ritual* (2014), when a man possessed by a demon stabs himself in the chest with a sharp talisman.

References

Antonucci, Barbara (2007), 'Mediatic metamorphosis and postmodern novels by Chuck Palahniuk, Bret Easton Ellis and Nick Hornby,' in Maddalena Pennacchia Punzi (ed.), *Literary Intermediality: the Transit of Literature Through the Media Circuit*, Bern: Peter Lang, pp. 163–82

Bai, Meijadai (2013), 'Gothic monster and Chinese cultural identity: analysis of *The Note of Ghoul*,' in Murali Balaji (ed.), *Thinking Dead: What the Zombie Apocalypse Means*, Lanham: Lexington Books, pp. 105–26.

Baird, Robert (2000), 'The startle effect: implications for spectator cognition and media theory,' *Film Quarterly*, 53 (spring), pp. 12–24.

Briefel, Aviva (2015), *The Racial Hand in the Victorian Imagination*, Cambridge: Cambridge University Press.

Chan, Brian Hok-shing (2007), 'Hybrid language and hybrid identity? The case of Cantonese-English code-switching in Hong Kong,' in Chan Kwok-bun, Jan W. Walls and David Hayward (eds), *East-West Identities: Globalization, Localization, and Hybridization* Leiden: Koninklijke Brill, pp. 189–202.

Chu, Yingchi (2003), *Hong Kong Cinema: Coloniser, Motherland and Self*, New York: Routledge.

Costanzo, William (2004), *Great Films and How to Teach Them*, Urbana: National Council of Teachers of English.

Desser, David (2000), 'The kung fu craze: Hong Kong cinema's first American reception', in Poshek Fu and David Desser (eds), *The Cinema of Hong Kong: History, Arts, Identity*, Cambridge: Cambridge University Press, pp. 19–43.

Ebert, Roger (2001), 'Review: *Time and Tide*', *RogerEbert.com* (18 May), <http://www.rogerebert.com/reviews/time-and-tide-2001> (last accessed 25 August 2017).

Gelder, Ken (2000), 'Introduction to Part Eleven', in Ken Gelder (ed.), *The Horror Reader*, London: Routledge, pp. 349–51.

Grant, Barry Keith (1996/2015), 'Introduction,' in Barry Keith Grant (ed.), *The Dread of Difference: Gender and the Horror Film*, Austin: University of Texas Press, pp. 1–13.

Hallenbeck, Bruce G. (2003), *Comedy-Horror Films: a Chronological History, 1914–2008*, Jefferson: McFarland.

Hammond, Stefan and Mike Wilkins (1996), *Sex and Zen & a Bullet in the Head: the Essential Guide to Hong Kong's Mind-bending Films*, New York: Fireside.

Heffernan, Kevin (2009), '*Inner Senses* and the changing face of Hong Kong horror cinema,' in Jinhee Choi and Mitsuyo Wada-Marciano (eds), *Horror to the Extreme: Changing Boundaries in Asian Cinema*, Hong Kong: Hong Kong University Press, pp. 57–68.

Hutchings, Peter (2008), *The A to Z of Horror Cinema*, Lanham: Scarecrow Press.

Koszarski, Richard (1994), *An Evening's Entertainment: the Age of the Silent Feature Picture, 1915–1928*, Berkeley: University of California Press.

Langford, Barry (2005), *Film Genre: Hollywood and Beyond*, Edinburgh: Edinburgh University Press.

Le Fanu, Joseph Sheridan (1964), *Best Ghost Stories of J. S. LeFanu*, New York: Dover Publications.

Mitamura, Keiko (2002), 'Daoist hand signs and Buddhist mudras', in Livia Kohn and Harold D. Roth (eds), *Daoist Identity: History, Lineage, and Ritual*, Honolulu: University of Hawai'i Press, pp. 235–55.

Morton, Lisa (2001), *The Cinema of Tsui Hark*, Jefferson: McFarland.

Ndalianis, Angela (2012), *The Horror Sensorium: Media and the Senses*, Jefferson: McFarland.

Nguyen, Ed (2002), 'Review: *Iron Monkey*', *DVD Movie Central* (26 March), <http://www.dvdmoviecentral.com/ReviewsText/iron_monkey.htm> (last accessed 25 August 2017).

O'Brien, Daniel (2003), *Spooky Encounters: a Gwailo's Guide to Hong Kong Horror*, Manchester: Headpress.

Pettigrove, Cedrick (2005), *The Esoteric Codex: Supernatural Legends*, Creative Commons Attribution 2.0.

Pinedo, Isabel Cristina (2004), 'Postmodern elements of the contemporary horror film', in Stephen Prince (ed.), *The Horror Film*, New Brunswick, NJ: Rutgers University Press, pp. 85–117.

Prawer, Siegbert Salomon (1980), *Caligari's Children: the Film as Tale of Terror*, New York: Da Capo Press.

Rickels, Laurence (2016), *The Psycho Records*, New York: Columbia University Press.

Showalter, Elaine (2000), 'Dr. Jekyll's Closet', in Ken Gelder (ed.), *The Horror Reader*, London: Routledge, pp. 190–7.

Sipos, Thomas M. (2010), *Horror Film Aesthetics: Creating The Visual Language of Fear*, Jefferson: McFarland.

Szeto, Mirana May and Yun-chung Chen (2015), 'Hong Kong cinema in the age of neoliberalization and mainlandization,' in Esther M. K. Cheung, Gina Marchetti and Esther C. M. Yau (eds), *A Companion to Hong Kong Cinema*, Chichester: John Wiley & Sons, pp. 89–115.

Tombs, Pete (1998), *Mondo Macabro: Weird and Wonderful Cinema Around the World*, New York: Macmillan.

White, Dennis L. (1971), 'The poetics of horror: more than meets the eye', *Cinema Journal*, 10:2 (spring): pp. 1–18.

Williams, Tony (1996), *Hearths of Darkness: the Family in the American Horror Film*, Cranbury, NJ: Associated University Presses.

Yue, Audrey (2000), 'Preposterous Hong Kong horror,' in Ken Gelder (ed.), *The Horror Reader*, London: Routledge, pp. 364–73.

Žižek, Slavoj (1997), *The Plague of Fantasies*, New York: Verso.

CHAPTER 8

Tsui Hark's *Detective Dee* Films: Police Procedural Colludes with Supernatural-Martial Arts Cinema

Kenneth Chan

Introduction: Transfiguring Genre

In this chapter's examination of the Chinese supernatural-martial arts film (*wuxia shenguai pian*) and its contemporary iterations, I approach Hong Kong horror at a tangent, specifically as a border-crossing cinematic modality that haunts other popular genre forms. What I have in mind as a case study are Hong Kong director Tsui Hark's most recent reinventions of the *wuxia shenguai* genre: *Detective Dee and the Mystery of the Phantom Flame* (2010) and *Young Detective Dee: Rise of the Sea Dragon* (2013). As Christine Gledhill rather artfully argues, 'The life of a genre is cyclical, coming round again in corkscrew fashion, never quite in the same place' (Gledhill 2000: 227). This visual metaphor of the recycling patterns in genre history which Gledhill conjures is a critically productive one, in that it forestalls the reductive assumption of genre repetition as a mark of popular cinema's predictability and creative ennui. The helical motion of genre reinvention mobilises a temporal schematic of cinema's historicity – an acknowledgement of a genre's cultural and historical precedence – while materially shifting its form to meet the exigencies of contemporary politics and cultural concerns. Or, as Gledhill puts it, 'Revealing patterns or usages lost to view . . . enables us to trace the movements of cultural history, carried forward or intruding into the present, revealing hidden continuities and transformations working under new or disguising names' (Ibid.). These continuities and transformations of the *wuxia shenguai pian*, as evident in early Shanghai film and in Hong Kong cinema, I address briefly in the next section as a way of contextualising the Detective Dee films as hybrid fusions of martial arts cinema, Chinese supernatural horror, and, even, the recent American fascination with detective dramas and police procedurals, all in an era of Chinese transnational co-productions.

In updating the *wuxia shenguai pian* for twenty-first-century audiences through creative genre transfigurations, Tsui Hark is doing what he has always done best in Hong Kong cinema since the 1980s: maintaining the cultural currency of the martial arts film for mainstream Chinese (and now global) audiences and, hence, retaining the box office viability of the genre. But beyond this rather obvious observation, which one could make of most financially successful blockbuster films, I also argue, through a close reading of *Detective Dee and the Mystery of the Phantom Flame*,[1] that the Detective Dee films' successful appeal to local and global Chinese audiences is based on an updated rendering of the familiar cultural trope of modernity versus tradition, as mirrored in the supposed tensions between the police procedural and the horror/supernatural elements. I problematise these tensions precisely because their narrative and rhetorical purpose is, ironically, to shore up the deterministic logic of Chinese cultural history, the interpellative call of Chinese political power, and the cultural nationalist logic of being Chinese. In other words, even as lighter mainstream entertainment, these films can be read as ideological twins of the more didactic and overtly problematic *Hero* (2002) by Zhang Yimou. But I conclude this chapter by modulating my critique of Tsui's film to suggest a more generous counter-reading of its politics by recasting this action spectacle as a global cinematic text of political irony and, even, oppositional resistance.

Reinventing the *Wuxia shenguai pian*

The *wuxia shenguai pian* has a long and complicated history in Chinese culture, elements of which stretch back far beyond cinema and modern Chinese literature. As part of his historical recounting of the *wuxia pian* (Chinese martial arts cinema), Stephen Teo notes that the martial arts film's 'early association with the historical period-costume film (*guzhuang pian*) evolved into further associations with another genre, *shenguai*, which has historical literary roots as deep as *wuxia*'. The term *shenguai* 'denotes gods and spirits (*shen*) and the strange and the bizarre (*guai*: which could also refer to monsters and creatures of legend and the imagination)' (Teo 2009: 11). Clearly, the fusion of martial arts (in the *wuxia*) and horror elements of the supernatural (in the *shenguai*) was probably inevitable, considering how visual spectacle constituted the very foundation of Chinese cinema's beginnings, as it has cinema in general.

It is this visual spectacularity and its relation to the notion of magic that has led Zhang Zhen, scholar of Shanghai cinema, to name the *wuxia shenguai* productions of the period as '"martial arts-magic spirit" films'. From 1928 to 1932, these magic spirit films and other *wuxia* films constitute some 240 titles emerging out of approximately fifty production outfits

(Zhang 2005: 199; 387, note 1). Mingxing studio's *The Burning of the Red Lotus Temple* (1928–31) is popularly regarded as the pioneering film series of the genre, but Zhang identifies an earlier title, *Red Beauty and Skeleton* (1922), which incorporated numerous generic forms including the detective film. Additionally, she argues that 'the film may be a progenitor in combining elements of both the "martial arts" and "magic spirit"' and 'it also prefigured the emergence of the horror film' (Ibid.: 208–9), potentially making this the earliest cinematic predecessor of Tsui's Detective Dee films, at least in terms of multi-genre formulations.

The mass appeal of this martial arts subgenre in Shanghai cinema consequently generated divergent responses, which Zhang describes in the following manner:

> On the one hand, the audience and critics marveled at the spectacular pyrotechnic display and the entertaining suspense produced by dramatic or supernatural elements . . . The valiant fortitude and physical prowess in martial arts-magic spirit films were regarded as particularly empowering by a people who had internalized the image of the 'sick man of the orient' (*dongya bingfu*) since China's defeat in the Opium Wars and the subsequent suppression of the Boxer rebellion by Western powers. On the other hand, when the genre quickly expanded in quantity and variation, attacks were launched at its outlandish use of 'superstitious' motifs, cinematic tricks, sexual promiscuity, and gender ambiguity. (Zhang 2005: 205)

Though there are quite a number of theoretical lessons one can learn from this early historical moment of the *wuxia shenguai* film, I would like to highlight just two key points that will be critical to my later analysis of the first Detective Dee film. First, the anti-Western imperialist potential was made possible by looking at these films through a nationalist lens, hence affirming Stephen Teo's contention that '[t]he *wuxia* film was and is regarded as a national form, fulfilling nationalist desires for self-strengthening at a time when China was weak' (Teo 2009: 8) – with the *shenguai* elements offering an added valence of magical and supernatural fantasy to elevate further that mode of nationalist empowerment and triumph. But in today's transnational cinematic environment, what does it mean for filmmakers to sustain the genre's (cultural) nationalist appeal? By specifically referencing Zhang Yimou's *Hero*, Teo asserts that the genre still serves 'to justify the modern concept of the nation-state' (Ibid.), a thesis with which I do not disagree, particularly in my own interpretations of the Detective Dee films. But I suggest, too, that the necessity of a global appeal injects political anxiety into Tsui's transnational productions, thus modulating the nationalist position into a much more conflicted and complicated one, as my analysis later in the chapter will demonstrate.

Second, the perennial tension between modernity and the traditional in Chinese nationalist discourses functions as the standard framework to understand the supernatural and the magical. Historians and cultural theoreticians have struggled with what it means to conceptualise a Chinese modernity, to think about China as a modern nation, while grappling with the tremendous weight of an ancient Chinese cultural tradition. With China then facing the competition of Western scientific progress and advanced military technology in the late nineteenth and early twentieth centuries, and now arriving in the new millennium to confront a digitally technologised and globally democratised future – or at least the hopes of a democratic global politics of anti-oppression, human rights and equality – this binary cultural conception of modernity versus tradition resurfaces in Chinese popular culture in significant ways. In an ironic fashion, cinema as the embodiment of technological advancement – and in this case the *wuxia shenguai* genre and its spectacular visual effects – was capable of inciting what was construed as culturally regressive notions of the supernatural. Zhang Zhen tells the oft-repeated tale of how, during the screening of the film *The Birth of Ne Zha* (1928), 'some viewers would start burning incense and bowing to the image of Ne Zha (a mythic child hero in *Fengsheng bang*) appearing on the silver screen' (Zhang 2005: 199; 388, note 5). At the time, the Kuomintang government accused the films of 'spreading superstition and unscientific thinking' but, politically, it 'also had its own reservations against the *wuxia* genre, being wary that the films could induce anarchy and rebellion among the young' (Teo 2009: 41). These cultural–rhetorical formulations and their ideological tensions do not disappear in the contemporary *wuxia shenguai pian*; they only assume new guises to address China's resurgence in the global cultural politics of the new millennium.

The martial arts-magic spirit films of the Shanghai period had a significant impact on the genre's re-emergence and growth in Hong Kong cinema. The cultural themes, literary adaptations, visual effects, narrative structures and action sequences of the older cinema lent themselves readily to the processes of remaking and reinvention in the energetic film industry of Hong Kong. The genre's popularity is clearly evident in any cursory survey of the archival catalogues of the major studios. For instance, Shaw Brothers devoted much of their production resources to not just *wuxia* films but also to the *shenguai* variety, which include titles like *The Monkey Goes West* (1966), *The Cave of the Silken Web* (1967), *Na Cha and the Seven Devils* (1973), *The Legend of the 7 Golden Vampires* (1974; a Shaw–Hammer co-production), *Na Cha the Great* (1974), *The Fantastic Magic Baby* (1975), *The Web of Death* (1976), *The Spiritual Boxer, Part Two*

(1979), *Heaven and Hell* (1980) and *Buddha's Palm* (1982).[2] While many Hong Kong film-makers have taken on the genre, no one has done so with greater transformative impact and influence than director Tsui Hark in the 1980s and 1990s.

Tsui Hark: Magic Maestro of the Contemporary *Wuxia shenguai pian*

In 2004 Tsui Hark joined the feature film jury of the Cannes Film Festival, an honour that reflected a distinguished career of numerous accomplishments in directing, screenwriting and producing.[3] Upon the directorial debut of *The Butterfly Murders* (1979), Tsui Hark embarked on an astounding film-making trajectory that transformed him from a Hong Kong New Wave auteur to one of the industry's most successful mainstream directors and producers. Hailed as 'the Steven Spielberg of Asia' (Hendrix 2003), Tsui's innovative work in popular Hong Kong film did not come at a better time than during the blockbuster era of the New Hollywood Cinema. Stephen Teo correctly notes that 'Tsui inducted the [*wuxia*] genre into the age of *Star Wars* by using that movie's special effects experts to bring the conceptual fantasy world of *Zu* [: *Warriors from the Magic Mountain* (1983)] into life on the big screen' (Teo 2009: 161).[4] Tsui's dexterity with reinventing and revitalising the *wuxia pian* and the *wuxia shenguai pian* has earned him the credit for launching important action films in the Hong Kong cinematic canon, such as *Once Upon a Time in China I–V*, *The Swordsman* series and the *Chinese Ghost Story* films. So connected is he to the action genre that Mainland Chinese critics have labelled action cinema from Hong Kong 'Tsui Hark Films' (Dai 2005: 81). This epithet is not unimportant in that his reputation has generated the kind of cultural capital that now allows him to assume, with ease and confidence, control of the helm of recent transnational co-production projects involving Mainland Chinese companies – for example, Huayi Brothers Media Corporation and Film Workshop Co. Ltd (a Hong Kong company) share production credit for *Phantom Flame*, with all the financing coming from Chinese sources (Thompson 2011).

What is also significant, as Teo points out, is Tsui's ebullient embrace of new cinematic technology, which becomes especially helpful when working in an effects-driven genre. His initial attempt with the Red One Camera in *Phantom Flame* signals his deep comfort with digital innovation (Ibid.). *Young Detective Dee: Rise of the Sea Dragon* saw Tsui using stereoscopic cameras to shoot his 3D epic, prompting one critic to describe the film as 'a visual spectacle from beginning to end . . . cramming chases, fights and monsters into most of its 133-minute duration' (Tsui 2013). But the director is very carefully reflective about how his deployment of technology ultimately serves the goals of filmic narrative and aesthetic quality:

> Whenever we in the industry use CG or a technique, software or hardware, we must be very careful to design in such a way to give the audience something unexpected and unpredictable, not always the same thing. It's about how to make a story interesting and fun to watch . . . I like to create the kind of effects shot that's relevant to the story and style of the movie. (quoted in Thompson 2013)

While one may quibble about the efficacy of this approach in his latest films, it is an aesthetic principle that will not only serve him well in the age of Chinese digital cinema, but will also enable him to continue to reimagine and reconfigure the *wuxia shenguai* genre for a new generation of viewers, which, I argue, he has already begun to do in the Detective Dee movies.

Tsui Hark's mainstream appeal and technological savvy are instrumental in laying the groundwork for the kind of storytelling that engages the cultural and political themes the *wuxia shenguai* genre has historically offered. But Tsui's glossy use of special effects, computer-generated imagery (CGI) and 3D technology is not the only way he updates the genre; he revamps some of the genre's key themes in intricate ways that resonate with audiences of transnational Chinese cinema. One of the central thematic tensions that I have identified earlier in my brief focus on Shanghai cinema is the genre's ability to embody both a Chinese nationalism (against Western imperialism) and a primitivistic fascination with the supernatural. In his analysis of the director's earlier *wuxia* films, Stephen Teo points out that 'Tsui depicts China as a mythic land whose potential strength remains in limbo, bounded by tradition and curbed by the refusal of talented individuals to come to terms with a new world' (Teo 2001: 152). In other words, Tsui's cinema is his mode of Chinese nationalism, his way of dragging China, kicking and screaming, into the twentieth century (and, in the case of *Phantom Flame*, the twenty-first century). But to conceptualise China as a modern nation is a complicated affair, especially when the term 'modern' needs to be defined and nuanced on multiple levels – culturally, philosophically and politically – a task that is clearly beyond the representational scope of the *wuxia shenguai pian*. But try Tsui does, in two specific ways: first, in marrying the contemporary detective film/police procedural to the *wuxia shenguai pian*, *Phantom Flame* foregrounds positivistic and scientific rationalism as the modern and preferred epistemological approach to arriving at facts in the legal and criminal justice system. But Tsui allows, intentionally or unwittingly, for Chinese cultural practices to disturb the processes of this mode of rationalism. Second, while the film's protagonist expresses a historically deterministic notion of China as nation to explain his motivations – a rather problematic cultural nationalistic logic that we see emerging in recent transnational Chinese cinema – Tsui, rather strategically, leaves enough room in the narrative for one to reread the film as an ironic text in critique of the state of both Chinese and global politics.

Detective Dee and the Mystery of the Phantom Flame

The character Detective Dee is a fictional rendition of a historical figure, Di Renjie, a celebrated judge of the Tang dynasty, who also assumed the role of prime minister during Empress Wu Zetian's reign (Kuhn 2013; Thompson 2011). Judge Dee found pop cultural incarnation in the West through Robert van Gulik's English translation of a nineteenth-century Chinese novel about the famed judge (Kuhn 2013). The premise of reinterpreting *Judge* Dee as *Detective* Dee is that everyone loves a good mystery, especially when enhanced atmospherically by a mysterious 'Oriental' setting. In fact, the US television network ABC adapted one of van Gulik's novels *The Haunted Monastery* into the television movie *Judge Dee and the Monastery Murders* (1974), where the eponymous judge had to confront violent killings and supernatural 'hauntings' in a Taoist monastery. This American production clearly saw the audience appeal of the Judge Dee figure as an 'Oriental' detective reminiscent of Charlie Chan.[5] By retaining this configuration of the Di Renjie character in the Detective Dee films (played by Andy Lau in *Phantom Flame* and Mark Chao in *Young Detective Dee: Rise of the Sea Dragon*), Tsui Hark is able to tap into this continued mainstream interest in the detective mystery genre as best represented in the literary, televisual and filmic traditions of Charlie Chan and Sherlock Holmes. The pleasure that audiences derive from a Chan or Holmes mystery is not only the suspenseful thrill of a whodunnit plot twist, but also the ability to accompany the brilliant detectives on their deductive quests to ascertain the truth. In the almost superhuman reasoning abilities of Chan and Holmes do audiences find the vicarious intellectual pleasure of logical, scientific rationality as a route towards explaining the inexplicable.

In recent years this scientific rationalism in detective stories and police procedurals has been further enveloped by a stylised aura that renders the arcane, meticulous and generally mind-numbing processes of detective work and forensic science with a mediatised, pop cultural stylishness, as seen in the American network CBS's highly popular television series *CSI:*

Crime Scene Investigation (2000–15) and its various spin-offs, and BBC's *Sherlock* (2010–17) starring the inimitable Benedict Cumberbatch. One could describe this phenomenon as 'the *CSI* effect', which happens to be the title of a collection of essays edited by Michele Byers and Val Marie Johnson. Byers and Johnson make the following observation:

> The shows have extremely high production values and use special effects technologies extensively. Most significantly, these technologies allow viewers to ride bullets and blood splatter forwards and backwards in time . . . [T]hey take us into bodies and in so doing suggest a venue through which the dead can speak. At the same time, the series are hyper-oriented toward a display of forensic technologies that is clearly fetishistic. (Byers and Johnson 2009: xv)

Expertly edited with rapid jump cuts, and accompanied by pop music soundtracks, the *CSI* series pulsates like a trendy music video, making the important, but tedious and slow, work of forensic investigators look exciting, flashy and sexy.

The animating speed of this new aesthetic is a perfect match for the dizzying kinetics one finds in Tsui's reinvention of the *wuxia shenguai pian*, which the director adopts and integrates into *Phantom Flame* (and later in *Young Detective Dee: Rise of the Sea Dragon*) with panache.[6] The slick martial arts-action set pieces effectively parallel the sharp narrative turns of the murder mystery. But even more, the use of certain cinematographic and editing techniques allow Tsui to adopt the stylised atmospherics present in *CSI*. Strategically placed flashbacks (to jog audience memory of crucial but previously underappreciated or ignored scenes), zoom focus (to close-ups of significant material evidence), and wide-angle shallow focus shots (to conjure targeted identification of critical action on the part of the victims or the perpetrators) are only some of the cinematic methods Tsui employs. The camera eye literally becomes the private eye, so to speak, with Detective Dee providing the point-of-view perspective to lead the audience through his analysis of the evidence. This fetishistic forensic focus – to borrow Byers and Johnson's terminology – stylistically modernises the Judge Dee figure even further through an established American media format.

The scientific process of crime scene investigation, in the form of this new aesthetic, provides the formalistic framework to elevate logical rationalism as the preferred modern epistemology to deal with the problems of the nation, vis-à-vis the superstition and religion with which the bizarre and the supernatural have traditionally been approached. To accentuate this point, the mystery of the phantom flame is no ordinary murder case – Empress Wu (Carina Lau) is so mystified by the strange deaths of her court officials that she agrees to commute Detective Dee's prison sentence by having him help her solve the case. The murders defy logical explanation in that the victims die from internal combustion: the fires start burning from the inside of their bodies when they are exposed to direct sunlight. The circumstances of the crimes and the investigative process provide Tsui the opportunity to populate the narrative and the *mise en scène* with the bizarre and the strange, as requisite in any good *wuxia shenguai pian*.

The socially accepted explanation for the first two phantom flame deaths is a religious one, considering how only the supernatural can explain the supernatural. Master Jia, the official in charge of building the giant Buddha, which serves 'to revere the Empress's divine glory' and to celebrate her coronation, dies after moving the amulets during a routine inspection.[7] 'These are amulets bestowed by the [Imperial] Chaplain. They can dispel evil and thwart disaster,' Jia himself explains to the foreign diplomat visiting the Buddha tower. But as his building manager Shatuo (Tony Leung Ka Fai) also warns Jia, 'Moving the amulets will bring bad luck, so ever since you moved them, everybody has been scared. Our work has been suffering.' This mass superstitious hysteria amongst the workers is validated when Jia dies at the top of the Buddha; and Master Xue, the chief official of the Supreme Court who is in charge of the case, also incinerates to death, when he defies the religious taboo of moving the amulet by ripping it off the tubular column and tempting the gods: 'Let divine intervention strike me now!'

But as one would expect of any good murder mystery, our intrepid and eagle-eyed Detective Dee intervenes by exposing the irrationality of that superstition, and by pointing to his former compatriot and friend Shatuo as the murderer. Inflamed by revenge and hatred for the Empress, who had his hand chopped off for the crime of rebelling against her political ambitions, Shatuo used the fire beetles to poison Jia and Xue in order to enact the absurdly complicated plan of toppling the giant Buddha during the coronation and then leading an armed rebellion against the Empress. Hence, he uses the superstition of his fellow workers and the masses as a ruse to attempt to throw off the investigators. In other words, logic and scientific deduction rule the day, even in seventh-century Tang Dynasty China.

I want to complicate this modern/traditional framework of logical deduction further by turning to the fire beetles as an evidentiary point. The entire logic of the case as devoid of the supernatural pivots on a 'natural' direct cause of animal poisoning, which is, ironically, a fantastical cinematic creation reliant on the mysterious and mystical taxonomy of traditional Chinese medicine. In their essay 'Magic, Medicine, Cannibalism', authors Emilie Yueh-yu Yeh and Neda Hei-tung Ng note how Peter Chan's macabre short film *Going Home* (2002) depicts its protagonists as needing 'to descend from the "legitimate" medical sphere to the underworld of ancient Chinese medicine'. The film places, they argue, 'the initial perception of the Chinese doctors into question. Are they human or demon? Or something in between?' (Yeh and Ng 2009: 150–1). The Imperial Physician Wang Bo heard about the legendary fire beetles and acquired them to cure the Emperor's illness, but to no avail. Fearing for his life, he transformed himself with acupuncture needles into Donkey Wang and hides out in the Phantom Bazaar.

My argument here is that the fire beetles, Wang Bo/Donkey Wang as Chinese physician, and physical transformation through acupuncture all constitute a piece in Chinese horror cinema's fantastical use of ancient Chinese medicine. The film integrates Chinese medicine into the investigative rationality of Detective Dee, by accepting its epistemology as scientifically consistent with crime scene investigative procedures. I am not here to adjudicate the scientific legitimacy of Chinese medicinal practice; instead, I am suggesting that the film embraces the bizarre and the fantastical as consonant with stereotypical perceptions of the Chinese medical world. For instance, Donkey Wang is the classic caricature of the voodoo doctor of the underworld. Because of his physical transformations, he is not who we think he is. The first encounter the audience has with him sees the doctor eating a live giant centipede. He inhabits the Phantom Bazaar, an underworld 'black market' where misfits, criminals and undesirables find refuge and thrive there. When Detective Dee and his team descend into that sphere, they are ferried to the doctor by a woman reminiscent of the Greek goddess Styx. The eerie underground river unveils its hellish denizens: a six-armed sitar player and zombie-like beings who appear to be cannibalistic. This *mise en scène* set piece could have come out of the *Pirates of the Caribbean* (2003), and the Phantom Bazaar could have easily been populated by the unsavoury characters of the Mos Eisley Cantina in the original *Star Wars* (1977). In short, my point is that Tsui blurs the boundaries of scientific logic and modernity by culturally roping in Chinese medical practices and their fantastical associations to disturb the modern/traditional framework and to complicate the notion of China as a modern nation. In this chapter's conclusion, I will draw out the political potential for a subversive oppositionality that the concept of cultural and social illegitimacy, as envisioned in the Phantom Bazaar, ultimately holds.

My second and final point about *Phantom Flame* targets the concept of the rising cultural nationalism that has seeped into a number of transnational Chinese co-productions. I am thinking specifically of Stanley Tong's *The Myth* (2005), which stars a growingly Chinese patriotic Jackie Chan, and, of course, Zhang Yimou's *Hero*, where Jet Li's character Nameless sacrifices himself – in the iconic scene where he faces a flying barrage of arrows – so that the first emperor of China can unite the country.[8] One could potentially argue that *Phantom Flame* falls into this grouping. This kind of cultural nationalism in Chinese popular cinema may be attributable to the contemporary rise of China not only as a world economic powerhouse, but also as a formidable player in the global film industry. It is, therefore, unsurprising to see film-makers pragmatically appealing to their Chinese financial overseers and their numerous Chinese fans. Of course, I am not trying to cast aspersions on the authenticity of the film-makers' nationalism, but to suggest that there is a convenient confluence of factors at work in making the cinematic presentation of a Chinese nationalism popular and palatable.

The detective mystery in *Phantom Flame* functions almost like an extended MacGuffin, initially distracting audiences from what is the more important story, which is a political one. Shatuo's motivation to commit multiple murders, beyond his desire to seek revenge against the Empress, began as a political resistance to the cruel methods that the Empress deploys against dissidents and her opponents in order to suppress them. In fact, Detective Dee and Shatuo were once fellow rebels against the Empress because, as Dee puts it to the Empress's confidante Jing'er (Li Bing Bing):

> In order to ascend the throne, the Empress eliminated clansmen and old officials, blaming everything on the Chaplain. In order to shut people's mouths, she even brought me back to solve the case, never expecting that I would suspect her. She told me the Chaplain would disappear after her coronation. That has been her way of doing things all along. To achieve greatness, everyone is expendable!

In other words, the Empress's ruthless quest for power is all that matters in her worldview. But even then, Detective Dee continues with the case because he believes that violence does not justify more violence – Shatuo's committing murder for a politically good cause is unjustifiable. Dee is also sympathetic to the plight of the Empress when she points out to him that 'men are just not used to women in power', which he notes is not the reason for his opposing her in the past. (It is important to observe here that the modern gender politics of this moment is definitely Tsui's way of appealing to contemporary audiences.[9]) Most significantly, Dee's loyalty to China as a nation is to accept the Empress as a means toward national unification, as he tells the Empress at the end of the film:

On the pretense of magic, you wantonly killed clansmen and officials. This is unpardonable. But society is on the brink of extinction, so your punishment is hereby suspended. Ruling requires power and strategy, but right and wrong cannot be confused. May the Empress know her every move, and let Tang clansmen succeed her, so that everything will return to the way it should be.

The film presents a historically deterministic view of the Empress in that Dee has the prescience to know that she would indeed serve China in bringing the country together – the film's postscript confirms Dee's faith:

In 690 AD, Empress Wu became the first and only female Emperor in the history of China. Fifteen years later, in 705 AD, Empress Wu retired from the throne, returning the title to the Crown Prince, in honor of her promise to Detective Dee.

But, like Nameless in Zhang Yimou's *Hero*, this nationalism came at a personal cost: in his defense of the Empress, Detective Dee is poisoned by the fire beetles and, as a consequence, must retreat to the darkness and the social margins of the Phantom Bazaar in order to keep himself from burning to death.

Conclusion: the Phantom Bazaar

Tsui Hark is a politically tactical film-maker. He foregrounds in his film a nationalistic identification with China as a historical and cultural polity, which plays well with most Chinese audiences globally. But he leaves himself just enough wriggle room and ambiguity in the narrative to inject an oppositional politics of critique and resistance to the national and global systems of oppression and exploitation. As Donkey Wang opines to Dee before they descend into the Phantom Bazaar to escape the sunlight, 'The truth has come to light. The world is finally at peace. But Detective Dee is in the Phantom Bazaar. Whether your fire beetle poison is curable will depend on the will of heaven.' To which Dee responds, 'The will of heaven is bright and clear, but I'm travelling alone. Heaven and earth have no space for me, but my heart is at peace.' In this moment of Zen, Tsui and the scriptwriters embed the affective horrors of disempowerment, displacement, loneliness and invisibility that can characterise life as one of the 99 per cent in this age of crony and vulture capitalism and widespread political corruption. Cultural, economic and political power has increasingly been amassed at the very top, and 'heaven and earth have no space for' us. But the narrative open-endedness in *Phantom Flame* leaves hope for a cure, not only for Detective Dee but also for this world.

Notes

1. In the rest of the chapter, I shall refer to the film as *Phantom Flame*.
2. Some of these films I recall watching in theatres as a teenager, or have seen on recently released DVDs. For a comprehensive listing of the Shaw catalogue, see Wong (2003: 346–414).
3. Available at <www.festival-cannes.fr/en/archives/artist/id/316848.html> (last accessed 28 April 2016).
4. For a detailed analysis of the film, see Schroeder (2010).
5. The casting of renowned Chinese American actor Keye Luke in the role of the villain Lord Sun Ming in *Judge Dee and the Monastery Murders* deepens the Charlie Chan connection. Luke starred next to Warner Oland in the Charlie Chan film series of the 1930s, as the detective's son and sidekick.
6. Another Hong Kong–China co-production example is Peter Chan's *Wu Xia* (2011; released as *Dragon* in the US). In an interview with Gary Bettinson, the director attributes *Wu Xia*'s narrative and stylistic formulations to the impact of television shows like *CSI* and *House* (Bettinson 2016: 143, note 3).
7. While relying mostly on the Blu-ray version's subtitle translations for all dialogue and textual elements (*Detective Dee* 2010), I have occasionally used my own translations from the original Mandarin for further accuracy and clarity.
8. I offer close analysis of these two films elsewhere (Kenneth Chan 2009). See also Evans Chan's trenchant and necessary critique of Zhang's film (Evans Chan 2009).
9. The gender politics of the Detective Dee films deserves an entire essay of its own, a topic to which I cannot do justice within the tight spatial constraints of this chapter.

References

Bettinson, Gary (2016), 'Hong Kong puzzle films: the persistence of tradition', in Gary Bettinson and James Udden (eds), *The Poetics of Chinese Cinema*, New York: Palgrave Macmillan, pp. 119–45.

Byers, Michele and Val Marie Johnson (2009), '*CSI* as neoliberalism: an introduction', in Michele Byers and Val Marie Johnson (eds), *The* CSI *Effect: Television, Crime, and Governance*, Lanham: Lexington Books, pp. xiii–xxxvi.

Chan, Evans (2009), 'Zhang Yimou's *Hero*: the temptations of fascism', in Tan See-Kam, Peter X. Feng and Gina Marchetti (eds), *Chinese Connections: Critical Perspectives on Film, Identity, and Diaspora*, Philadelphia: Temple University Press, pp. 263–77.

Chan, Kenneth (2009), *Remade in Hollywood: the Global Chinese Presence in Transnational Cinemas*, Hong Kong: Hong Kong University Press.

Dai Jinhua (2005), 'Order/anti-order: representation of identity in Hong Kong action movies', Zhang Jingyuan (trans.), in Meaghan Morris, Siu Leung Li and Stephen Chan Ching-Kiu (eds), *Hong Kong Connections: Transnational Imagination in Action Cinema*, Durham, NC: Duke University Press, pp. 81–94.

Detective Dee and the Mystery of the Phantom Flame (2010), Film (Blu-ray), directed by Tsui Hark, China: Huayi Brothers Media Corporation.

Gledhill, Christine (2000), 'Rethinking genre', in Christine Gledhill and Linda Williams (eds), *Reinventing Film Studies*, London: Arnold, pp. 221–43.

Hendrix, Grady (2003), 'Tsui Hark', *Senses of Cinema*, 27, <sensesofcinema. com/2003/great-directors/tsui/> (last accessed 28 April 2016).

Kuhn, Anthony (2013), 'Before Sherlock: an ancient Chinese sleuth's enduring appeal', *NPR*, October 25, <www.npr.org/sections/parallels/ 2013/10/25/240685259/before-sherlock-an-ancient-chinese-sleuths-enduri ng-appeal> (last accessed 30 April 2016).

Schroeder, Andrew (2010), *Tsui Hark's Zu: Warriors from the Magic Mountain*, Hong Kong: Hong Kong University Press.

Teo, Stephen (2009), *Chinese Martial Arts Cinema: the* Wuxia *Tradition*, Edinburgh: Edinburgh University Press.

Teo, Stephen (2001), 'Tsui Hark: national style and polemic', in Esther C. M. Yau (ed.), *At Full Speed: Hong Kong Cinema in a Borderless World*, Minneapolis: University of Minnesota Press, pp. 143–58.

Thompson, Anne (2011), 'Tsui Hark talks *Detective Dee and the Mystery of the Phantom Flame*, goes 3-D', *Indiewire.com*, 6 September, <blogs.indiewire. com/thompsononhollywood/tsui_hark_talks_detective_dee_and_the_myst ery_of_the_phantom_flame_goes_3-d> (last accessed 29 April 2016).

Tsui, Clarence (2013), '*Young Detective Dee – Rise of the Sea Dragon (Di Ren Jie Zhi Shen Du Long Wang)*: film review', *The Hollywood Reporter*, 17 September, <www.hollywoodreporter.com/review/young-detective-dee-rise-sea-6306 70> (last accessed 29 April 2016).

Wong, Ain-ling (ed.) (2003), *The Shaw Screen: a Preliminary Study*, Hong Kong: Hong Kong Film Archive.

Yeh, Emilie Yueh-yu and Neda Hei-tung Ng (2009), 'Magic, medicine, cannibalism: the China demon in Hong Kong horror', in Jinhee Choi and Mitsuyo Wada-Marciano (eds), *Horror to the Extreme: Changing Boundaries in Asian Cinema*, Hong Kong: Hong Kong University Press, pp. 145–59.

Zhang, Zhen (2005), *An Amorous History of the Silver Screen: Shanghai Cinema, 1896–1937*, Chicago: University of Chicago Press.

Part III

Transnational Trends: Globalisation and Politics in Contemporary Hong Kong Horror

CHAPTER 9

Cross-border Implications:
Transnational Haunting, Gender
and the Persistent Look of *The Eye*

Enrique Ajuria Ibarra

The calligraphy lesson in the Pang Brothers' *The Eye* (2002) presents a haunting that differs significantly from the other spectral encounters in the film. While protagonist Wong Kar Mun is concentrating on following her teacher's instructions, she suddenly hears a female voice asking her why she has taken her seat. Mun is scared and looks back at the old teacher to see if he has also noticed the haunting voice. She turns around and the reverse shot reveals a pale woman floating on the other side of the room. Once again, she demands to know why Mun is sitting on her chair before charging towards her and suddenly dissolving before Mun's perplexed and horrified countenance. Unlike the rest of the spectres in this film, this ghost is heard before it is seen. By focusing first on the aural qualities of the haunting, this scene gains significance: Mun realises she can also hear supernatural voices, thus making her encounter much more frightening. Since the source of the voice is off-screen, the haunting possesses an acousmatic quality. In Michel Chion's terms, this heightens the immaterial and invisible quality of this ghost, rendering it ubiquitous (Chion 1999: 24–5), yet unheard and unseen but for Mun. The scene is thus unusual because the haunting is never presented this way again throughout the rest of the film. Instead of further experimenting with different cinematic techniques to portray a spectral apparition, *The Eye*, as the title suggests, solely uses vision to identify ghosts. Also, once the spectre has been visually perceived, its ubiquity changes to a deictic configuration: the ghost is standing *there* before it comes at Mun *here*.

The success of the Pang Brothers' film prompted two sequels, *The Eye 2* (2004) and *The Eye 10* (also known as *The Eye Infinity* and occasionally as *The Eye 3*, 2005), in which the directors once again explore other terrifying forms of seeing ghosts: the second film focuses on a depressed pregnant woman, and the third instalment follows a group of friends playing several traditional Thai games that claim to allow people to see spectres. The series' predilection for visual elaborations of ghostly hauntings works as a structural catalyst for further debates in the determination of a transnational, Asian Gothic horror aesthetic that confronts concepts of identity, nationality and subjectivity, mostly framed by a distancing – whether geographical or spatial – that this privilege of vision suggests. Indeed, *The Eye* series is a repository for critical debates about pan-Asian film production and cultural identity. On the surface, the films seem to embrace a transnational outlook that attempts to fit a shared cinematic agenda. Nevertheless, their expression of globalisation discloses cultural tensions, concerning in particular Hong Kong's regional identity, its relationship with the rest of Southeast Asia, and its mixture of Western and Eastern traditions (Knee 2009). As horror films, the *The Eye* and its sequels focus on the transpositional qualities of ghostly haunting that prompt the subject to question their perceptions of reality. With transplants, suicide attempts, and geographical and metaphysical border crossings, these films examine problems at personal, social and political levels. This chapter offers an enquiry into the critical debates of the films' pan-Asian look in relation to research in Asian Gothic horror, and then questions how the films' privilege of the sense of vision confronts an idealised global and transnational discourse that is challenged by distancing the belief in the supernatural from modern Hong Kong to other locations in Southeast Asia.

The Eye tells the story of acquiring new sight and of coping with extravisual capabilities. Blind since she was a small girl, Mun finally gets a cornea transplant and works with visual therapist Dr Wah to (re)learn how to see. Nevertheless, Mun realises she now constantly sees ghosts and the shadow of Death that takes these spirits away. With the help of Dr Wah, she discovers that her corneas were donated by Chiu Wai-ling, a Thai girl of Chinese origin. Together, Mun and Wah travel to Thailand to learn the cause of Mun's supernatural visual abilities and put an end to her visual haunting. In *The Eye 2*, Joey Cheng is a young woman who has just ended an affair with a married man, and decides to commit suicide in a hotel in Bangkok. She does not realise she is already pregnant, and it is later revealed that her physical condition and near-death experience allows her to see spirits too. Joey realises she is being haunted by a mysterious female ghost, who, according to Buddhist tradition, is attempting to reincarnate as Joey's soon-to-be-born child. *The Eye 10* takes a more comic turn, as a group of Hong Kong friends – Kofei, April, Ted and Amy – decide to play a series of games suggested by their friend Chong-kwai during their visit in Thailand. Soon, the comic frights turn into horrifying disappearances, and the characters are still being haunted even though they are back in Hong Kong. The three films not only look at different ways of seeing spectres; they also embrace a pan-Asian setting where a regional attempt to display horror does not necessarily imply locality but transnationality.

The Pang Brothers' trilogy belongs to a group of films that have been advertised and commercialised with a pan-Asian appeal, especially since they have been distributed in American and UK markets through the Tartan Asia Extreme brand. Instead of focusing on films from select Asian countries, the term 'Asian horror' seeks not only to recognise regional films, such as those from Japan or South Korea, but also to help boost the production and distribution of films from other countries and territories like Hong Kong, Singapore, Thailand or Malaysia. Nikki J. Y. Lee argues that 'the genre of Asian horror is an intraregional and equally a transregional construction that functions as a mediator between national film industries and both regional and global markets' (Lee 2011: 104). Lee notes that this proposed category reflects a desire for more successful transregional and global promotion in the effort to share production costs, as well as to boost the film industries of smaller Southeast Asian countries and regions. Likewise, in terms of marketability and distribution in the West, Chi-Yun Shin has noted that Tartan's 'Asia Extreme' brand has allowed a 'viable East Asian film niche' in international Anglophone markets, and that the label, 'based on the discourses of differences and excess, fit[s] comfortably into the widespread notion about the East' (Shin 2008). This suggests that film productions could potentially homogenise cultural and social qualities across a wide regional panorama, which, according to Steven Rawle, 'has often obscured the diversity of films produced within East and Southeast Asian countries', thus singularising most of these films as just 'Asian,' both thematically and visually (Rawle 2009: 168). Applause Pictures, the production company responsible for *The Eye* series, was central in fomenting this kind of transnational collaborative work, and was further situated in the Asian Extreme catalogue with the distribution of the films through Tartan.[1]

Nevertheless, what these transregional films evidence is a commercial endeavour that encapsulates a look at Asianness that is specifically designed for distribution purposes worldwide. Bliss Cua Lim claims that these films – including *The Eye* – play along the lines of generic pan-Asian naming for the sake of a marketing strategy (Lim 2007: 119). Generic convention is paired with cultural expectations of Asianness in the elaboration of a film narrative that aims to encompass an Asian cultural generality. Lim notices that 'this rhetoric betrays a play with cultural/regional identity that, in the same breath, discounts cultural specificity, claiming a universal, culture-neutral appeal' (Ibid.: 118) that is geared more towards the creation of this pan-Asian identity through horror. In *The Eye* series, privileging vision as the favoured sense to perceive horror hints at the failure of the pan-Asian look. With an obsession to witness spectres visually, the idealisation of a general brand of Asian horror discloses particular and regional concerns about what is it to be pan-Asian. This is further represented in the films with a distanced geographic positioning of ghosts that ultimately reveals the complex identity that befalls these particular Southeast Asian regions: the distancing of the supernatural and the traditional reveals an uncanny tension between the present and the past in the determination of what is it to be Asian, and more specifically to be from Hong Kong within Asia.

Visual Haunting

Even though the calligraphy scene described above presents a ghost acousmatically, the rest of the ghosts in *The Eye* are always seen first and sometimes heard afterwards. Mun sees spirits of fellow patients at the hospital ward, of neighbours in her apartment building, and the ghosts of the eatery owner's dead wife and child when nobody else does. She is also terrified of the ghost of the old man inside the elevator. The latter particularly focuses on vision mediated through lenses. The security camera does not record the haunting presence the way Mun's eyes do. Additionally, the ghost in the elevator does not emit a single sound. The scene is horrifying because the ghost is a purely visual threat. It is a presence that should not be there. Mun is afraid of what else she can see: the ghost's crushed face is barely shown as a supplementary visual confirmation of this horror. In short, in *The Eye* the haunting is primarily and preferably visual. The protagonist recovers her sight and is able to hear ghosts too. Even if she were hearing ghosts when she was blind, she needs vision to be able to acknowledge them. This also involves a disturbing realisation of the proximity of the haunting: the supernatural occurs in a constricted space that forces an acknowledgement of the past that cannot be entirely overlooked.

Throughout the film series, elevators become central locations for spectral hauntings. In *The Eye 2*, Joey and a fellow patient in labour are trapped in the hospital elevator, when a spectral figure floats down towards the woman who is struggling with her emergency birth. Joey screams in horror at the sight of this dark figure descending and entering the woman's womb. The act of penetration is hidden from view, but is clearly suggested by a series of medium close-up shots of the spirit of a young woman with long hair gliding in between the pregnant woman's legs. Joey's supernatural vision is only confirmed by a series of shots/ reverse shots that only feature the spectre by means of the protagonist's point of view. Similarly, in *The Eye 10*, Ted is chased down by a spirit that inhabits the hallways of the apartment building where his cousin May resides. Despite Hong Kong's technological improvements, ghosts are keen to inhabit these spaces, and be seen (or not seen) through apparatuses of vision, such as surveillance cameras or handheld cameras. These scenes also point to a relationship between life and death that envisions ghosts and spirits as part of everyday life in Asia. Katarzyna Ancuta claims that 'modernization did not necessarily mean the eradication of older spiritual beliefs', and that 'Asian ghosts have no problem adapting to the demands of the modern world and its new communication technologies, abandoning their graveyards and crumbling mansions for the sake of the high-speed railway, commercial elevators, mobile telephony, or the Internet' (Ancuta 2014: 211). As noted by Ancuta, Asian horror films like *The Eye* series expand on a cultural determination of living with ghosts, an assimilation of old cultural assumptions that cannot be done away with, even though society has advanced technologically. The Pang Brothers may not explore the vicissitudes of digital media – as happens in the Japanese films *Ring* (1998), directed by Hideo Nakata, and *Pulse* (2001), directed by Kiyoshi Kurosawa, or the South Korean *Phone* (2002), directed by Byeong-ki Ahn – yet their films continue exploring systems of belief that are developed in the encounter between tradition and modernity. Additonally, *The Eye* series is determined by a core structure in the notion of spectrality: that haunting is a visual experience and that it is therefore also involved with spatial perceptions of proximity and distance.

Ghosts challenge the triad of vision, perception and knowledge. They are objects without materiality that can only be grasped by a quick glance to their flickering non-corporeal existence in a world of objects. Ghosts are visual, they are meant to be looked at – unexpectedly, that is. In *The Eye* series, the perception of spectres follows a traditional Westernised concept of vision to acknowledge and experience the world. Mun, Joey, and Ted and Amy see ghosts where no other member in the community is able to see them. In Mun's case, her efforts focus on learning to recognise the material world around her now that she has recovered her vision with the cornea transplant. What truly disturbs her is the fact that she is able to see more than she is supposed to. Her mental process of perception must learn to cope with the visual spectrum, but her recovered sight is supplementary: she sees that which lies beyond the natural; her vision is supernatural.

Thus, visual haunting points to this central tendency for perception and reason. Martin Jay claims that 'the visual has been dominant in modern Western culture in a wide variety of ways', what he calls a 'scopic regime' that is the 'hegemonic, visual model of the modern era'

(Jay 1998: 66–7). Jay recognises a philosophical, theological and artistic trend in Western culture that privileges vision as the principal form of knowledge and apprehension of the world. Similarly, W. J. T. Mitchell argues that 'vision is in itself invisible, that we cannot see what seeing is' (Mitchell 2002: 166). Even though *The Eye* series attempts to question the process of vision, of visuality as the core perception of reality, it is still bound by the precise assumption that perception depends on the eye itself. Mitchell notes that the study of visual culture 'entails a meditation on blindness, the invisible, the unseen, the unseeable, and the overlooked' (Ibid.: 170). As such, vision becomes the privileged sense for understanding and categorising that which cannot be seen or the lack of vision itself. In a strict dialectical sense, vision frames the notion of the supernatural as that which can be seen selectively, a supplemental experience that should be disturbing because it is not typical to be able to see immaterial beings or to not be able to see at all, particularly within one's closest surroundings.

In *The Eye*, Mun's inability to see is considered an impediment that must be rectified to become a fully perceiving subject, and not a blind Other. On the contrary, her perception of the supernatural still points to otherness mainly based once again on reality and materiality sustained by the eye and its gaze upon objects and surroundings. Mun learns to understand her haunting vision as a curse. Likewise, the film emphasises that this perception is exclusively limited to the feminine, as Dr Wah, the rational man of science, is at odds trying to help Mun overcome her fear to see again. This gendered perception is further developed in *The Eye 2*, where the ability to see spirits of the dead is heightened by the fact that the protagonist is pregnant.

Gendered Haunting

The first two instalments in the *The Eye* series feature female protagonists. Whilst the first film mainly focuses on Mun's newly acquired sight by means of technological and medical advancement, in the second film Joey's depression aligns pregnancy – or life – with death. Spectres eagerly await their return to the physical world, and haunt pregnant women in their efforts to be reborn during childbirth. This persistent association between supernatural perception and the feminine is further enhanced by the notion of the fear of the body, her own body itself. For Joey, the haunting spirits become a dreadful corporeal affront in their interest to possess the body of her child. Life and death once again merge at a significant border – the moment of birth – but also come too close, both physically and spiritually, that their presence has to be inevitably acknowledged and associated with an excruciating bodily process.

Barbara Creed's notion of the monstrous feminine seems appropriate to explore the experience of horror in *The Eye 2*. According to Creed, there is an 'ancient connection between woman, womb and the monstrous' that is frequently invoked in the horror film (Creed 1993: 43). This connection implies a sense of abjection that results from the association between woman and the natural, animal world. As such, 'awareness of his links to nature reminds man of his mortality and of the fragility of the symbolic order' (Ibid.: 47). The experience of birth is thus perceived in its utmost corporality: the expansion and deformation of the female form accompanied by pain and blood, which may not necessarily spring forth life but may in some cases deliver a still body, just like any other bodily fluid that is expelled and done away with. Creed concludes that the monstrous womb addresses abjection 'in terms of inside/outside', elements that cannot be clearly separated in strictly symbolic terms (Ibid.: 48–9). *The Eye 2* hints to this idea of the abject, but adds a traditional Buddhist notion of spiritual rebirth to further complicate this division: body and spirit, modernity and tradition, life and death, past and present, here and there converge in pregnancy, the horror of the constant haunting presence of spirits in ways that seem penetrative, intrusive and utterly horrifying, as evidenced in the elevator scene from *The Eye 2* mentioned above.

The film constantly develops a certain dread for feminine perception, a perception that cannot be extricated by any means other than death. Joey seeks death twice in the film in order to deal with rejection by her lover and the rejection of herself as the potential carrier of the new receptacle of the recently deceased wife of her lover. Abjection is presented here in terms of a constant struggle between modernity and tradition in the female body: a body that constantly reminds man of his origins prior to the symbolic. In this case, it is the difficulty of achieving a successful hybrid relationship between past origins and present modernity in terms of postcolonial, social and cultural standing. Supernatural vision is cast out and rejected along with the experience of pregnancy, as they make us see traditional beliefs that should be surmounted in contemporary society. Female vision is rejected as well in both films, since Mun and Joey are the only ones who are able to see and perceive more than the physical world appears to show. A hierarchical preference over a more masculinised – rationalised – sense of seeing is favoured throughout the film series.

This visual hierarchical preference flaunts the cultural confrontation of Hong Kong's contemporary world. More than embracing the marketable, idealised global and modern vision for Southeast Asia, this issue foregrounds the discursive differences that constitute Hong Kong's identity. Donna Haraway has pointed out the cultural persistence of vision for the sake of knowledge and objectivity. She claims that eyes have been used to signify 'a perverse capacity – honed to perfection in the history of science tied to militarism, capitalism, colonialism, and male supremacy – to distance the knowing subject from everybody and everything in the interests of unfettered power' (Haraway 1988: 581). Haraway speaks of a privileged sense of vision that supports a phallocentric supremacy, one that is rational and positivist, and that relies on visual difference to name the Other. The failure of the film series to provide a horror effect that deviates from the visual experience foregrounds the complex cultural dynamics that characterise this region.

In *The Eye*, once Mun recovers her vision, she must learn how to see, how to tell the real from the supernatural and the self from the other, in order to claim her identity and the privileged cultural discourse. Seeing ghosts terrifies her, and she feels unable to cope with a world that provides her with such supernatural vision. Haraway encourages a vision grounded in feminism, a vision that is situated. For her, 'the split and contradictory self is the one who can interrogate positionings and be accountable, the one who can construct and join rational conversations and fantastic imaginings that change history [. . .]. Subjectivity is multidimensional; so, therefore, is vision' (Ibid.: 586). In a sense, Mun's sight points to a different way of seeing that would allow her to locate herself in a multidimensional plane of existence and of identity. With her eyes, time and place become fluid in an encounter of different positions of the other (foreign, feminine, spectral, handicapped). But Mun is being instructed to see in a positivist, scientific way that tends to distance or overlook certain visual evidence: thus she reacts with fear at what she is able to perceive. She is determined to free herself from what she considers a curse, and therefore does not regret losing her vision at the end of the film. The narrative condemns a situated and more dynamic vision that is specifically embodied in feminine experience. In the end Mun recovers her position of other in the modern world and is now constantly aided by her partner Dr Wah, a man of reason and science.

A Transnational Asian Gothic Look?

The three films in *The Eye* series feature a troubling relationship between Hong Kong and Thailand in terms of the need for a geographical distancing between modernity and folklore. This results in an uncanny and disturbing look at the coexistence of modernity and tradition that is inevitably present in a Southeast Asian region like Hong Kong. By displacing tradition and folklore 'there' in Thailand, the films disclose that, far from acknowledging this cultural discourse sustained by the mutual presence of the past and the present, it reveals an identity in conflict: a here/ there that, when separated into specific geographical settings in the films, unleashes an anxiety towards beliefs that also belong to Hong Kong.[2] Furthermore, this also confirms that the regional identity of Hong Kong and its place and status in China, as well as in Southeast Asia, is far from simple or resolved. In her analysis of the songs of Luo Dayou, Rey Chow argues that 'Chinese urban culture, like urban culture elsewhere in the non-Western world, involves tension and conflict between "traditional" and "Western" values' that is further complicated by specific geographical areas that demand their own local recognition and 'their rights to governance' (Chow 1998: 152). Chow notices that this is an even more difficult issue in Hong Kong because of its singular colonialist history that has involved a move from one power (the UK) to another (China). As such, 'Hong Kong culture has always been dismissed by the Mainland Chinese as too Westernised and thus inauthentic' (Ibid.: 154). Chow also suggests that this region 'must move beyond not only British but also Chinese habits of historiography [. . .] to combat from the inside [. . .] the total-izing nativist vision of the Chinese folk' (Ibid.: 154–5). What the Pang Brothers' films do is evidence that this troubling process may also be a cause for anxiety over regional identity through the horror genre and the specification of geographical settings in the narratives.

In *The Eye*, Mun and Dr Wah travel to Thailand to find out who donated the corneas that allow Mun to see ghosts. The setting suggests that the lack of modern features has stalled time in this Thai commu-nity, prompting the notion of superstition and fear for the unexplained. Although this portrayal of Thailand is not repeated in *The Eye 2*, there is a contrast between high-rise buildings, fancy shopping centres, and comfortable and modern hotels in Bangkok and the religious belief that spaces need to be blessed by monks before they can be occupied again. After her suicide attempt, Joey goes back to her hotel to discover the manager has moved her to another room. She is told that her actions have brought death too close to the realm of the living, so a purifying ceremony is necessary before her room can be booked again. Joey is drawn by curios-ity to this ceremony, but stands in the distance as she watches the monks perform the ritual. Joey is alienated by this procedure, further emphasis-ing the distance of geographic spaces the film series is keen on elaborating.

In *The Eye 10*, the portrayal of Thailand in contrast with Hong Kong is consistent with the previous two films. Chong-kwai invites his Hong

Kong friends to playfully perform a series of actions to see spirits of the dead, suggested by a book he purchased in an old bookstore. Although incredulous, all five characters participate, and each one is able to perceive furtive shadows approaching the group with each game. Like in the other two films, Thailand is portrayed as the land of traditional beliefs, of revenants, of mediums and of hauntings. As the group of friends play along, Kofei suddenly disappears because the realm of the dead opens to the living and he happens to step inside. April is also drawn into this other world when she tries to look for Kofei, and Ted and Amy realise they keep being haunted back in Hong Kong by the spirit of a girl they saw had been run over on the road during their stay in Thailand.

This last scene attempts to embrace the notion of a transnational cinema: the Thai ghost is able to follow her haunted subjects all the way to Hong Kong's urban sprawl, beyond borders and fixations of spectres to particular places. The girl realises she is dead when she looks in disbelief at the footage Ted had filmed whilst on the road in Thailand. As such, the haunting is not limited to locality, but rather downplays geographical and cultural distance in favour of a blurring of culture and tradition across Southeast Asia. Nevertheless, the ghost has a source of origin that is alien to Hong Kong, so its movement across regions results in a dreadful encounter for the characters. Despite the film's efforts to emphasise a sense of transnational haunting and horror, the narrative plot keeps on distancing the source of superstition and the supernatural in Thailand, making any ghostly approach to Hong Kong incompatible. The gates of the spirit world are always open in Thailand: Ted and Amy must go back and seek Chong-kwai to rescue their friends Kofei and April. Hong Kong residents are once again alienated and distanced from these supernatural experiences in an urban and technological environment that should do away with the old and look forward to the new.

The first film manifests a transnational cooperation in terms of its production. The film was produced not only by Hong Kong, but also by Singapore, and was shot both in Hong Kong and Thailand. The film has been interpreted as an expression of a globalised pan-Asian identity, where *The Eye* represents what Laikwan Pang argues are 'many attempts among Hong Kong filmmakers to break into new markets, and [. . .] a tendency where Hong Kong films are targeting the audiences of other regions' (Pang 2007: 414). The Pang Brothers' productions offer a clear example of the intensification of 'interactions between Hong Kong cinema and Thai cinema' in response to Hong Kong's postcolonial views of globalisation that locate identity in the transnational and the dispersed (Ibid.: 413–14). *The Eye* then, presents a cinematic expression of a globalised, pan-Asian identity that seems to respond to Hong Kong's current film production endeavours and to the region's search for identity under the shadow of China, in an expanding modern world.

Despite its idealised pan-Asianness, *The Eye*'s discursive structure indicates a representation of identity that relies on vision and mythicised othering. Adam Knee has convincingly argued that this film 'points to a range of tensions underneath the relatively stable surface of present-day East and Southeast Asia' (Knee 2009: 81). Knee develops an analysis that suggests a clear dialectical configuration in the film – between the past and the present, the old and the new, the local and the foreign, the masculine and the feminine – 'a yin-yang structure to the universe, a set of dynamic oppositions which, while having immediate, topical resonances, are also part of certain eternal and inevitable conditions' (Idem). Even though the films attempt to embrace a transnational approach to Southeast Asian identity, their plot and distanced settings fail to achieve such a global approach. More than visualising this global and current image of Southeast Asia, *The Eye* series focuses on elaborating an idealised image of Thailand in opposition to modern and global Hong Kong.

In an earlier essay Knee identified this 'remarkable level of consistency in Hong Kong's cinematic representations of Thailand', which 'suggests that Hong Kong's neighbor to the South holds a distinctive symbolic value, a particular fascination for the Hong Kong imagination' (Knee 2007: 78). *The Eye* series is certainly a good example of this consistency. Here, Thailand is presented in stark contrast with modern Hong Kong. In the latter, urban modernity and positivist and rational healthcare are contrasted with the former's rural settings and superstitious beliefs in the supernatural. A cornea transplant, a pregnancy and trips to Thailand set in motion an uncomfortable breach in Hong Kong's contemporary, global space. Despite this irruption of the past in present time, the narrative drives away the supernatural from Hong Kong to Thailand, in an attempt to cope with the supernatural and superstition elsewhere, away from home. Knee insists that

> Thailand arguably becomes an allegorical closet in which reside the true and hidden desires of Hong Kong and an entire realm of mysteries and alliances repressed in modern life. Thailand offers a way to get back to what has been paved over in contemporary, urban Hong Kong existence, connections to nature, past, family, and diaspora. Ibid.: 89)

Even though the recurrence of Thailand seems to bring these closeted desires to light, *The Eye* decides to turn away from them. Thus, the film seeks for an uncanny distancing that constantly threatens the myth of pan-Asian identity.

Knee's analysis of *The Eye* bears close resemblance to Gothic approaches to Asian film, literature and culture in general. To speak of Asian Gothic is to speak of a constant confrontation between tradition and modernity. The modern reconstructions of cultural spaces and popular culture face the unearthing of what has been discarded for the purposes of social, economic and cultural development. This confrontation also references encounters of the local versus the global and the East versus the West. It also highlights issues of representation and imagery, perennially tainted by Orientalism and a colonial past. It seems as if the apparently thriving postcolonial culture in Asia is persistently haunted by its own struggle for identity, the coming to terms between past, present and future, collapsing into the space–time instant of the pan-Asian ideal. In this sense, the representation of haunting and the supernatural in Hong Kong's imagery of Thailand refers to issues that are of Gothic interest. Nevertheless, the Gothic approach is not without its problems.

Katarzyna Ancuta acknowledges that it is difficult to speak of Asian Gothic, since it is an outsider term that can further Orientalise the region and culture (Ancuta 2012: 428). But instead of condemning this Gothic approach, Ancuta encourages an 'understanding of Gothic' that 'has to be adjusted to suit local cultural contexts' (Ibid.: 429). She identifies a series of Asian writers that are 'doing Gothic', that is, 'consciously acting upon an established generic convention' (Ibid.: 430). This means that Asia embraces a globalised Gothic outreach and incorporates such elements to approach particular social and cultural concerns. In this sense, the Gothic representation of otherness – both alien and horrifying – is doubled when located in an Asian context. Ancuta claims that 'unlike in traditional Gothic narratives that made much of oriental otherness, while conveniently silencing Asian others, when we shift our focus to Asian Gothic, these "other things" need to be accounted for' (Ibid.: 435). Thus, an Asian Gothic horror text manifests the other's vision of otherness – an imagery that unearths the Asian struggle for identity as it confronts the modern, global world. The Pang Brothers' film certainly depicts Gothic in the way Ancuta argues. Moreover, the audio-visual structure of the haunting and *The Eye*'s obsession with vision also question this attempted transnational, pan-Asian look.

This privilege of the visual over the aural and other senses hints at a hierarchical discursive structure of perception that threatens pan-Asianness. As a dialectic, visual/aural can be placed along the same structural line that conforms the postcolonial Hong Kong discourse of identity. In her analysis of Fruit Chan's *Dumplings* (2004), Glennis Byron argues that the film

> sets up only to challenge the familiar categories of East and West, tradition and modernity; around which Hong Kong identity politics centred, terms which the conditions of globalisation render meaningless. Simultaneously, through the trope of cannibalism, *Dumplings* critiques globalisation, showing Hong Kong and China merging together, equally driven by the prevailing imperative of the global economy: consumption. (Byron 2013: 134)

Byron clearly establishes Hong Kong's attempt for an identity based on syncretism, where both past and present, self and other (and the other other), modernity and tradition successfully determine its identity. Nevertheless, *Dumplings*' allusions to cannibalism show that this is single-handedly driven by a global economy solely based on consumption. In the end one element will be consumed, whilst the other will successfully prevail. If *Dumplings* exercises cannibalist consumption, then *The Eye* series performs a privilege for vision. The visual hierarchical preference flaunts the ever-constant cultural and discursive confrontation of Hong Kong's contemporary world. More than embracing a global and modern vision for Southeast Asia, this audiovisual issue foregrounds the constant social, cultural and discursive differences that constitute Hong Kong's identity.

There is one scene in *The Eye* in which Mun wakes up late at night after having a stressful nightmare. When she approaches the mirror her room suddenly changes into a different space, that is, Ling's room in Thailand. For Knee,

> the shift in spaces is not singular and distinct, but subtle and wavering, the dark imagery dissolving back and forth between one space and the other repeatedly, and thus evoking a consciousness that is neither solidly here nor there, now nor then, but rather hovers uncertainly among realms, never on solid ground. (Knee 2007: 83–4)

This fluid confrontation of space and time leads Knee to suggest that the film speaks of a 'floating identity' (Ibid.: 84), thus attempting to envision a transnational, global look. Even though Knee believes this floating identity can be perceived in the film, *The Eye* keeps avoiding this possible situated flexibility. In the end, the protagonist loses her newly acquired sight, falling back into a blind safety that does not threaten her own sense of fixed objectivity. The Pang Brothers' films might suggest an outlook for a global Southeast Asian identity in terms of their production and consumption, but the series nevertheless keeps failing to achieve such idealisation. In the end, the films' narrative structure keeps coming back to a discursive and cultural preference for vision that distances experiences geographically. Chow claims that

> what is unique to Hong Kong [. . .] is precisely an in-betweenness and an aware-ness of impure origins, origins as impure. A postcoloniality that marks at once the untenability of nativism and postmodernism distinguishes Hong Kong's 'Chinese' self-consciousness and differentiates it from other 'Chinese' cities. (Chow 1998: 157)

It is this constant struggle that becomes salient in the aforementioned scene: the collapse of space, time and beliefs in Mun's room demonstrates the complex and sometimes terrifying identity that Hong Kong is constantly dealing with. If vision cannot cope with the tension that arises in the recognition of fixed knowledge and othering to speak of cultural and regional identity, it is better to do away with it, perhaps with blindness.

Notes

1. Jennifer Feeley has explored pan-Asian horror in another similar production: *The Maid* (2005). Filmed in Singapore, the film looks at the convergence of different local identities in this island city state – Malayan, Cantonese, Indian – as these traditions face the contemporary, global and technological world. Feeley notices how the image of Chineseness in the film is primarily elaborated. According to her, '*The Maid* employs pan-Asian cultural motifs to link local identity to a regional Chinese identity. This fabricated Chineseness gives the illusion of a coherent culture that stands in for the nation (Singapore) and the region (Asia) to global audiences, especially through the film's circulation in Western markets' (Feeley 2012: 52). Once again, commercial aims determine the representation of a Chineseness that Feeley deems to be 'flattened-out' and 'outdated', (Ibid.: 60) and not in line with the complex issues that arise with Singapore's multicultural policies. As a label, Asian Horror moves across the region for the sake of global commercial competition in the continent and around the world. Instead of directing the films towards a shared cultural experience, this becomes a fabricated and borrowed experience of Asianness.
2. The films do recognise that traditional beliefs are present in Hong Kong. In the first film Mun is able to see the spirit of a boy who is doomed to haunt the corridors of her apartment building. He committed suicide after his parents chided him over his school grades. Mun's grandmother detects that there is a troubled ghost, speaks with the boy's parents and performs a ritual ceremony to cleanse the building. Nevertheless, Mun is kept away from this traditional act by her sister Yee, who considers she must not be troubled by this during her visual recovery.

References

Ancuta, Katarzyna (2012), 'Asian Gothic', in David Punter (ed.), *A New Companion to the Gothic*, Oxford: Blackwell, pp. 428–41.

Ancuta, Katarzyna (2014), 'Asian Gothic', in Jerrold E. Hogle (ed.), *The Cambridge Companion to the Modern Gothic*, Cambridge: Cambridge University Press, pp. 208–23.

Byron, Glennis (2013), 'Cannibal culture: serving the people in Fruit Chan's *Dumplings*', in Glennis Byron (ed.), *Globalgothic*, Manchester: Manchester University Press, pp. 133–43.

Chion, Michel (1999), *The Voice in Cinema*, New York: Columbia University Press.

Chow, Rey (1998), *Ethics After Idealism: Theory, Culture, Ethnicity, Reading*, Bloomington, IN: Indiana University Press.

Creed, Barbara (1993), *The Monstrous-Feminine: Film, Feminism, Psychoanalysis*, London: Routledge.

Feeley, Jennifer (2012), 'Transnational spectres and regional spectators: flexible citizenship in new Chinese horror cinema', *Journal of Chinese Cinemas*, 6:1, pp. 41–64.

Haraway, Donna (1988), 'Situated knowledges: the science question in feminism and the privilege of partial perspective', *Feminist Studies*, 14:3, pp. 575–99.

Jay, Martin (1998), 'Scopic regimes of modernity', in Nicholas Mirzoeff (ed.), *The Visual Culture Reader*, London: Routledge, pp. 66–9.

Knee, Adam (2007), 'Thailand in the Hong Kong cinematic imagination', in Gina Marchetti and See Kam Tan (eds), *Hong Kong Film, Hollywood and the New Global Cinema: No Film Is an Island*, London: Routledge, pp. 77–90.

Knee, Adam (2009), 'The Pan-Asian outlook of *The Eye*', in Jinhee Choi and Mitsuyo Wada-Marciano (eds), *Horror to the Extreme: Changing Boundaries in Asian Cinema*, Hong Kong: Hong Kong University Press, pp. 69–84.

Lee, Nikki J. Y. (2011), '"Asia" as regional signifier and transnational genre-branding: the Asian horror omnibus movies *Three and Three . . . Extremes*', in Vivian P. Y. Lee (ed.), *East Asian Cinemas: Regional Flows and Global Transformations*, Basingstoke: Palgrave Macmillan, pp. 103–17.

Lim, Bliss Cua (2007), 'Generic ghosts: remaking the new "Asian horror film"', in Gina Marchetti and See Kam Tan (eds), *Hong Kong Film, Hollywood and the New Global Cinema: No Film Is an Island*, London: Routledge, pp. 109–125.

Mitchell, W. J. T. (2002), 'Showing seeing: a critique of visual culture', *Journal of Visual Culture*, 1:2, pp. 165–81.

Pang, Laikwan (2007), 'Postcolonial Hong Kong cinema: utilitarianism and (trans)local', *Postcolonial Studies*, 10:4, pp. 413–30.

Rawle, Steven (2009), 'From *The Black Society* to *The Isle*: Miike Takashi and Kim Ki-Duk at the intersection of Asia Extreme', *Journal of Japanese and Korean Cinema*, 1:2, pp. 167–84.

Shin, Chi-Yun (2008), 'Art of branding: Tartan "Asia Extreme" films', *Jump Cut: a Review of Contemporary Media*, [online] 50, <https://www.ejumpcut.org/archive/jc50.2008/TartanDist/text.html> (last accessed 27 January 2017).

CHAPTER 10

Food for Thought: Cannibalism in
The Untold Story and *Dumplings*

Lisa Odham Stokes

Food features prominently in Hong Kong cinema, from the infamous 'Eat my rice' scene in Woo's heroic bloodshed *A Better Tomorrow 2* (1987) to special recipes of dueling restaurants in the Hui Brothers' comedy *Chicken and Duck Talk* (1988). While in many genres, food brings people together, in Hong Kong horror films, food carries ominous overtones. Cannibalism serves as main course in Herman Yau's *The Untold Story* (aka *Human Meat Buns*) and Fruit Chan's *Dumplings* (the former drawn from a real case and the latter a short and feature). Both explore political and social underpinnings of their time. *Untold* (1993) is an excellent example of crisis cinema – low budget, high anxiety over Hong Kong's return to China. *Dumplings* (2004) addresses post-postmodern global fascination with youth culture at any cost. Each marks class distinctions and reflects food's cultural importance in Chinese society. Food for thought!

Directors Yau and Chan have much in common. Both have backgrounds as experienced cinematographers who became prominent directors, writing/co-writing their own movies. Each is associated with the independent film-making movement, due to their documentary-style shooting. Chan has used chiefly non-professionals while Yau had notably collaborated with Anthony Wong. Yau lent his hand to Category III films like *Ebola Syndrome* (1996) and *Whispers and Moans* (2007), and Category II films such as *Taxi Hunter* (1993) and *From the Queen to the Chief Executive* (2001) that emphasise class divides. Chan likewise addressed class in *Made in Hong Kong* (1997), *Little Cheung* (1999), *Durian, Durian* (2000) and *Hollywood Hong Kong* (2001). Both film-makers have developed ghost stories, with Yau directing six of the *Troublesome Nights* series and Chan making *Finale in Blood* (1993).

Yau and Chan share similar visions. They address social issues and economic inequities. Their ideologies are steeped in class consciousness, with underclass main characters, from abused prostitutes and illegal immigrants to underage, hence voiceless, criminals and labour-intensive workers that undergo escalating injustices. Even Yau's Category III movies have this subtext. These outcasts earn viewers' sympathy, even, to a degree, *Untold*'s insane serial killer and *Dumplings*' freelance former abortionist. Yau avoids a distinctive visual style, instead allowing narrative and characters to move the film ahead, resulting in a quasi-documentary approach; Chan follows suit in his early films, but by *Dumplings* favours a voyeuristic look that prioritises formalistic style. Yau follows in Cassavetes' or Fassbinder's footsteps, while Chan evokes Hitchcock or Wong Kar-wai. Yau's class consciousness is also evident in his activism beyond film-making. In his own words: 'I earn money from the film industry, [and] I subsidized some social movements and protests, and publishing books on social issues' (Yau 2016).

The lenses of these two film-makers reflect the changes that have occurred in Hong Kong's underlying social issues, all driven by the colony's extreme class consciousness. Through the common cultural motif of food, the films reflect, among other things, the increasing importance of women in society, the fragility of their newly found position, and the shift from a fear of the Hong Kong underclass uprising to a fear of Mainland Chinese taking over. While the causes of these tensions may have changed, the underlying subtext, a threat to ruling-class male Hong Kong, remains the same.

Food

Hong Kong's historical and cultural diversity is represented by its number and variety of restaurants, currently 10,207 of them, more than any other city worldwide; its population spends roughly 20 per cent of its total expenditures dining out (Ng 2016; Thorborn et al. 1996). Cheng Yew-meng notes that, 'Apart from patronizing cinemas, Hong Kongers are keen on eating out. Restaurants often provide an alternative venue for socializing, given that most homes are not spacious enough to entertain large numbers of guests' (Cheng 1996: 474–5). Director Stanley Tong surmises that food's prominence in Hong Kong cinema is due to the former colony/Special Administrative Region's (SAR) status as a gourmand's paradise, in addition to film industry people's desire for a good meal. Says Tong:

> Hong Kong is known to be the best food center in the world. For Chinese food, Hong Kong is the best place. People in the industry, because they work so hard, they always go for good food and are willing to spend a lot of money . . . Hong Kong is called 'the heaven of food' center. You can have any kind of food from anywhere

in the world – Greek, Indian, American, French, Italian, German, Dutch, Swiss, Taiwanese, Indonesian, whatever. (Tong 1998)

Food is frequently used in Hong Kong movies to distinguish and type characters. It signifies *jing* (basic survival) and *qing* (emotive feelings). It also represents trans-Chinese national pride. For example, in *A Better Tomorrow 2*, Chow Yun-fat plays Ken, twin brother of Mark from the first film. A restaurateur in New York City, he takes on a Mafioso diner's blackmail attempt by forcing him to eat his mother's rice. Ken is immediately characterised as righteous, dignified and heroic. Food preparation also figures prominently, and elaborately choreographed cooking sequences appear in films like *Shogun and Little Kitchen* (1992), *The Chinese Feast* (1995) and *God of Cookery* (1996). In these films, food draws people together, especially variously made-up 'families'.

Yau likewise includes numerous food scenes in his films. In *Whispers*, 'working girls' are routinely seen gathered together after hours to eat, just as the parents in the comedy *Happy Family* (2002) are regularly served breakfast outdoors. Everybody eats, whether Triads or cops, in *Sharkbusters* (2002) or *On the Edge* (2006). *Herbal Tea* (2004) is set in a tea shop where the young owner romances a customer through her fare. The puissant protest film *From the Queen to the Chief Executive* features a penultimate ending scene in which a daughter forgives and reunites with her abusive mother, who shows her regret by preparing her daughter a meal. Even in the extreme shocker *Ebola Syndrome*, Anthony Wong's restaurant worker rapes an Ebola victim, beginning the virus's spread by serving up 'African burgers' consisting of tainted human meat; bodily functions include decaying organs and projectile vomiting.

Cannibalism

The act of cannibalism, a practice throughout human history, whether as cult, during warfare, or for basic survival, is considered by the majority as taboo, perceived as disgusting and perverse. Numerous sixteenth-century Jesuit priests, including Manoel da Nóbrega, José de Anchieta, Juan de Aspilcueta Navarro and Pero Correia, reported and were appalled by incidents among Tupian-speaking Indians along coastal Brazil, including the eating of enemy captives, children and infants (Forsyth 1983:151). In more recent history, the nineteenth-century ill-fated Donner-Reed Party, snowbound in the Sierra Nevada, resorted to cannibalism, and the 1972 Andean crash survivors of Uruguayan Flight 571 fed on deceased passengers, in both cases to survive. In Milwaukee, infamous serial killer Jeffrey

Dahmer abused and killed seventeen men and boys over two decades, performing necrophilia and cannibalism on many; this mental illness case closed in 1994 when the imprisoned Dahmer was beaten to death by another inmate.

Of course, in *Untold*, diners are unwitting cannibals, not the killer, but in *Dumplings* both Mei and the Li couple willingly participate. The film-makers expect audience revulsion and exploit this reaction by using this peculiar form of horror. But in movies, the discomfort is safe, as audiences vicariously experience what's on-screen, and their disgust registers cognitive dissonance – audiences don't want to see but can't help but look at – simultaneous revulsion and attraction. Viewers can be repelled and horrified by the portrayal of cannibalism, but the experience is ultimately cathartic, as the movie ends and real life resumes. The commercial success of the former movie, and its persistent cult following, stands in contrast to the modest returns of the latter. This outcome can be attributed to local audience 'tastes.' Hong Kong has been and remains a commercial film industry, first and foremost. Since the 1980s and 1990s heyday, the industry has 'cannibalised' Hollywood products – its sure-fire trends and blockbusters. Case in point, Jonathan Demme's *Silence of the Lambs* (1991), based on Thomas Harris's titular novel and introducing the Hannibal Lecter character, perhaps the most infamous fictional cannibal ever, inspired Danny Lee's *Dr. Lamb* (1992), which in turn is in the same genre as *The Untold Story*. In contrast, as Fruit Chan abandoned gritty realistic disaffected youth drama for a more artistic vision, he suffered locally while courting an international art house audience. Hong Kong diners are well known for being picky eaters and as moviegoers, they prefer the main course satisfies the palates.

Untold was a smash at the Hong Kong box office, with box office earnings of HK$15,763,018.00 in its theatrical run from 13 May to 2 June 1993 (The Yearbook Committee 1994: 18). As a cult classic internationally, it has several DVD and Blu-ray videos available (Hong Kong Movie Database 2016). Chan shot the short version of *Dumplings* first, for the omnibus *Three . . . Extremes* (2004), then expanded the forty-minute short into a ninety-minute feature. The feature was theatrically released on 19 August 2004, while the omnibus followed shortly afterwards, on 2 September 2004. The *Dumplings* feature played numerous international festivals in 2005, including Berlin and Melbourne. Food in the former film is associated with a male purview – the chef is male, the restaurant cheap, dirty and dingy, and there is a lack of attention to detail. His progeny, 'human pork buns', is delivered brusquely, carelessly and simply. In the latter film, food is associated with a female realm – beautifully displayed, as a delicacy, with intricate feminine touches of garnish and presentation. The food representations not only exhibit the dominants of each story, but also reflect the films' respective receptions, large and small.

The Untold Story

Despite Category III ratings for sex and violence, in *Untold* Yau has avoided the usual qualities typical of Category III exploitation, and his extreme cinema challenges a mainstream film industry. In *Whispers and Moans*, for instance, there is very little graphic sex. Likewise, *Untold* is not a typical slasher movie, and while made with the intent to satisfy audiences, it provides a subtext lacking in much contemporaneous 'extreme' cinema. First is the look of the film. Yau is often overlooked for his cinematography, which is ironic, because he has served as Director of Photography (DP) on many films and photography is important to him. Perhaps this critical oversight is due to his extreme cinema's subject matter, with a focus on underclass and often unsavoury characters. Furthermore, adding to its sensationalism, *Untold* is based on a 1985 real crime in Macau, where a criminal murdered an entire family over restaurant ownership. Actor Danny Lee initiated 'the idea to adapt the actual crime into a film', and Yau 'came on as director and began to work on the research and script in mid-1992 and the film was shot in 1993' (Yau 2016). Yau and actor Anthony Wong conducted extensive research, studying numerous newspaper articles; Yau also received much information from interviewing an inmate incarcerated with the real killer, and used his imagination to re-envision cinematically how the crimes were committed. Whether the killer actually made 'human meat buns' remains unverified, but rumour and hearsay circulated.

Handheld camerawork defines *Untold*'s style, indicating the killer's confused psychology and the audience's horrified reaction to the acts. Bryan Chang reports that 'Yau has said that if the material concerns social issues and the narrative itself has something to say, he would not impose a strong visual approach' (Li 2007: 71). Chang also notes that 'Yau's belief in following characters developed into a guerilla style . . . taking into consideration the environment and the characters . . . Each shot, each cut, represents narrative progression' (Ibid.: 72–3). A quasi-documentary style makes *Untold* raw and realistic, especially its violent scenes. This does not mean Yau lacks technique. He says: 'I care about camerawork very much' (Stokes and Hoover 2002: 38). Yau is modest when it comes to showing the brutality itself. What a film-maker chooses to actually show and leave unseen can determine the success, both commercially and artistically, of a movie. Yau often cuts from gruesome acts of killing to a medium or close-up shot of the killer, with the mutilated bodies out of frame. Instead, the frenzied obsession of the butcher at work heightens the scare. Yau also avoids low-key lighting for the killings, something his DP Cho Wai-kei had suggested (the exceptions are the Hong Kong killing and the murder of the newly hired waiter). Yau instead wanted bright fluorescent lighting: 'I thought it would be more horrible and different from the usual treatment' (Ibid.: 35). Conventional horror films, such as the *Saw* franchise (2004–17) and *The Texas Chainsaw Massacre* franchise (1974–2013) are splatter-fests, often lit with low key lighting, and as punitive on their audiences as their characters.

Consider *Untold*'s opening sequence, the first murder. According to Yau:

> I thought the use of stop-motion (or step-printing, actually I shot with 12 frames per second for that scene) would give the movie a catchy beginning. Also, the opening scene was a flashback, so I wanted images in some ways different from normal images. Besides, I believe step-printing can create a tempo inside the shots. Since I shot at 12 frames/second, the images would blur and that's interesting and seemed more horrible in a visual sense. (Stokes and Hoover 2002: 38)

The movie's opening sequence is exemplary of Yau's style. *Untold*'s first shot is a 360-degree pan of the blue-darkened sky with tops of buildings, and the identifying title 'Hong Kong 1978'. Audiences overhear an ensuing argument between Chan Chi-leung and his boss over a mah-jong game before a quick cut to a close-up of the box of tiles and players' hands. Step printing and numerous cuts are unnerving. In this first killing a skillet is the choice of weapon, with wall head-banging, culminating in a gasoline fire. As the boss's burning body writhes in pain, a quick cut to a close-up of Chan burning his Hong Kong identification card links the two shots by fire. The next shot shows Chan's fingerprinting in Macau, assuming his new identity as Wong Chi-leung. Very concisely, Yau establishes the themes to be explored in this film – the setting of the first murder is a restaurant, and the murder weapon of choice a kitchen utensil. Another cut leads to establishing shots, Macau, 1986. Children find body parts on the beach. At first, unsure who may be the victim (or victims), audience confusion is intentional. Some time passes before the explanation, and the revelation is postponed until near the film's end. While there is no food to be seen in the opening sequences, its presence thematically is there – the reason for the killing is that 'Wong' believes he has been cheated out of a restaurant, and revenge is best served in 'human pork buns'.

Following is the introduction of the police who will be investigating these crimes; the four detectives (including one female) are types, and Danny Lee as chief inspector is characterised as an absentee womaniser. For most of the film the cops are presented as incompetent, irresponsible and lazy. Sexism reigns in the Macau police department, a male domain except for a single female cop, belittled by the others. Following this insert, via a jump cut, the next scene shows Wong at work, with a disturbing close-up of him expertly chopping up a pig, at his Macau restaurant, The Eight Immortals. Not just the chopping, but its forcefulness and sound effects, as well as Wong's crazed expression, have a visceral effect. How does director Yau show the explosion of built-up frustrations of the underclass? Through constant close-ups of Anthony Wong's frenzied and determined facial expressions and selective close-ups of the mutilations of meat, whether of the animal or human variety. Even when the character Wong visits an attorney who refuses to legalise his restaurant ownership, his expression carries the same intensity.

Untold includes five violent scenes – the aforementioned Hong Kong murder (death by skillet and fire); Wong's separate desperate killings of two employees – a recently hired waiter and the cashier/waitress (he groundlessly fears they have exposed him to the cops); the flashback in which he kills The Eight Immortals' owner and his entire family; and, the severe beatings of the imprisoned Wong. The new hire, the second victim, notices Wong cheating at mah-jong (death by spindle and ladle). The next victim is the cashier/waitress, who refuses to comply when questioned by the cops. Perhaps the second most gruesome scene is when Wong rapes and murders this woman, after he is mistakenly convinced she has betrayed him (vaginal penetration and death by chopsticks). Actor Wong remembers that Yau required them to reshoot the rape scene, because he didn't think it was violent enough; the result is horrifying. Yau also wanted to avoid clichés. Certainly the most disturbing, repellent scene is the family's murder, including five children, followed by the owner's mother (deaths by broken bottle, knife and cleaver). The film is structured for each act of violence to be more horrifying than the previous one, and the action builds to the climactic flashback of the Cheng Lam family's murders.

While the scenes are indeed grisly, Yau withholds the worst, mostly. The unseen becomes more potent than what is actually seen. Sound effects of chopping, along with dissonant soundtrack, are scary indeed. Says Wong, 'We had to think about how to scare people every day' (*Untold* DVD 1996)[1]. Yau favours showing the aftermath, as the character takes out the trash, the audience knowing that the remains of the victims are inside – that is, the refuse not put into the barbeque 'pork' buns. *Untold* also shows in detail the preparation of the buns, as the character discards bones, saving meat, run through a grinder, adding sauce, sifting flour and kneading dough, shaping and stuffing buns and steaming them. The drawn-out process, the audience knowing what is being fashioned, is nauseating, and the queasiness intensifies when the buns are served.

Yau's technique, novel to the genre, is to exploit the ordinary. Everyday objects found in a restaurant kitchen are used for weapons – a skillet, the bill receipt spindle, a ladle, chopsticks, a broken bottle, a big knife and a meat cleaver. The commonplace becomes unsettling. Yau includes numerous shots where these potential weapons are foregrounded . . . ready and waiting for uncommon use. By the time the restaurant becomes well known for its steamed pork buns, the audience has long been aware of their ingredients. When the police visit for questioning, Wong insists they take boxes of buns with them, gratis ('Pay next time'); they willingly do so, gorging on human remains, a funny stomach-churner. Yau relishes showing their enjoyment close up as they gobble down the buns and greedily emote – all except their boss, who offhandedly remarks, tellingly, 'You never know what's in the filling.' Here an instance of conspicuous consumption combines both elements of the film (Wong's atrocities and the cops' incompetence) into the darkest of humour.

Untold is recognised as one of the first in a spate of slasher movies including Danny Lee's *Dr. Lamb* (1992). Unlike this 1990s trend, Yau's film breaks more new ground; he cross-cuts continuously between extremely violent scenes and episodes of comical police activity (or inactivity, as the case may be). Police scenes, unlike those in the rest of the film, seem to be from another movie entirely, and are used, for the most part, as comic relief from the horror. Roughly two-thirds through, however, the detectives turn serious, brutalising and torturing the suspect; the contrast ends and the abuse intensifies. Yau believes that 'in real life, that [police brutality] really happens. Not just in Hong Kong and Southeast Asia, but in western countries too.' He explains that Lee, also the film's producer, who has made a career playing stand-up movie cops, had to be reassured 'they were playing *Macau, not Hong Kong, cops*' (emphasis mine, *Untold* DVD 1996). That Yau continues going against the grain of the typical psycho killer films and popular police procedurals is apparent upon Wong's capture, in which his human rights are not only violated, but he is set up for worse in prison – and the audience, rather than being relieved at the criminal's capture, side, to a degree, with the murderer, not the cops. The remaining violent scenes in *Untold* (the exception being the Cheng Lam family murder) illustrate the violence perpetrated on the killer. First, the cops beat him upon arrest, then Cheng Lam's incarcerated brother (played by a giant of a man, Shing Fui-on) and other inmates beat him unmercifully in prison. Food is withheld, both in prison and the hospital. Wong resorts to drinking his own urine. The killer is further abused while hospitalised, by staff and cops again, with various instruments of torture (long needles, water injections causing blisters, bright lights and no sleep, drug induced insomnia), so much so that the killer confesses under extreme duress and when returned to prison, commits suicide. Yau's take on the character is exemplary of his social commitment and this film, presented as a horror film, challenges both the contemporaneous genre as well as mainstream Hong Kong cinema.

To claim that Wong Chi-leung is a sympathetic character (credit Wong's performance and the unrelenting police brutality depicted in the film) perhaps goes too far – Yau reiterates 'that would be irrational' – but that the character is depicted as oppressed is without doubt. He believes himself cheated by two restaurant owners, betrayed by his employees, and can get nowhere with the law. Furthermore, he finds that both prison guards and medical staff collaborate with the cops to force his confession. The only way he is heard is through violence. Wong describes the character as 'a hero' and an 'anti-hero', because

> he fights [for himself] . . . if you create a character like this, you have to believe you're normal. You're not crazy, you're not mad. What you are doing is totally normal. Otherwise you're just like a madman . . . You have to believe what you're doing is right. He asks for his money. He thinks other people are stupid. Everything in his mind is right.

Wong reiterates that 'for the character there is only one way – violence.' He explains capturing the 'feeling' of the character, stating, 'The character can talk to you.' He labels his performance as 'a distortion of acting', comparing it to putting on a CD at full volume, with the sound turning into distortion. Wong won Best Actor at the Hong Kong Film Awards for his performance, and he shares that he and Yau discussed the character daily: 'Even when we finished for the day, I would go home, wake up, and call him immediately when an idea popped into my head' (*Untold* DVD 1996).

The character Wong Chi-hang 'feels' he has been treated unjustly, deprived of what he believes to be rightfully his, and is powerless by legal means to resolve his situation. In his struggle to survive, he turns to the basest of instincts – revenge and murder – turning the tables on the unsuspecting who become cannibals, eating and enjoying his selective victims. Both psychiatrist/theorist Franz Fanon and educator/theorist Paulo Friere, the former in *The Wretched of the Earth* and the latter in *Pedagogy of the Oppressed*, have described the phenomenon that oppressed peoples have the tendency to themselves become oppressors (Fanon 1963; Friere 1970). This is one way of looking at the case of Chan Chi-leung/ Wong Chi-hang; disenfranchised, he is helpless against males more privileged and preys on the unsuspecting.

Yau has commented that his intention in *Ebola Syndrome* was to 'create an anarchical situation, a world out of control' with a 1997 subtext (Stokes and Hoover 2002: 36). Likewise, *Untold*, rather than a simple exploitation slasher movie is at heart crisis cinema, reflecting Hong Kongers' anxiety at the impending 1997 return of the colony to the Mainland. Yau himself accepts this interpretation, emphasising, 'As Fredric Jameson said, "everything, in the end, is political." I agree with Jameson' (Yau 2016). Hong Kong's historical acceptance as a British colony and its much noted political apathy began to change with the handover's approach. In the 1970s the PRC rejected a 'three legged stool' approach to the Hong Kong question that would have involved the three entities. Colony residents were excluded from that discussion, and the 1984 Joint Declaration between China and Britain, which cemented the handover and established 'one country, two systems' for fifty years, ostracised Hong Kong representatives from diplomatic discussions. The 1989 Tiananmen tragedy magnified Hong Kongers' fears about their future. The last British colonial governor, Chris Patten, instituted the 1992 'Patten Reform', providing for elected members to the Legislative Council. This resulted in pro-democracy, grassroots and trade union councillors holding a majority of seats in its first session under British rule. The assembly passed legislation that included collective bargaining rights, protection against job discrimination, and an increase in welfare spending. In other words, the working class was finally being given a voice. It is in this environment that Yau made *Untold*, an angry film in reaction to the times.

Dumplings

Based on Lillian Lee's novella, and adapted by her for the film, *Dumplings*, a local August 2004 release, earned a moderate HK$6 million (Elley 2004). Chan expanded and added scenes to his short, but the basic plot remains the same. Li Qing (Miriam Yeung), a married woman and retired TV star, endures her husband's philandering, as long as he 'doesn't flaunt it'. However, as their Peak house is undergoing renovation while the couple is temporarily quartered in a luxury hotel, Mrs Li discovers that her husband, Li Si-je (Tony Leung Ka-fai), is keeping his mistress in a nearby room. She's lost 'face' in two ways: (1) her husband is disrespectful, and (2) her age shows on her countenance. A lonely and tarnished trophy wife, she laments her lost youth, recalling how her producer husband had been attracted to her youth and beauty. Now he plays the absentee who thinks money is an adequate substitute for attention. To attract her husband, specifically sexually, she turns to 'Auntie' Mei (Bai Ling), a mysterious dumpling maker, who guarantees results ('I'll bring back your youth and his heart'). The film's horror hook, revealed in its opening minutes, is that by consuming human foetuses in specially prepared, expensive dumplings, diners can recapture youth and beauty, due to the properties of this not-so-secret ingredient. Rather than a big reveal, as in *Untold*, this horror film delicacy delights in making consumption the routine and questions what people will do to maintain youth. Holding a foetus in her hand, Mei shows Mrs Li and comments, 'This is what I chopped up.'

Fruit Chan explains:

> The film is related to popular beliefs in South China. There, some people still believe that if you eat liver, your liver function will improve, if you drink blood – animal, of course (*laughter*) – your blood will improve. Gall bladder is good against cough, monkey brain is good for brain, and a fetus can, some believe, give permanent youth to those who eat them. (Trbic 2005)

Noting these practices can be found in Southern China, Chan has his chef/former surgeon/abortionist Mei travel between Hong Kong and her former hometown, Shenzhen, to collect aborted foetuses. Guangdong Province functions as an economic resource that satisfies the supply and demand relationship, exploited by entrepreneurs like Mei, and operating outside the legal system – anything goes. Chan adds:

> People started to eat embryos a long time ago. Average housewives tended to eat the placenta for regaining health after giving birth to a baby. In Chinese tradition it's a common way for rejuvenation. In real life it really does exist. (*Three . . .* DVD 2004)

In the film, Mei provides a thumbnail history of Chinese cannibalism:

> We Chinese have a long history. Who can tell if it is illegal to eat flesh? About eating humans ancient medical texts say human flesh and organs can heal diseases. During famine people could not bear to eat their own children, so they traded and ate other people's children. An ancient chef heard that his Emperor wanted to taste human flesh. To please his emperor he cooked and served his own son to the monarch . . . Tales abound of caring sons and daughters cutting off flesh for their parents' medicine. In *The Water Margin*, heroes ate human organs with their wine. One even opened a bun shop using flesh as filling. The Japanese ate the Chinese. China had civil unrest and famines. Did they avoid human flesh? . . . A patriotic poem describes 'eating barbarian flesh . . . drinking their blood'.

A mouthful of a speech, she makes it as she serves Li Si-je his first taste of her dumplings.

While eating human embryos remains undocumented, the eating of animal embryos (as occurs with baby chicks in the film) and of human placenta, not only in other places and times, but in recent history, has been duly noted. Human placenta consumption, it is thought, provides nutrients and energy, and according to some, can encourage breast milk production and prevent post-partum depression (Devlin 2014). Cannibalism, whether medicinal, mortuary or survivalist, has been traced back 100,000 years to Neanderthals, was performed by Crusaders in the Middle Ages, and was (until recently) practised by various tribes in the South Seas, West and Central Africa, and North and South America (Encyclopedia Britannica 2016). While 'cannibalism' is the common term, 'anthropophagy' was the first word used for the eating of human flesh by human beings. *The Oxford English Dictionary* dates the first usage of 'anthropophagi', – 'men eaters' – to 1585, while comparative literature scholar Carmen Nocentelli argues for an earlier appearance in a 1538 dictionary defining 'anthropophogi' as 'people in Asia, which eate [sic] men' (OED 1981; Everts 2013).

The film shows the complete process of the dumpling preparation in many scenes, as well as extensive dumpling eating. Close-ups, unusual angles, including oblique and Dutch-angled camera, and from below and through a transparent dish, as well as eerie sound effects, from crunches to slurps, in addition to a high-pitched, grating soundtrack effect, are disconcerting. According to award-winning sound engineer Robert Reider, it is the sound of a gate, or anything with a metal hinge, that has been 'doubled or tripled and just played at different speeds and edited to make a cohesive sound' (Reider 2016). Numerous scenes of Mrs Li's dumpling dining not only show the passage of time but are essential to her developing character. Initially, upon seeing her first foetus, she runs away in horror, but returns for her distasteful first meal, during which she almost vomits. Gradually, as she experiences good results and the attention of her husband, her dining becomes routine. Finally, she devours the foetus with greedy consumption. As Li Qing, Miriam Yeung delivers a developing character who undergoes psychological changes, believably transforming from desperate, weak, uncertain and hysterical to obsessive, manipulative, concentrated and cruel. Besides the film's chilling penultimate shots (to be discussed below), Li Qing's transformation is apparent in an eating montage, which, like other eating scenes, not only indicates the passage of time but her acquired taste for dumplings. Li Qing's character arc is also expressed in the scene where the mistress undergoes an abortion. Mrs Li coldly instructs the obstetrician: 'Don't let her miscarry. Do not use drugs to induce birth. I don't want drugs in its system. Use a catheter and adrenaline to stimulate the vagina. Then the foetus will be perfect.' She dismisses the doctor's concern that this process will take longer and be painful. When the mistress asks why she wants the foetus, Mrs Li coldly replies, 'Trophy. A souvenir. It's the world's most expensive souvenir.' She wants to watch. The scenes are darkly humorous in some respects as Hong Kongers can be famously fussy about what they eat. Film critic Tony Rayns describes the film as 'Jonathan Swift's *A Modest Proposal* updated to post-Marxist realities' (Rayns 2005).

Chan collaborated with cinematographer Chris Doyle, at the time known primarily for his work with Wong Kar-wai. Doyle gives the film a distinctive, art house look, quite different from Chan's previous movies. Doyle combines the oblique angles with voyeuristic shots around walls and doorways, and a slowly creeping camera that moves in on a character to create an unsettling effect. Numerous pans across Auntie Mei's apartment add to the 'peeping tom' effect; similar pans of body parts suggest a scopophilic effect. Often objects are foregrounded in a scene with extreme close-ups of what viewers don't want to but can't help seeing – pinkish foetuses in almost translucent dumplings or, as the *pièce de résistance*, a blood-red second trimester foetus with hair, eyebrows, eyelashes and fingernails. Doyle's voyeuristic camera is similar to his work in many Wong Kar-wai movies, but here with a difference – as a horror film, the camera lurks, hesitates, often blocked by semi-sheer curtains, slightly breeze-blown, before deciding to see, creating an immediate, unrelenting tension.

The film's dialogue also emphasises the horror of cannibalism, in this case magnified because of the abortion issue and general connotations of babies. Over and over, Mei, preparing dumplings or conversing as Mrs Li eats, matter-of-factly makes her case. Explaining the product's source, Mei explains,

> It's best in the fifth or sixth month. Extract it by breaking the water sac and slide it. It's covered by a layer of creamy fat. The colours are defined and you can see the cranium. And the little hands and feet moving around. [Laughs] The fifth month is perfect, kitten-like and most nutritious.

As Mrs Li dwells on the current mistress, she demands of Mei: 'I can't wait. I need your best.' When Mei procures the incestuous foetus from a teen's abortion, in a mirror two shot uniting the women, Mei tempts Mrs Li, 'It was a boy. [Laughs] See that? So beautiful and rare. It is also a first born, more nutritious. It is the most nutritious thing in the world.' Doyle matches the dialogue by following with a disgusting close-up trick shot from underneath the table which shows the bloodied foetus through glass.

Dumplings, in contrast to *Untold*, is primarily a woman's picture, and reverses the sexism and misogyny of the latter's characters. Tony Leung Ka-fai, cast as the philandering husband, simply hovers at the edges of the story and appears largely as a sexual animal and object (of course, he is Li Qing's reason for rejuvenation). He is featured in three sex scenes with different women – one on the floor with his mistress (lots of skin is shown), one with his wife when he's laid up with a broken leg (Li Qing is the aggressor), and one of pure animalistic sex across a table with Mei (he takes her from behind across a table). Instead, Li Qing and Auntie Mei dominate as polar opposites in regards to age, class, nationality and culture; they share, however, a willingness to do anything to maintain youth and beauty. At first antagonistic and distrustful, Mrs Li is desperate and browbeaten by Mei, who tells her, 'Women like you are everywhere. Be glad you know me. Otherwise . . . second wife in five years . . . third wife in ten years . . . and fourteenth wife in fifteen.' Both are literally and metaphorically fleshed out by their environments and clothing. Auntie Mei lives in a small, crowded apartment in a deteriorating 1950s Kowloon public housing tenement inhabited by underclass people; its decor suggests an even earlier time period, key to her age. (Other age identifiers for Mei are the appellation 'Auntie', used as a sign of age and respect, as well as a song from a bygone era she sings, identified by Chan Kwong-wing, the film's music composer, as 'Waves in Hongu Lake' (Chan Kwong-wing 2011). By contrast, Li Qing, who refuses to sing, but hums once her rejuvenation begins, is linked to the more immediate past by her TV shows. The Lis' under-construction Peak mansion (also symbolic of the Lis' marriage), which impresses Mei 'is a house, not a home', Li Qing admits. The unusual bonding of these women, so unalike, erases class distinctions as they share confidences, but this too is impermanent – class and men apparently win. Mei chooses Si-je over Qing and her money, just as Si-je's mistress chooses Qing's money over Si-je. Auntie Mei ends up as a fugitive, and Mrs Li has taken from Mei the Auntie's expertise, procuring her husband's own foetus and presumably making her own dumplings – for herself, not for her husband. Her expression in the penultimate scene, as she prepares her first meal, is as crazed as Wong's in *Untold*.

Mrs Li's level of luxury, demanding service and privilege, is in direct contrast to the hard-working Auntie Mei. The two female protagonists are also represented by their clothing, Li Qing dressed in expensive jewels and designer outfits and shoes, carrying matching Hermes handbags and wearing their scarves, her face hidden by designer sunglasses. Mei, with frizzled hair and revealing, tacky mismatched outfits and cheap shoes, lacks 'class'. Both are striking women but in different ways. Li Qing's romanticised origin story of her relationship with her husband suggests her youthful beauty brought out the best in him. 'I fell during a stunt,' she tells Mei, and 'he held me.' Mei, on the other hand, through her provocative dress, brings out his worst. The husband betrays his wife in two ways: first by his infidelity, and second by usurping her access to Mei's product and service. 'Men are all the same,' Mei replies to Qing, 'all they want is sex.' This conversation takes place at the house renovation, and unlike the visual vaginal metaphors elsewhere in the film, here the images are phallic, with squirting hoses and spurting fountains standing out.

Still, women dominate the film and males are ultimately emasculated. In contrast to the rape/chopstick murder in *Untold*, *Dumplings* also takes on rape, but from a woman's point of view. Mei reluctantly agrees, at a mother's insistence, to an abortion for a fifteen-year-old victim of incest; what seals the deal is that Mei needs the 'most potent stuff' for her exclusive client Mrs Li ('So fresh!'). Visiting the more modern high rise public housing complex where the girl resides, Mei finds herself disoriented in a circular maze. 'What is this place?' she asks herself. Shot with a jimmy jib from above, the upward spiralling corridors create a vaginal space, repeated in a reverse shot when the police invade said space after a homicide. Vaginal visuals repeat during the abortion ('We must protect ourselves or they [men] will bully us,' Mei tells mother and daughter), with crotch shots that reveal little but seem graphic. Ultimately, the girl's mother murders her rapist husband. And one of the closing sequences shows a fugitive 'coolie' – like Mei, struggling with her worldly goods, trekking through an arched covered walkway, remaking herself once more in Shenzhen, as she visually penetrates the vaginal imagery. Mr Li is out of the picture.

In recent history, beauty products and cosmetic surgery were directed solely towards women, although this phenomenon is currently changing. Yet the double standard of ageing, whether it be in movies or in life, between men and women, persists – as men's hair greys and wrinkles develop, they are regarded as mature, while women are still considered old. *Dumplings* mostly focuses on the women's problem, but that ageing is also problematic for men is acknowledged briefly. Li Si-je eats chick embryos for breakfast and has young mistresses; he willingly pursues Mei for her cure, and after animalistic sex is confused and shocked, even disgusted, to learn she is in her sixties; as Mei tells Li Qing: 'I'm my own best advertisement', and she wears her youthful appearance as a mask she hides behind. Li Si-je quickly rethinks his situation, seemingly to his advantage. Little does he realise, with Mei's flight, his wife has the upper hand. Li Qing likewise is desperate to reverse time and defy age and perseveres. She agrees with Mei: 'For youth and beauty, women must fight time!' Rather than accepting ageing gracefully, she is obsessed with not just retarding ageing, but reversing it, a sign of her vanity, self-delusion and low self-esteem. The film's coda illustrates this, a black and white flashback to Qing's wedding day, as she looks at herself in the mirror, a promising future ahead. Numerous mirror shots in the film suggest she still has a vision of herself the way she looked on her wedding day. But there's no denying the inefficiency of an ageing body, from reduced skin elasticity to the weakening of such body to self-repair. As scientists relate, 'It's an inescapable biological reality that once the engine of life switches on, the body inevitably sows the seeds of its own destruction' (Olishensky 2002).

Fruit Chan surmises, 'What if human placenta, apart from its healing value, does deliver everlasting beauty? Then cannibalism might somehow be revived in a place like Hong Kong, and most probably, not only in Hong Kong' (HKIFF 2005: 108). He describes the quest for rejuvenation as 'a psychopathic craving so widespread that [it] is approaching a universal level . . . I don't think we can simply sit on this – about how much more, we, as human beings, are going to defy [ageing] and at what cost!' (HKIFF 2005: 108). Producer Peter Chan concurs: 'I do hope that it [the movie] scares those who are always endlessly searching for beauty. Self-esteem is the actual key. You've got to accept the way you look' (*Three . . .* 2004). The film therefore shakes a finger at a sick, superficial society and serves as a warning to those who value surface over depth.

There's more underneath the cosmetics of *Dumplings*. Bai Ling as Mei is the only character speaking Mandarin and the only featured Mainlander. Locals think of Hong Kong as a sophisticated, twenty-four-hour city, especially in contrast to the Mainland. Hong Kong films, from the 'North–South Trilogy' of the 1960s (comedies include *The Greatest Civil War on Earth*, *The Greatest Love Affair on Earth* and *The Greatest Wedding on Earth*) to Peter Chan's *Comrades, Almost a Love Story* (1996), address differences between transplanted Mainlanders and Hong Kong Cantonese. Numerous films have portrayed Mainlanders in Hong Kong as second-class citizens – bumpkins and yokels. *Dumplings*, through the figure of Mei, presents Mainlanders as an invasive threat, a corrupting force. The irony, of course, is that most Hong Kongers have come from elsewhere – it is an island of immigrants. The first generation of true Hong Kongers came of age in the 1970s; that is, they thought of Hong Kong as 'home', even though many were born elsewhere. Today, Mainland presence is palpable in Hong Kong, and Mandarin is spoken more frequently.

As viewers learn Auntie Mei's background, the film emphasises that the foetuses Mei has aborted were due to China's one-child policy. When the Shenzhen clinic doctor supplying her with foetuses asks her about her past break-up with a fellow doctor she responds: 'He disliked the one-child policy. But I was aborting over ten foetuses a day, or over 3,000 a year. Over 30,000 for ten years. Because I had done so many abortions, he was afraid we would be cursed.' The doctor replies, 'It was national policy.' Mei's past experience explains both her expertise and her attitude towards men. And not only is a glaring difference between life in colonial Hong Kong and the current Special Administrative Region (SAR) contrasted with Mainland law and practice, but also reinforced is Mainland superstition, even among the educated. Situating Mei in Kowloon also adds negative connotations, and the background activity glimpsed in the exterior housing scenes indicates underclass survival. Says Chan:

> If you live on the Hong Kong Island, there's a chance you might perceive people from Kowloon as low class, rough, uneducated. Some people I know live in Hong Kong Island and go to Kowloon once a year. Some like to avoid it, but it's difficult. Approximately 50 percent of Hong Kong's population live in 'low-class' government housing. And there are different types of government housing. (Trbic 2005)

Furthermore, with the Severe Acute Respiratory Syndrome (SARS) outbreak in 2003, Hong Kong (coincidentally now called the SAR) was often blamed in the Western press for the outbreak, even though the epidemic began in China, perhaps from someone eating a sick civet cat. Considered a delicacy and prized for its health-giving properties (improved male potency, curing of skin diseases and other ailments), civets were captured, caged, slaughtered and served fresh at *yewei* (wild taste) gourmet restaurants in the south and near Guangzhou (NBC 2004). The coincidences between *The Untold Story* and *Dumplings* and real life are uncanny – Mei refers to a bun shop serving filling of human flesh in her thumbnail history of Chinese cannibalism (see above), which references *Untold*. Here, a belief in the health-giving properties of raw meat is not far afield from faith in the restorative properties of Mei's dumplings. And, here again, Chinese scapegoating (Hong Kong blaming China for its own scapegoating in the Western press) and superstition are conflated.

On the other hand, just as Hong Kongers distrust Mainlanders, Mainlanders blame Hong Kong for their tenuous but ingrained relationship. The Shenzhen clinic doctor complains to Mei, 'I worked so hard to get these [foetuses]. It is hard to keep secret. I hear reporters want pictures. The problem is from Hong Kong. Don't come for the next two weeks. Even the locals can't get ahold of the stock.' Her statement also implies that foetus-eating is commonplace in Shenzhen. The Chinese are depicted as 'omnivorous, pragmatic and utterly ruthless' (Rayns 2005: 53). Aida Yuen Wong sees the film as

> a metaphor for the primal fears that many Hong Kongers have towards the Mainland. Its message seems to be that the co-dependency of Hong Kong and the motherland can spell disaster – the mindless pursuit of money and vanity. Neither the cold-blooded Mainland merchant nor the affluent Hong Kong consumer can claim the moral high ground; they are mutually implicated in the disastrous outcome. (Wong 2005: 238)

Another film metaphor becomes apparent as one peels away *Dumplings'* cosmetic layers. Beauty, of course, is only skin deep, as the saying goes. Fruit Chan relates the co-dependency of China and Hong Kong to the film industry's current state of affairs; whether its 'co-dependency' will be 'disastrous' remains to be seen:

> Hong Kong cinema has been extremely productive since the mid-1980s, but now we have a stagnation period that has been going on for almost five years. There are many reasons for this: economic factors, DVD industry, problems with distributors, and DVD releases. With the rise of Korean and Thai film, Hong Kong lost its mainstream market. The market is now smaller, and one can make it bigger only by combining finance from China, Hong Kong, and Taiwan. [The] Hong Kong film industry is trying to open the Chinese market, but it's tough, because the system is different. (Trbic 2005)

Food for Thought

Using cannibalism in their films, Yau and Chan twist the easily recognisable food motif into a cinematic brew of horror, tapping into primal universal fears of otherness and the unknown, violent death and suffering. Are human beings built to enjoy being scared or horrified? In childhood there's a thrill to the scary stories we hear, but also dread. Is it evolutionary baggage humans carry? As early as 1792 German philosopher Friedrich von Schiller observed:

> It is a phenomenon common to all men, that sad, frightful things, even the horrible, exercise over us an irresistible seduction, and that in presence of a scene of desolation and of terror we feel at once repelled and attracted by two equal forces. (Schiller 1792)

Schiller's description applies equally to audience response to *Untold* and *Dumplings*. Horror can provide insightful commentary on the times, and both films give us something to chew on. Yau's film exemplifies the situation of the voiceless as 1997 approached; Chan's movie illustrates an obsession with the cult of youth and beauty at any costs. Both films present male fears and challenge the status quo of the film industry itself. Anyone for seconds?

Note

1. Bonus materials, *The Untold Story* (1993), film (DVD [1996]), directed by Herman Yau, Hong Kong.

References

Chan Kwong-wing (2011), *Hung Lake – Dumplings (2004)*, YouTube, 17 July, <www.youtube.com/watch?v=eESOzPJ42Zw&noredirect=1> (last accessed 12 Jan 2016).

Cheung, Yew-ming (1996), 'Culture and lifestyles', in Nyaw Mee-kau and Li Si-ming (eds), *The Other Hong Kong Report 1996*, Hong Kong: Chinese University Press, pp. 474–5.

Devlin, Laura (2014), 'Why do people eat placentas?', *BBC News*, 11 May, <www.bbc.com/news/uk-england-27307476> (last accessed 1 February 2016).

Elley, Derek (2004), 'Dumplings', *Variety*, 9 November, <www.variety.com/index.asp?layout=print_review&reviewid+VE1117925507&categoryid=31> (last accessed 6 March 2005).

Encyclopaedia Britannica (2016), 'Cannibalism', <www.britannica.com/topic/cannibalism-human-behaviour> (last accessed 1 February 2016).

Everts, Sarah (2013), 'Europe's hypocritical history of cannibalism', *Smithsonian*, 24 April, <www.smithsonianmag.com/history/europes-hypocritical-history-of-cannibalism-42642371/?no-ist=&fb_locale=ja_jp&page=1> (last accessed 1 February 2016).

Fanon, Franz (1963), *The Wretched of the Earth*, New York: Grove Press.

Forsyth, Donald W. (1983), 'The beginnings of Brazilian anthropology: Jesuits and Tupinamba cannibalism', *Journal of Anthropological Research*, 39:2, pp. 147–78.

Friere, Paulo (1970), *Pedagogy of the Oppressed*, New York: Seabury Press.

Hong Kong International Film Festival (HKIFF) (2005), *The 29th Hong Kong International Film Festival* (Programme), Hong Kong: Hong Kong International Film Festival Office.

Hong Kong Movie Database (2016), <hkmdb.com/db/movies/view.mhtml?id=7630&display_set=eng> (last accessed 1 Jan 2016).

Li, Cheuk-to (ed.) (2007), *Herman Yau, Director in Focus*, Hong Kong: Hong Kong International Film Festival Society.

NBC News (2004), 'SARS Outbreak', 8 January, <www.nbcnews.com/

id/3908790/ns/health-infectious_diseases/t/civet-cat-becomes-sars-scape goat/#.VpcEN1kTBhY> (last accessed 13 Jan 2016).

Ng, Chi-kwan, Director of Food and Environmental Hygiene, Hong Kong Government (2016), personal correspondence.

Olishensky, S. Jay, Leonard Hayflick and Bruce A. Carnes (2002), 'No truth to the fountain of youth', *Scientific American*, (June), pp. 2–5.

[*The Compact*] *Oxford English Dictionary* (1981), 'Anthropophagi', Oxford: Oxford University Press.

Rayns, Tony (2005), 'Dumplings', *Sight and Sound*, 7, p. 53.

Reider, Robert (2016), Personal correspondence with Tim Anderson, 27 January.

Schiller, Friedrich von (1792), 'On the tragic art', in *Aesthetical and Philosophical Essays*, *The Guttenberg Project*, <www.gutenberg.org/files/6798/6798-h/6798-h.htm#link2H_4_0046> (last accessed 21 June 2014).

Stokes, Lisa and Michael Hoover (2002), 'An exclusive interview with Herman Yau', *Asian Cult Cinema*, 35, 2nd quarter, pp. 33–45.

Thorborn, Garth, C. Yuen and S. Lee (1996), 'Hong Kong food market reports,' *Tradeport*, <www.tradeport.org> (last accessed 30 March 2003).

Tong, Stanley (1998), personal interview, 8 December.

Trbic, Boris (2005), 'The immortality blues: talking with Fruit Chan about *Dumplings*', *Bright Lights Film Journal*, 1 November, <brightlightsfilm.com/immortality-blues-talking-fruit-chan-dumplings/#.VpE50VkTBhY> (last accessed 9 January 2016).

The Untold Story (1996), film (DVD), directed by Herman Yau, Hong Kong.

The Yearbook Committee, MPIA (Motion Picture Industry Association) (1994), *Hong Kong Films 1993*, Hong Kong: Hong Kong and New Territories Motion Picture Association, Ltd.

Three ... Extremes (2004), Film (DVD) '"The making of" featurette', Hong Kong Media Asia, distributed by Megastar Video Distribution Hong Kong Ltd.

Wong, Anita Yuen (2005), 'Three films about food by Fruit Chan: allegories of Hong Kong–China Relations after 1997', *Asian Cinema*, 16:2, pp. 229–41.

Wong, Anthony (2016), personal correspondence, 21 April.

Yau, Herman (2016), personal correspondence, 23 February.

CHAPTER 11

Sympathy for the Slasher: Strategies of Character Engagement in Pang Ho-cheung's *Dream Home*

Gary Bettinson

Among the most controversial scenes in *Dream Home* (2010) is one in which the ostensible heroine, Sheung (played by Josie Ho), brutally slays a heavily pregnant housewife. Director Pang Ho-cheung depicts this bloody assault in unflinching, visceral fashion. Sheung, having forced her way into the victim's upscale Hong Kong apartment, has already disposed of the property's domestic worker in gruesome fashion, recalling the extreme luridness of Category III cinema. With predatory venom, Sheung rams a screwdriver into the domestic servant's skull, forcing the woman's left eyeball to burst from its socket and spin across the hardwood floor.[1] Now Sheung corners the hysterical housewife, wrestling her to the ground. Though her victim lies stricken, Sheung refuses to relent. She binds the woman's wrists, ties a plastic vacuum bag over her head, and attaches a live suction hose, cutting off the woman's oxygen. As the asphyxiating housewife squirms on the wooden floor, Sheung passively observes her pathetic, agonising death throes.

As one critic puts it, this is 'a scene sure to disgust many' (M. Lee 2010); and predictably enough, various critics expressed high dudgeon at this and certain other scenes in *Dream Home*. Perhaps surprisingly, however, what these critics found objectionable was not the film's violence per se (which some routinely dismissed as 'gratuitous'),[2] but that much of the film's violence is initiated and executed by an apparently sympathetic protagonist. A typical grievance finds Sheung to be 'a character whose motives and behaviour are so difficult to sympathize with' despite the film's efforts to portray Sheung sympathetically (Ibid.). A stronger version of this perspective holds that 'Sheung's brutal asphyxiation of a pregnant woman, who aborts her child while dying, *destroys* any residual empathy [with Sheung]' (Floyd 2010; my emphasis).[3] Furthermore, Sheung's acts of violence are perceived to be not only repugnant but unjust: 'None of Sheung's woes . . . are dire enough to justify killing innocent people in cold blood' (M. Lee 2010).[4] In essence *Dream Home*'s detractors identify what they take to be an aesthetic and moral defect. They perceive the film to inadvertently undercut its own attempt to generate sympathy for the main protagonist.[5] From this perspective, *Dream Home* commits what Noël Carroll would call an 'aesthetic error' (Carroll 1996: 233).

I am concerned in this chapter to dispute both the specific criticisms invoked above and the broad implication that *Dream Home* is an aesthetically defective text. I begin by demonstrating that *Dream Home* elicits and sustains a sympathetic allegiance with its protagonist (thereby discrediting the claim that the film 'destroys' our allegiance with Sheung). I then go on to suggest why the film allies us with a murderer. By investigating these concerns, I aim to clarify the nature of *Dream Home*'s strategies of character engagement; to argue that these strategies are meaningfully imbricated with the film's moral and rhetorical systems; and, not least, to disqualify the premise that *Dream Home* commits an aesthetic and moral error.

Since I am centrally concerned with *Dream Home*'s strategies of character engagement, my discussion focuses principally on the areas of story, characterisation and narration. At a broad level, I am indebted to Murray Smith's (1995) narrational concepts of *alignment* (which pertains both to the degree of *access* we are given to a character, and to the extent of our *knowledge* about a character's interior states) and *allegiance* (the nature of the spectator's moral judgement of a character, for example sympathy or antipathy).

Sustaining Sympathy

Dream Home depicts the travails of Sheung, a young working-class woman whose prime ambition is to buy an apartment of her own in Hong Kong. Sheung sets her heart on one apartment in particular, a coveted unit within a luxury complex that boasts a spectacular view of Victoria Harbour. Undeterred by astronomical property prices, unscrupulous developers and market volatility, Sheung quits school and works diligently until, finally, she can afford the deposit on the apartment. But a hike in the market sends property prices soaring, and Sheung's dream apartment is cast beyond her reach. Embittered, Sheung resolves to invade the high-end complex, slaughter the inhabitants of the neighbouring apartments, and thereby reduce both the apartment's desirability and its market price. Among Sheung's chance victims are a pregnant housewife and her adulterous spouse, a coterie of debauched male youths, two stupefied prostitutes, a drowsy security guard and a pair of armed police officers summoned to the scene.[6] Sheung's diabolical scheme succeeds, but as she moves into her dream home, news of a global financial crisis spells further instability to come.

The film's central action comprises Sheung's invasion of the trendy apartment complex, and it is this extended sequence – stretched across most of the film's duration and punctuated, periodically, by expository flashbacks – that is the chief object of critical reproach. One aspect of this reproach, as noted above, concerns the validity of Sheung's lethal rampage. Insofar as her act of violence is indiscriminate, it is devoid of moral or retributive justification. Sheung metes out harms to apparently innocent strangers, none of whom have personally wronged her, and whose misfortune in being in the 'wrong place at the wrong time' renders them so much collateral damage. On the other hand, the narration's pattern of alignment is organised so as to suggest that, fortuitously, some of Sheung's victims are somehow 'deserving' of moral punishment or comeuppance. Crucially, the plot aligns us with the degenerate youths before Sheung subjects them to graphically brutal harm. Likewise it attaches us to the philandering husband in the moments preceding his murder. In both cases, what we observe of these characters invites our moral disapprobation. The carnally rapacious youths commit rape, the adulterous husband betrays his wife, and by the time these men succumb to Sheung's brutality they have been strongly established as moral defectives. In the punitive terms of the genre, these are 'obvious' horror-film victims: their moral turpitude is bound up with sexual transgression, hence they are ripe for savage retribution. (To some degree, then – but to some degree only – *China Daily*'s reviewer is correct to assert that each of Sheung's victims 'deserves it' (Kerr 2010).) By means of an alignment structure that limns these victims as worthy of condemnation, *Dream Home* constructs an internal moral hierarchy whereby Sheung attracts our greater sympathy almost by default. Thus, even as she commits repellent acts of violence, she does not arouse our unalloyed moral animus. Rather, we continue to cast our allegiance with Sheung, in part because of her relative desirability and also because her actions seem to enact a kind of morally satisfying, if inadvertent and extreme, form of poetic justice.[7]

The fact remains, however, that while the spectator is granted knowledge of the victims' moral bankruptcy, Sheung herself is not. Indeed, she could not care less about executing retributive justice. From Sheung's standpoint, her violence is impersonal and amoral (in contrast to that of the woman–vigilante protagonist in films such as Park's *Lady Vengeance* (2005) and Tarantino's *Kill Bill* (2003)). If some of her victims 'deserve it', this is simply due to brute chance.[8] However, not every character terrorised by Sheung is shown to merit such treatment. Here, for some critics, is the source of *Dream Home*'s aesthetic defect: because the pregnant housewife, the domestic helper, the security guard, the on-duty cops and even the prostitutes may be construed as innocents, the film undermines its own attempt to involve the viewer in sympathetic engagement with the main protagonist's actions and projects. This perspective, though not entirely wrong-headed, misconstrues *Dream Home* as an aesthetically and morally defective text. My present purpose is to show that the film in fact does not wholly undermine or destroy the spectator's allegiance with Sheung, but rather marshals a host of strategies that mitigate the heroine's crimes and consolidate the viewer's sympathy with her. The narration's arraying of characters on a moral hierarchy, by which Sheung assumes relative desirability, is one such strategy; but there are other tactics, too, that importantly sustain sympathy for the slasher–killer protagonist.

Dream Home opens with Sheung's slaying of the security warden, one of the 'undeserving' among Sheung's quarry. Here the grotesque physical horror that will characterise much of the film is put vividly on display. Sheung snaps a zip-tie around the warden's neck, depriving him of oxygen; the warden, grabbing a nearby box cutter to sever the rigid snare, succeeds only in mortifying his own taut flesh. A flurry of close-up shots magnifies his horrific paroxysm (dilating, bloodshot eyeballs; self-inflicted incisions that slash into his jugular artery, accelerating his death). Certainly we are meant to find this grisly spectacle physically and morally repugnant, but our moral revulsion does not redound to Sheung's discredit. Why not? The prime reason is that the scene's visual narration is strategically restricted in ways that obscure and ambiguate the killer's identity. By means of oblique aerial compositions, blocked framings, back-to-camera staging and other repressive strategies (such as the obfuscating baseball cap that masks the killer's face), this pre-credit sequence denies the viewer a legible purchase on the assailant, and thereby retards the primacy effect (the term given to the spectator's initial orientation toward a character). In short, this repressive expositional strategy actively precludes our ability to identify, much less to form a negative preliminary appraisal of, the central protagonist.

Following the opening credits, the flashback narrative activates the primacy effect proper, introducing Sheung in legible and roundly sympathetic terms. Indeed, the film's initial flashback segment is geared to foster a saturated emotional allegiance with Sheung, whose pitiable situation embodies all the pathos of classic melodrama. She is quickly established as being among the have-nots of society, scratching a meagre living in two low-wage jobs (in telesales banking and retail); she maintains an emotionally sterile affair with a married man; and, having suffered the loss of her mother, she inherits the burden of a self-pitying father and freeloading brother. In addition, she harbours a 'dream' – of a domestic idyll – that would be merely idealistic were it not so seemingly impossible; instead, given her financial and personal straits, the dream constitutes a pathetic chimera and thus another stimulus for our compassion. At the same time, the preliminary flashback encourages admiration for her 'melodramatic' traits of self-sacrifice and stoicism. When Sheung displays forbearance toward abusive clients at the bank where she works, our sympathy is aroused not only by her fortitude but by the perceived unfair treatment to which she is subjected. Enlisting the full force of the primacy effect, the preliminary flashback establishes a positive moral orientation toward Sheung that subsequent scenes, no matter how countervailing, will not easily efface.

Dream Home interpolates flashbacks throughout its plot in fairly complex fashion. Past events arrive unpredictably, achronologically, not merely juxtaposed against Sheung's present-day frenzy but deepening our comprehension of that event somehow. Most importantly for our inquiry, the flashbacks play a cardinal role in sustaining and intensifying our allegiance with Sheung, even as the juxtaposed 'home invasion' scenes threaten to undermine it. What these anterior scenes lay bare – gradually, in the manner of stair-step construction[9] – is Sheung's slow-burning arc of moral dissolution. In other words, the flashbacks reveal Sheung as having once been an embodiment of moral virtue. In one scene, we observe her as a child conceiving an altruistic goal: hoping to assuage her beloved grandfather, a former sailor nostalgic for the sea, Sheung dreams of relocating her family to an apartment overlooking Victoria Harbour. These scenes of youthful benevolence are pivotal, for they establish that Sheung is not by nature monstrous. The catalyst for her heinous actions therefore lies elsewhere than in innate, irrational drives or compulsions (like, say, cannibalism or necrophilia) – a point upon which I shall expand in the next section. For now, let it suffice to note that the kernel of Sheung's 'perversity' is less biological than societal, and the flashback narrative functions, in part, to chart Sheung's slow yet steep moral decline. It is here that the film's moral horror resides. For what could be more horrific, in human terms, than the decay and eventual abandonment of one's own moral identity? *Dream Home* dramatises precisely this: the protagonist's innate moral fibre is abraded by external forces, eventuating in nothing less than the loss of the human. It is through the erosion of Sheung's humanity, I suggest, that *Dream Home* most compellingly evokes sympathy for its ostensibly deranged protagonist.

But what of the film's physical horror? Are the primacy effect and ameliorating flashbacks an adequate bulwark against viewer antipathy toward Sheung, particularly in those moments when we witness her performing gross acts of violence on undeserving victims? Surely such ferocious displays vanquish whatever goodwill or sympathy the film has generated on Sheung's behalf? Here again I submit that the spectator maintains a 'pro' attitude toward Sheung even as the protagonist runs amok. For one thing, as Murray Smith contends, the primacy effect is apt to engender a kind of emotion 'drag' which 'results in a lingering sentiment for unattractive characters with whom we were once (at least somewhat) sympathetic' (Smith 1995: 217). A similar process obtains in *Dream Home*. So emotionally saturated is the preliminary flashback's appeal to our sympathies that it seems implausible that we simply 'switch off' our concern for Sheung when she acts in ways we cannot condone. Moreover, the distributed flashback segments, interspersed throughout the central massacre action, at once attenuate Sheung's vicious behaviour in the present and periodically refresh her claim upon our sympathy.

Rather than being torpedoed, our foregoing sympathy with Sheung may shade into other emotion types when she undertakes the series of murders. We are likely, for example, to experience what Ed Tan terms 'fascination', whereby 'one is caught up in the spectacle' of the unfolding action (Tan 1996: 175). The spectacle of the apartment murders in *Dream Home* acquires a saliency and an interest in its own right; specifically, it is apt to trigger an amoral attention to the film's aesthetic dimension. As most reviewers of *Dream Home* have observed (more or less favourably or disapprovingly), the film's scenes of physical horror compel attention by virtue of the outrageousness of their design and execution, inviting an appreciation (or at least an awareness) of the film-maker's inventiveness. At such moments, the spectator experiences what cognitivists call 'artefact emotions', impelled by 'a sense of admiration for the ingenuity of the film-maker' (Ibid.: 242). Fascination and artefact emotions are types of non-empathetic emotions (Ibid.: 175), so-called because they do not primarily stem from our involvement with characters but rather from our interest in the film as an aesthetic object. The key point is that *Dream Home*'s depictions of murder do not so much sever our sympathy with Sheung as deflect possible antipathy toward her, chiefly by engaging us in other types of emotional activity. (And here we might include the targeting of our hardwired, physiological reflexes, as when we involuntarily flinch or wince at an unexpected and especially nasty piece of action.)

It is important to note, too, that the home-invasion fracas plunges Sheung into a position of peril; one of her own making, to be sure, but perilous all the same. Thus any disapprobation that we may feel toward Sheung's acts of aggression (particularly when her target is morally undeserving of aggression) is tempered by concern for her welfare; we don't wish harm to befall the figure with whom we are most strongly allied. To a certain extent, moreover, Sheung's gender may contribute to the spectator's conferral of sympathy. Such was Pang Ho-cheung's hypothesis during the film's pre-production phase: 'In the first draft of the script, the main character was male,' Pang recalls. 'I thought that if we changed it to a female, the audience would feel more sympathy for her.'[10] By reworking the character thus, Pang conceivably augments the physical vulnerability of the protagonist, particularly when the film pits her against virile or aggressive male agents (the red-blooded youths; the gun-toting cops). Here again Sheung's welfare becomes the object of sympathetic concern. More subtly, perhaps, the fact of Sheung's gender problematises her Darwinian struggle for position. That is, her primary goal of upward social mobility would, within the capitalist Hong Kong milieu, be hard enough achieved by a working-class man but becomes still more formidable for a disenfranchised woman, faced as such women are with gender inequality, sexism, class prejudice and other social obstacles to success. Seen in this light, Sheung's gender may serve to reinforce our sympathy with respect to her concerns and projects. The disparity between Sheung's modest social status and her material aspirations seems, on the face of it, too great to be reconciled, hence worthy of sympathetic compassion.

If I have thus far held in abeyance the question of *Dream Home*'s imputed 'aesthetic error', I hope to have demonstrated that, despite critics' claims to the contrary, the film does elicit and sustain allegiance with its slasher-killer protagonist, and does so quite emphatically.[11] But why should Pang Ho-cheung want to ally us with such an apparently perverse figure? And does the film's strategy of sympathetic engagement, and its internal system of values, engender in the work a moral and aesthetic defect?

Properties and Polemics

Broadly stated, I want to argue that the structures of character engagement and moral orientation discussed above function, integrally and inextricably, to manifest a trenchant critique of Hong Kong's late-capitalist, neo-liberal hegemony. This critique is not latent within the text but redundantly foregrounded from the outset. In this respect, *Dream Home* departs from the ideological and expressive norms of the Hollywood slasher film, which, as Cynthia Freeland (2003) points out, typically obscure or displace the social triggers of violence. By refusing to target the 'actual social conditions' that beget violence, Hollywood slasher films fail to 'prompt . . . action and resistance' (Freeland 2003: 209). *Dream Home*, by contrast, makes no bones about it: the causes of the violence perpetrated by Sheung are deeply social, and demonstrably so. The film's interest lies not in Sheung's moral disintegration per se, but in how her moral decline designates a wider corrosion of values within Hong Kong's social formation. It is no exaggeration, then, to state that *Dream Home* is as much social protest film as high-end slasher movie; or, put differently, the film is no less political than it is popular. It pushes beyond the ideological evasiveness of the Hollywood slasher movie to mount an overt anti-capitalist polemic, even as the film itself exemplifies, to a considerable degree, one strain of capitalist enterprise (mass-marketed film-making). In such ways, director Pang betrays an acute albeit modest ambition to impel social reflection, if not actual political change.

How, then, does *Dream Home* anchor its structure of sympathy and moral framework to its social polemic? In what ways does Sheung's moral dissolution manifest the film's condemnatory stance toward Hong Kong hegemony? Here it is necessary to rehearse the events that induce Sheung's moral debasement. As a child, Sheung harbours ambitions of social ascension. If this goal is aspirational, it is also (at least initially) salutary – Sheung covets a luxury apartment on behalf of her grandfather and immediate relatives, all of whom have spent years squeezed into the kind of tiny public housing unit ubiquitous in Kowloon. (Here is the film's most explicit polemical target, namely the unjust housing strategy by which the poor are jammed into run-down, high-density tenements while the wealthy reside in privately owned upscale high-rises.) Several years pass, and Sheung pursues her goal into adulthood. Toiling away in two fields of work, she squirrels her wages and foregoes recreation. Then, personal tragedy strikes – first, with the death of her mother and, second, with the encroaching ill health of her father, whose medical bills further increase Sheung's woes (and here the Hong Kong Special Administrative Region's (SAR) public healthcare system is held up for critical disdain). No amount of personal sacrifice, hardship or industry brings Sheung's inveterate goal to fruition. As the rich grow richer, the working-class citizenry – to which Sheung belongs – encounters a conspicuous lack of upward mobility.

By laying bare this social inequity, *Dream Home* skewers the fictional milieu (and, implicitly, the real-world Hong Kong hegemony) on the grounds of economic polarisation and moral hypocrisy.[12] The false meritocracy of late capitalism, in direct contradistinction to capitalist doctrine, travesties the promise of personal achievement and fulfilment through hard work and social obedience. Sheung naively buys into this specious system of values. If she covets an idealised 'dream home', this chimera consists, for

Sheung, not only of bricks-and-mortar real estate but of familial stability, unity and contentment. The point I wish to advance here is that, by no means coincidentally, Sheung's far-fetched 'dream' precisely echoes the so-called Chinese dream, an explicit ideology prevalent within Sinicised society during the film's narrative epoch (the 1980s–2000s). As Gerard Lemos observes, the Chinese dream encapsulates civic hopes for 'prosperity and security' (Lemos 2013: 82) – precisely the comforts desired by Sheung. Yet in reality this seductive ideology, which promulgates social cohesion and egalitarianism, soon evaporated for all but the super-elite. The Chinese dream 'was a dream for others,' Lemos writes. 'For most people, the dream, so quick to take shape . . . just as swiftly died' (Ibid.: 81). *Dream Home* invokes precisely this kind of counterfeit ideology. For all her efforts, Sheung encounters a social realm that rewards neither industriousness nor moral probity nor obeisance to social mores. We can begin to see, I think, that the film's strategies of character allegiance are intimately bound up with its social critique. Allied with Sheung, the spectator adopts a critical stance toward that which encumbers her, works unjustly upon her, and causes her distress – a negative stance, in other words, toward the hegemonic processes to which Sheung is subjugated.

A decisive stage in Sheung's moral downfall comes with the death of her father, an event for which she is not strictly responsible but which she passively, purposefully facilitates. Bedridden and ailing, her father struggles for breath. Sheung, however, refuses to provide aid, slighting the oxygen mask that lies ready to hand. Sheung's inaction is calculated: her father's life insurance will enable her, at long last, to enter the property market. Yet we are in no doubt that Sheung's wilful negligence constitutes, on her part, a profound personal sacrifice. If the scene's sympathetic strategies are vulnerable to criticism (after all, Sheung's father is basically another undeserving victim), it must be stressed that we are not encouraged to endorse Sheung's role in this death. But nor does the scene prompt us to condemn Sheung. For one thing, it makes redundantly clear her acute emotional conflict over what unfolds. Furthermore, the incident arrives at a fairly advanced plot stage, by which time our sympathies are firmly rooted with Sheung.[13] The scene, then, neither aborts our sympathy with Sheung nor cues us to applaud her wrongdoing.[14] If this amounts to an equivocation on the film's part, it is a strategic equivocation, not an accidental one. (Nor is it inept, as proponents of the aesthetic-error thesis might aver.) By sustaining our allegiance with Sheung, and by implicating her in deeds that we (and the film's internal moral system) cannot justify, *Dream Home* opens up a critical perspective from which we are to evaluate the nature and extent of Sheung's moral descent.

From this critical vantage point the spectator will be led to grasp that (1) Sheung's refusal to save her father's life marks the onset of her moral disorientation (therefore this is a key event in the film's representation of moral horror); and (2) the immoral activity that Sheung will proceed to enact (slaughtering the residents of an exclusive apartment complex) is wholly disproportionate to the intrinsic value of her goal (to own one of those apartments). Upon collecting her father's life insurance, Sheung sets off to purchase the property she has long hankered after. But to her dismay the incumbent owners, spurred by rising land prices, jack up the apartment's cost beyond Sheung's means. This latest setback triggers a stark anagnorisis. For all the years of sacrifice, dashed hopes and drudgery, no course of action – not even the agonising relinquishment of her father's life – effectually improves Sheung's material circumstances. The vacuity of capitalist ideology now becomes sharply apparent to Sheung, whose bereft subjective state Pang registers through dissonant nondiegetic music, disjunctive cutting and disconcerting staccato camerawork. These stylistic devices function to evoke and telegraph a kind of psychic fugue. Thereafter, Sheung's moral centre dissipates, and her once-laudable goal transmogrifies into a murderous scheme. Still the film maintains our allegiance with Sheung (we pity her plight), but it does not ask us to condone her behaviour. A degree of critical detachment enables us to recognise that her crime is out of all proportion to that which she covets, and the film derives horror (and no small measure of macabre humour) from this means–ends disparity.[15]

As implied by her recourse to homicide, Sheung's moral disintegration entails a reduction of the human with regard to her goals, motives and actions. Even before she lays siege to the apartment block, her fantasy of familial harmony has begun to recede. Indeed, 'disposing' of her father in mercenary (if ambivalent) fashion testifies as much; by then, all that remains of her original goal is the consumerist pursuit of property. By the same token, Sheung's attack on the individuals within the apartment complex is depersonalised and, as we have already noted, indiscriminate. Her activity here can be seen as an oblique protest against property prices, not people.[16] Nor does she act on behalf of persons other than herself. (The altruism she possessed in childhood is, by now, all but eviscerated.) Her quest to drive down property prices is less noble than self-serving, born of a concern for private gain rather than for civic duty. Ultimately, Sheung adopts a purely individualistic course of action, one in which 'the personal' plays no part.

Herein lays the crux of the film's polemic: Sheung's moral trajectory demonstrates the dehumanising effects of capitalism. Within the context of recognisable Hong Kong hegemony, Sheung's innate virtuousness devolves into abject consumerism. Eventually her whole existence revolves around material gain. The object of her desire becomes all-consuming, evacuating reason, empathy, morality. In other words, Sheung's moral decay culminates in true, absolute horror: the loss of the self. Crucially, the film's internal moral system and structure of sympathy ensure that we perceive Sheung not simply as a personification of capitalist excess but as a victim of capitalist machinery. Just as the film elicits sympathy for Sheung, so it promotes socio-moral indignation toward Hong Kong's capitalist regime, a hegemonic system that nurtures imbalances of power, gross inequality and the corrosion of moral values. Conceptually, *Dream Home* reveals its own humanist agenda by depicting the dissipation of Sheung's humanity, which the film presents as a direct corollary of dehumanising social forces.

On the face of it, perhaps, Sheung reigns triumphant at the film's climax. Her deadly scheme succeeds: her wanton killing spree brings stigma upon the apartment complex, the property prices drop and Sheung installs herself in the apartment of her dreams. But director Pang taints this apparent nirvana – the fulfilment of the Chinese dream – with a sardonic hint of disenchantment: Sheung discovers, much to her displeasure, that her bed will not fit inside the apartment's modestly sized bedroom. Over the radio, moreover, is forecast a bleak future. The economic downturn of 2007 (the year of the film's present-day action) hovers on the horizon, presaging further financial privation for Sheung. (Pang mordantly implicates Sheung in this global calamity, albeit distantly, by virtue of her employment at a corporate bank.) If we construe Sheung as a kind of inadvertent social activist – for certainly she undertakes a radical rebellion against perceived social inequity – then her apparent triumph over the hegemonic system is short lived. Though she successfully brings her childhood goal to fruition, Sheung's insurgency poses no meaningful threat to the status quo; and, with the economic crisis looming, she remains at the mercy of the capitalist behemoth. Here again *Dream Home* refuses to endorse Sheung's perverse behaviour. The film underscores that Sheung's immoral, radical action is not only excessive but fleeting and (given the economic tsunami heading for Hong Kong) probably futile. By extension – and here Pang's rhetorical point comes to the fore – the film implies the ineffectuality of rebellion (or activism), lawful or otherwise, against Hong Kong's contemporary political regime. (This has proven to be prescient commentary in light of the 2014 Umbrella Movement and its failure to effect actual policy change.)[17] The 'system' always prevails in spite of individual protest. If the prospects for Hong Kong citizens are to change for the better, *Dream*

Home suggests, then the capitalist paradigm itself must be dismantled in favour of a less unjust and exploitive form of social organisation.

So much for the film's polemical thrust. What of that nagging question framing this chapter, regarding *Dream Home*'s imputed aesthetic error? I hope it is by now apparent that the film can and should be defended against this charge. To recap the basic argument: *Dream Home* undermines spectatorial sympathy by engaging Sheung in acts of unjustified violence. Because the film actively seeks a sympathetic engagement with Sheung, it commits an aesthetic error by involving her in activity that the spectator finds both repellent and irredeemable. Now, one can concede that *Dream Home* qualifies the spectator's sympathy with Sheung at various junctures. Indeed I have argued as much above. On certain occasions we find ourselves unable to endorse her actions. However, I have also tried to demonstrate that the film does not wholly undermine or sever our sympathy with the character. Rather, Sheung remains an essentially sympathetic figure, and we have canvassed some of the strategies by which this sympathy is aroused and maintained. We can grant as well that Sheung commits several acts of unjustified violence. Sheung's father, the pregnant housewife, the somnolent security guard – these are all undeserving victims by the logic of the film's moral hierarchy. We can concede these premises, then, without consenting that they add up to an artistic blunder. Rather, the errors attributed to the film are intentional and purposive strategies, not accidents or artistic missteps.

Just because we sympathise with Sheung doesn't mean we endorse her every action. This, I think, is a distinction that the aesthetic-error position overlooks. Consider once again Sheung's role in her father's death. Her refusal to lend aid is morally unsupportable, and the film does not encourage us to affirm Sheung's behaviour in this moment. (Indeed, the affective tone of the sequence marks the incident as tragic rather than admirable.) Similarly, Sheung's attack on the pregnant housewife is unequivocally portrayed as blood-curdling and barbaric. In no sense, then, does either scene cue us to advocate Sheung's behaviour (though it might engage us in other types of 'affirmative' response, such as artefact emotions – in which case we admire the film-maker's activity, not Sheung's). The point to underline is that *Dream Home* does not seek to mobilise what Smith (1999) terms 'perverse' allegiance, in which alliance with a character is predicated on the act of wrongdoing. We do not sympathise with Sheung because she murders a pregnant person, but in spite of her doing so. At the same time, the film asks us to perceive Sheung's crimes critically. For only by grasping these actions as excessive, irrational, immoral and inhuman do we perceive the horrifying, dehumanising effects of capitalism. And by maintaining our ongoing sympathy with Sheung, the film solicits our negative appraisal of the (social) forces that cause her harm and that lead her to cause harm to others. Thus we sympathise with the killer not because she kills, but because of the suffering and subjugation that compels her to kill. The film's aesthetic errors, then, are nothing of the sort. Rather, they constitute the purposeful strategies by which *Dream Home* cues and crystallises its anti-capitalist critique.[18]

Home Truths

There remains one more level of *Dream Home*'s discourse that so far I have slighted: its satirical or ludic dimension. Pang himself refers to the 'black humour' permeating *Dream Home*,[19] and indeed the film's overarching tone is savagely, grotesquely comic. Of particular importance is the comic device of exaggeration, by which it is made clear that the film's moral 'lesson' is not to be taken literally. That is, *Dream Home*'s polemical story presents an extreme case; the film does not claim that capitalism spawns a whole society of mass murderers. (Rather, the degrading effects of capitalism may be subtler and more polymorphous, if no less insidious, than is depicted in the film.) I suspect, moreover, that *Dream Home*'s overt playfulness – in particular, its meshing of graphic physical horror with outlandish humour – strikes some critics as morally objectionable, if not altogether obscene. Yet humour is vital to *Dream Home*'s effects, serving not only to attenuate Sheung's outré acts of violence – and thereby both preclude antipathy and trigger the viewer's artefact emotions – but to heighten the film's appeal as a work of popular genre fiction. Indeed, it would be wrong for us to let our discussion of *Dream Home*'s politicised, subversive qualities obscure the film's principal function as commercial entertainment. For all its sociopolitical rhetoric, *Dream Home* is not an agitational work, nor is it openly didactic. In this regard, it should be distinguished from the so-called feel-bad film (Lübecker 2015). Like *Dream Home*, feel-bad films strategically elicit antithetical ('mixed') emotions with the explicit aim of stimulating social and ethical thought. But the films belonging to the feel-bad category (such as Haneke's *Funny Games* (1997) and Von Trier's *Dogville* (2003)) tend to exemplify rather more confrontational and, dare I say, exalted forms of cinema by comparison to *Dream Home*, whose roots in Category III exploitation cinema are palpably and proudly put on display.

This last point reminds us that *Dream Home* is a film deeply embedded in Hong Kong culture and traditions. Its sociopolitical and regional specificity marks it off as a Hong Kong horror film, as distinct from either a Mainland Chinese production or a Hong Kong–China co-production. Certainly the film contains several ingredients that, from the outset, militated against its viability as a Mainland-produced or co-produced venture: a highly 'egregious' portrayal of physical violence; an immoral yet sympathetic protagonist; and a narrative closure in which the protagonist escapes lawful arrest. No less contentious, from SAPPRFT's point of view,[20] is what Pang calls the film's core 'message', its fulmination against the Hong Kong SAR's inequitable housing market.[21] As Pang puts it: 'I don't think the Mainland censorship would allow this message to pass [the script-approval stage]; but if I cut this message out, then it is no longer the movie I want to make or the story I want to tell.'[22] *Dream Home* is domestic in ways that exceed its protagonist's pursuit of a harmonious family idyll. It is steeped in the Hong Kong film-making tradition, at once invoking and upgrading the Category III exploitation genre.[23] And its ideological polemic is inseparable from both Hong Kong's housing situation and, more generally, Hong Kong's capitalist hegemony. In all, the film gives the lie to the imputed apoliticism of popular Hong Kong cinema.

None of the foregoing discussion is to argue that *Dream Home*'s socio-moral commentary is novel or profound (though I do think the film imparts this commentary in inventive and facile ways). That capitalism is a morally contaminating phenomenon is hardly a foreign thesis. Furthermore, the film cannot specify its polemical target other than in broad terms, hence 'capitalism' stands in *tout court* for more nuanced alternatives such as 'neo-liberal capitalism' or 'neo-liberalism with Chinese characteristics.' Moreover, *Dream Home* proffers neither a solution to Hong Kong's social ills nor an alternative to neoliberal capitalism. But as Noël Carroll (1996) points out, popular narratives typically traffic in moral truisms already entrenched within the culture. Rarely do such artworks radically rework a priori moral precepts, or introduce new moral lessons (Carroll 1996: 229–31). So it is with *Dream Home*, which essentially recapitulates the well-known unjustness of capitalism. Carroll maintains, however, that popular artworks, though often 'trading in moral commonplaces,' nevertheless 'involve moral education' (Ibid.: 229–30), whether by deepening and reaffirming pre-existing moral tenets or by 'muddying' moral understanding somehow (for instance, by allying us with a murderer). Popular horror movies not only reaffirm our moral and social values; they exercise and enrich them too. In an era marked by pro-democratic activism against state powers, *Dream Home* offers a particularly timely, if sobering, exemplum of this propensity.

My thanks to Law Kar, Li Cheuk-to, Pang Ho-cheung and Veronica Bassetto for information and assistance; and to an audience at King's College London for helpful comments and suggestions.

Notes

1. This gruesome action finds a precursor in the Category III prison drama *Riki-Oh: the Story of Ricky* (1991), whose literally eye-popping scenes of physical horror (along with its general ethos of transgression) served as a model for the makers of *Dream Home* (see E. Lee 2010). Elsewhere in the *Dream Home* sequence lurks an allusion to French horror movie *Inside* (2007), which similarly stages scenes of home invasion and features action involving a terrorised, pregnant urban dweller. '*Inside*', Pang Ho-cheung has stated, 'was one of the movies that inspired me to make *Dream Home*' (author interview with Pang Ho-cheung, North Point, Hong Kong, 31 March 2016).
2. See for example E. Lee (2010) and Waddell (2015).
3. I am conscious of a slippage created by aligning the former critic's reference to spectator *sympathy* with the latter critic's allusion to *empathy*. As Murray Smith (1995) and other cognitive theorists have argued, sympathy and empathy are distinct responses; but as Smith has also pointed out, both terms are frequently conflated in everyday usage. The two critics cited here intend, I believe, to invoke basically congruent phenomena. At the very least, their remarks pertain to the spectator's 'pro' attitude toward the protagonist, including a broad comprehension – and (a more or less weak or strong) affirmation – of her motivations; a pro-attitude which is, in the view of these critics, jeopardised or jettisoned by Sheung's perverse actions.
4. A similar criticism is posited in Bitel 2010.
5. Producer–star Josie Ho articulated a similar concern while *Dream Home* was in production, prompting a hiatus in shooting. Ho surmised that Pang's highly explicit presentation of physical violence might negate sympathy for Sheung. Evidently, certain critics hold the view that *Dream Home* bears out Ho's misgivings (see Floyd 2010).
6. Technically, Sheung kills only one of the police officers in cold blood, but the second officer is killed in a melee caused by Sheung's actions.
7. An example of this brand of arch poetic justice comes when Sheung invades the bourgeois home of an adulterous husband and strikes him with his own golf club – a choice weapon given that a golfing trip is the alibi with which the husband deceives his wife. Sheung subsequently bludgeons him with an altogether different kind of iron.
8. Indeed, certain characters may be said to 'deserve it' but ultimately get off relatively lightly. If Sheung was truly set on a personal vendetta, her boorish lover (played by Eason Chan) would surely come in for greater discomfort than he does.

9. As defined by Kristin Thompson, stair-step construction 'implies stretches of action in which the events progress toward the ending alternating with other stretches in which digressions and delays deflect the action from its direct path' (Thompson 1988: 37).

10. Author interview with Pang, Hong Kong, 31 March 2016.

11. I have limited my discussion to what I take to be the most salient and pertinent aspects of character allegiance in *Dream Home*. I do not deny that other features within the text, and other processes of film viewing in general, serve as constituent factors in our responses of sympathy. At the general level, for instance, we might point out that spectators typically come to a narrative film predisposed or primed to engage sympathetically with the text's 'interest-focus' (Chatman 1990) – that is, its chief protagonist(s) – and that narrative fictions both rely and capitalise upon this viewer proclivity. And with specific regard to *Dream Home*, we might ask whether there is not some relationship between our moral evaluation of the characters, on the one hand, and the (mendacious) truth claims that preface the film, on the other. (The opening superimposed caption reads: 'This is based on a true story.') I think it likely that a modern, cineliterate audience will treat this gambit circumspectly. But if we are a trusting spectator, the truth-claiming caption does not, I suggest, actively *determine* the nature of our character engagements (sympathetic or otherwise), though it might serve to *intensify* our sympathy or antipathy one way or another. In this case, the opening truth claims may affect our engagement with Sheung in degree but not in kind.

12. Though spurious, the film's opening claim to historical fact ('This is based on a true story') once again warrants our attention: we might reasonably regard this device as a tactic by which Pang tethers the diegetic narrative to real-world referents, the better to encourage the spectator to identify the dramatised milieu (replete with its socio-economic inadequacies) with the actual contemporaneous Hong Kong society.

13. In addition, a plaintive music cue marks the incident as personally distressing for Sheung.

14. If Pang Ho-cheung had sought to elicit our affirmation of Sheung's actions here, the tonal qualities of this scene would be euphoric, not mournful.

15. Stylistically, too, Pang encourages a certain spectatorial detachment by furnishing Sheung's point of view (POV) only sparingly. By and large, the murder scenes are not focalised around Sheung's optical perspective. Pang briefly aligns us with Sheung's POV during the attack on the dissolute male youths; but such instances are too fleeting and infrequent to encourage the spectator's affirmation of Sheung's violent conduct. In any event, we should be mindful of what Smith calls 'the fallacy of POV' (Smith 1995: 156–65): perceptual alignment with a character does not automatically engender subjective access or allegiance, nor does it amount to a spectatorial validation of the character's activity.

16. As Pang puts it, 'What [Sheung] is killing is not a group of people; she's

killing astronomical property prices instead. She's trying to come up with the most bloody protest against the property developers who continuously inflate Hong Kong's housing market' (Anon 2010: 5).

17. Protesting for democracy, universal suffrage and the right for Hong Kong citizens to nominate and elect the city's chief executive, the Umbrella Movement activists blocked Hong Kong streets for seventy-nine days in 2014, but they ultimately failed to achieve their goals.

18. It is therefore flat wrong to assert, as one critic does, that 'The [film's] social context ultimately serves only as a pretext for blood and gore' (M. Lee 2010).

19. What Pang calls black humour is to be found not only within the text itself (for example, the outré scenes of violent horror, some of which are keyed to evoke amusement as well as disgust) but also at an extra-textual level. Pang enlisted Josie Ho as the film's producer and star, in large part, he says, for commentative ends. Ho is the real-life daughter of the celebrity magnate Stanley Ho, whose empire is partly anchored in the real-estate industry. 'This is the biggest source of black humour in *Dream Home*,' Pang states. 'The person [Josie Ho] who gained wealth from the real-estate industry ended up investing in a film that is a comic satire on the real-estate issue' (author interview with Pang, Hong Kong, 31 March 2016).

20. SAPPRFT is an acronym for the State Administration of Press, Publication, Radio, Film and Television. It operates through the China Film Bureau as the state government's official censorship authority.

21. *Dream Home*'s narrative emphasis on domestic horror finds a distant cousin in Soi Cheang's *Home Sweet Home* (2005), whose sinister action orbits around a Hong Kong apartment building and its network of air ducts, elevator shafts, service areas and parking lots. At a further cultural remove, Pang's film assimilates to the 'apartment horror' genre discriminable within Korean cinema (see Lee 2013); and to the international category of what might be called 'property horror', films whose plots are frequently organised around home-invasion scenarios, and whose post-war exemplars include Peckinpah's *Straw Dogs* (1971), Polanski's *The Tenant* (1976), Schlesinger's *Pacific Heights* (1990), Chabrol's *La Cérémonie* (1995) and Fincher's *Panic Room* (2002).

22. Author interview with Pang, Hong Kong, 31 March 2016. At the time this interview was conducted, Pang was at work on a new horror film mounted as a Hong Kong–China co-production. Pang is all too aware that a horror film made in China must be shrewdly packaged in order to satisfy the Mainland censors. For example, the 'horror' element must, first, be cloaked in another generic complexion (hence Pang has yoked his zombie-horror story to the romance genre) and, second, be removed from reality (thus Pang's script reveals the zombies to exist only in the protagonist's imagination). By such tactics, Pang maintains, 'I have solved the censorship problem [of making horror films with and within the Mainland].'

23. *Dream Home*'s link to the Category III genre inheres not only in the out-rageousness and 'bad taste' of its physical violence, but also in its thematic

emphasis on class oppression and its sympathetic portrayal of a killer. For more information on these aspects of Category III cinema, see Stringer 1999; Davis and Yeh, 2001; and Williams 2005.

References

Anon. (2010), *Dream Home* press kit, Fortissimo Films.

Bitel, Anton (2010), '*Dream Home*', *Sight & Sound* 20:12 (December), p. 60.

Carroll, Noël (1996), 'Moderate moralism', *British Journal of Aesthetics*, 36:2 (July), pp. 223–38.

Chatman, Seymour (1990), *Coming to Terms: the Rhetoric of Narrative in Fiction Film*, Ithaca and London: Cornell University Press.

Davis, Darrell and Yeh Yueh-Yu (2001), 'Warning! Category III: the other Hong Kong cinema', *Film Quarterly*, 54:4 (summer), pp. 12–26.

Floyd, Nigel (2010), '*Dream Home*', *Time Out*, 16 November, <www.timeout.com/london/film/dream-home> (last accessed 6 August 2016).

Freeland, Cynthia A. (2003), 'The slasher's blood lust,' in Steven Jay Schneider and Daniel Shaw (eds), *Dark Thoughts: Philosophic Reflections on Cinematic Horror*, Lanham and Oxford: The Scarecrow Press, pp. 198–211.

Kerr, Elizabeth (2010), 'Nightmare *Dream Home*', *China Daily*, 15 May, <www.chinadaily.com.cn/hkedition/2010-05/15/content_9852232.htm> (last accessed 6 August 2016).

Lee, Edmond (2010), 'Josie the killer', *Time Out Hong Kong*, 28 April, <http://timeout-admin-node1.candrholdings.com/film/features/33930/josie-the-killer.html> (last accessed 5 August 2016).

Lee, Maggie (2010), '*Dream Home* – Film Review', *The Hollywood Reporter*, 14 November, <www.hollywoodreporter.com/review/dream-home-film-review-29548> (last accessed 6 August 2016).

Lee, Nikki J. Y. (2013), 'Apartment Horror: *Sorum* and *Possessed*', in Alison Peirse and Daniel Martin (eds), *Korean Horror Cinema*, Edinburgh: Edinburgh University Press, pp. 101–13.

Lemos, Gerard (2013), *The End of the Chinese Dream: Why Chinese People Fear the Future*, New Haven and London: Yale University Press.

Lübecker, Nikolaj (2015), *The Feel-bad Film*, Edinburgh: Edinburgh University Press.

Smith, Murray (1995), *Engaging Characters: Fiction, Emotion, and the Cinema*, Clarendon, Oxford: Oxford University Press.

Smith, Murray (1999), 'Gangsters, cannibals, aesthetes, or apparently perverse allegiances', in Carl Plantinga and Greg M. Smith (eds), *Passionate Views: Film, Cognition, and Emotion*, Baltimore and London: The Johns Hopkins University Press, pp. 217–38.

Stringer, Julian (1999), 'Category 3: sex and violence in postmodern Hong Kong', in Christopher Sharrett (ed.), *Mythologies of Violence in Postmodern Media*, Detroit: Wayne State University Press, pp. 361–79.

Tan, Ed S. (1996), *Emotion and the Structure of Narrative Film: Film as an Emotion Machine*, Mahwah, NJ: Lawrence Erlbaum.

Thompson, Kristin (1988), *Breaking the Glass Armor: Neoformalist Film Analysis*, Princeton, NJ: Princeton University Press.

Waddell, Calum (2015), '*Dream Home*', *Neo*, 24 April, <www.neomag.co.uk/art/asian-film/review/2429/dream-home> (last accessed 6 August 2016).

Williams, Tony (2005), 'Hong Kong social horror: tragedy and farce in Category 3', in Steven Jay Schneider and Tony Williams (eds), *Horror International*, Detroit: Wayne State University Press, pp. 203–19.

CHAPTER 12

Ghostly Returns: the Politics of Horror in Hong Kong Cinema

Vivian Lee

This chapter seeks to unpack the politics of the local in Hong Kong horror films as a contested site of cultural production where different players – film-makers, producers, audience and the 'market' – perform in orchestrated dissonance. Cinematic horror in the cultural imagination of post-1997 Hong Kong gains in complexity as the film industry is increasingly integrated into the regulatory regime in Mainland China, which still harbours exceptional caution towards ideologically suspect films, which naturally include those that promote 'superstition' through the supernatural. In the heat of public debates over Hong Kong's purportedly endangered local identity and the erosion of the city's 'high degree of autonomy' after a series of political contentions (which culminated in the Umbrella Movement in 2014),[1] the repercussions of decolonisation have found their way into the city's cultural imagination. Cinematic horror, both as a vehicle of the popular cultural imagination and as a contested site of identity politics, is seen as both an artistic embodiment of the social psyche and a tool to unpack its latent or repressed anxieties and fantasies. As blockbuster-type Hong Kong–China co-productions have become a market dominant, making horror films amounts to a risky business. While this trend may continue to prevail, there have been some fresh attempts to revitalise this popular genre and inject it with new meanings in the changing context of cultural politics in the city. Between 2012 and 2014 several low- to medium-budget horror films were released. Local audiences responded enthusiastically and many saw these as a sign of the resilience of the local popular culture to counter or at least deflate the Mainland market's grip on Hong Kong's film culture, if not cultural imagination and identity politics more broadly. Whether as a calculated move to appeal to this general sentiment under which a 'niche' local market for Hong Kong horror films is taking shape, or as a cinematic gesture of deviance and subversion, these films embrace a self-conscious 'localness' at the textual and meta-textual levels with cathartic political satires against the ruling regime. The following discussion will first trace the trajectory of Hong Kong horror through the pre- and post-handover decades, situating horror within the evolving discourse of identity and the issues of local histories and collective memory. The second part will elaborate on the politics of horror as seen from more recent productions. Other than being calculated deviations from hegemonic practices to tap into a potential local market, these films, including their reception by critics and fans, give concrete expression to the politics of the local, and no less its predicaments, in present-day Hong Kong. This chapter will conclude with some reflections on film horror as a response to the cultural politics of delocalisation and relocalisation in post-colonial Hong Kong.

Horror in the Age of National Home-coming

Since the mid-2000s Hong Kong cinema has witnessed an industry-wide repositioning towards pan-Chinese co-production. Some critics pointed out that the accelerated economic integration of the Hong Kong Special Administrative Region (SAR) and Mainland China after the introduction of CEPA (Closer Economic Partnership Arrangement) in 2004 was the main catalyst for this 'home-coming' turn.[2] The implications of the co-production film (*he pai pian*) phenomenon go deeper than ideological conformism's limitations on creativity: the market dominance of co-production films epitomises the larger systemic adjustment of Hong Kong's economy, which also happens to be the city's biggest *political* capital, towards the China market. Arguably such an adjustment – which has been absorbed into the global city rhetoric captured in the official slogan, '*bei kao zuguo, mian xiang shijie*' (literally, backed by the motherland, embrace the world) – has a delocalising effect, at least as far as the filmmaking world is concerned.[3] Despite the growing unease over a withering local film culture (especially when it is nostalgically compared to the 1980s 'golden age'), recently, a number of films have challenged this new status quo by overtly deviating from this founding principle. In 2010 alone three box-office hits branded as 'local film for local people' were released: *Echoes of the Rainbow* (Alex Law, art house drama), *72 Tenants of Prosperity* (Eric Tsang, comedy-remake) and *Gallants* (Derek Kwok and Clement Cheung, retro-style kung fu). They span a wide spectrum of styles and subject matters, but all were applauded as long overdue tributes to local culture. Others in this category include *Vulgaria* (Pang Ho-Cheung, 2012), *Naked Ambition 2* (Lee Kung Lok, 2014), *The Midnight After* (Fruit Chan, 2014) and *Tales of the Dark* 1 & 2 (2013), two portmanteau horror films based on the popular novels of Hong Kong writer Li Bihua.

The audience's enthusiastic reception of these films did not say much about their uneven quality and occasional coarseness. Sometimes the viewer is left pondering the ultimate purpose of the film's indulgence in unrestrained vulgarity. Apart from artistic merit and sensational excitement, a more important determining factor of their popularity is perhaps the politics implicit in the production *and* consumption of these 'local' horror films: they signal an about-turn from the co-production paradigm, and the readiness of the local audience to purchase tickets to watch the film in the cinema (rather than waiting for DVD releases or simply turning to piracy channels) could also be seen as a sign of a deeper-running sense of crisis reminiscent of the *fin de siècle* scenario in the 1980s and throughout the political transition period (approximately 1984–97). A good example is Fruit Chan's latest political (some call it postmodern) allegory, *The Midnight After*, better known as 'red van' or 'hung van' in Hong Kong-style Cantonese, an adaptation of a popular online fiction. Set in post-apocalyptic Hong Kong, the film is saturated by in-your-face metaphors and political puns that hardly need decoding to understand their intended meanings.

Seen in the light of Fruit Chan's corpus, most notably his Hong Kong Trilogy from the late 1990s, the coarseness of the film strikes a similar chord with its predecessors: the ubiquity of the struggling, die-hard 'Hong Kong voice' against an impending (imaginary) 'end of history'. The striking image of the red van being crushed, abused and rampaged as it embarks on a journey to literally nowhere is an unmistakable metaphor of the city: decolonisation as a political process that began in the mid-1980s is fraught with contradictions as well as unresolved conflicts and dilemmas in society and culture. In the film, the passengers are an inchoate mix of age, gender, class and social background. They all feel trapped inside a dysfunctional vehicle controlled by a reckless driver, who compares himself to a pilot 'taking off' an airplane, which could possibly be an oblique and satirical reference to the 'Act Now' slogan (rendered 'set sail' in Chinese) used by ex-Chief Executive Donald Tsang during a controversial promotion of a hugely unpopular political reform package between 2009 and 2010. The main difference between this film and Chan's more subtle cinematic metaphors of Hong Kong, for instance *Little Cheung* (1999) and *The Longest Summer* (1998), is also what accounts for its stylistic rough edges: this film is a more concrete – though not exactly cogently written – statement about the here and now, an emotionally charged visualisation of an existential nightmare towards which one could no longer afford the same kind of contemplative intellectual distance as in Chan's earlier films.[4] In this sense, the red van and its driver are not only a metaphor of the film (and

Chan himself as the helmsman of this nightmarish cinematic vehicle), but also a dystopian vision of the postcolonial (post-apocalyptic?) city and the social pathologies that result. The celebration of the grotesque, the vulgar and the despicable are also found in some recent productions (all are in the 'Grade III' – eighteen years old or above – category), such as *Vulgaria*, *Naked Ambition 2* and *Tales of the Dark*.

No doubt, widespread apprehensions of the erosion of the city's high degree of autonomy under 'one country, two systems' has further politicised the discourse of the local. The post-CEPA decade saw a deepening sense of alienation and disempowerment due to the widening gulf not only between social classes and income groups, but also between conflicting perceptions of what constitutes the 'best interest' and 'core values' of the Hong Kong society. Amidst the heated political climate, the local (*bentu*) has been given new meanings and provocative interpretations in public debates and political campaigns. At the same time, resistance to the delocalising forces, especially among the young people (the so-called post-1980s and post-1990s generation), has been gaining momentum, as can be seen from the upsurge of social and political activism and conservation movements that, more than coincidentally, claim to defend the city's 'collective memory', 'local identity' and 'core values' such as liberty and human rights. Emerging from this social schism are various constructions of 'local culture' and 'collective memory' mobilised by different parties in political debates and protests, to the effect that their meaning is contingent upon the context of articulation and the political/economic interests at stake. The local therefore is a value-laden and highly politicised term in contemporary Hong Kong. Its complex meanings must be seen through not one but multiple lenses. Fruit Chan's film is only a more outrageous attempt to activate the horror imagination to give expression to a new (or renewed) 'crisis consciousness'[5] and the social and political tensions that are fast dissolving the official myth of 'stability and prosperity' under 'one country, two systems'.

Revisiting Hong Kong Horror

Whether as a literary or film genre, horror has fascinated both critics and audiences as a magnifying lens of the individual and social psyche, embodying both the universal 'fear of the unknown' and more culturally and historically specific elements that give form and substance to horror styles and expressions across time and space (Prince 2004: 1–14). In recent years, studies on non-Western horror films have yielded a rich discourse on the distinctive horror traditions in Asia, and new trade labels have been introduced to underscore their distinctions from Western counterparts. Specialised vocabularies in film publicity and popular reviews, such as 'J-horror' and 'Asia Extreme', are created to update and repackage the image of an Orientalised 'Asia' in the perception and representation of radical otherness and alterity.[6] Where the supernatural is invoked, horror establishes an intimate connection with the mythological and spiritual tradition that originates the 'ghost story'. Certain recurrent motifs and visual codes would also serve as style markers that give a film its distinctive look, as in the case of the *onryo* (aggrieved female ghost) in Japanese folklore and exotic shamanistic practices in Thai horror. This is not to overlook the genre's penchant for adapting 'urban legends' that constantly renew its vocabulary of fear to broaden its appeal to contemporary audiences. Even when one looks at the studio productions of the 1970s and early 1980s, Hong Kong film horror registers multiple cultural influences from China, Southeast Asia and Hollywood, absorbing, translating and sometimes transgressing received codes and conventions.[7] Like other popular genres, horror in Hong Kong cinema bears the traits of the city's historical trajectory and its linkages to China and other parts of the world as a British colony since the late nineteenth century. For the purpose of discussion in this chapter, a brief overview of the more noteworthy footprints of film horror in the last two decades will help unpack the politics of horror in the post-CEPA era.

The Longest Horror Series: *Troublesome Night* (1997–2007)

Any discussion of Hong Kong horror would not be complete without at least an acknowledgement of the record set by the *Troublesome Night* series, which literally spanned the first decade of Hong Kong's reunification with Mainland China.[8] Caution must be taken *not* to over-interpret the political implications of this temporal coincidence; yet the longevity of this series, the cult status it still enjoys and the celebrity it generated for the stars in leading roles speak volumes about the symbolic significance of the *Troublesome Night* films. The success of the series was not an isolated phenomenon: it derives one of its main (and most charismatic) characters from its immediate predecessor, the '*Lung Por*' series (1996–7). Lung Por (literally, Dragon Grannie), the title-role protagonist, is played by Helen Law Lan, a veteran TV star well known for playing antagonist and supporting roles in black-and-white Cantonese movies in the 1950s and 1960s. Her performance as a spiritual medium, a vengeful spirit or sometimes an unexplained haunting apparition, in both series has established her as the 'ghost lady' par excellence in film and television. 'Lung Por' subsequently became the actress's unofficial screen franchise (and nickname) thereafter. The *Troublesome Night* series also helped launch the film career of Louis Koo, at a time when the TV star's popularity was beginning to wane. The first five films were released during a general economic depression following the 1997 Asian Financial Crisis. The series' ability to score moderate market success on low-budget production[9] further testifies to the appeal of the local-flavour 'scary movie' *in its most generic form* to film audiences. A landmark of local horror film cycles before the genre went into decline after the mid-2000s, the *Troublesome Night* series presents an illuminating case study ten years after its discontinuation, when film horror is showing signs of a moderate comeback as an 'alternative' commercial genre.[10]

Similar to most cult film cycles, the series gained market credibility and a cult following upon the box office success of the initial instalments directed by Herman Yau,[11] a versatile director whose corpus includes critically acclaimed social dramas as well as commercial genre films. Yau's sensitivity toward gender politics and social injustice leaves discernible traces in his commercial horror films. In particular, women are empowered with greater agency compared to the oftentimes dismissive, if not abusive, treatment of women in much Hong Kong horror. In *Troublesome Night 5* (1999), for instance, the leading characters are two taxi drivers, whose ghostly encounters tell a moralising tale of retribution. While the women are in supporting roles, they are seen to be independent agents who act upon life. Throughout the film Yau manages to balance the gender roles through humorous treatment of the female ghosts. In the pre-credit sequence, Law Lan's nameless Old Lady character abruptly stops and boards a late-night taxi. When the driver (Louis Koo) looks into the back mirror, the lady is nowhere to be seen. The use of a quick cut to Koo's point of view is a familiar technique in horror films to create surprise and suspense. But when the sequence is repeated, we see the old lady back in her original position again, calmly explaining to the driver that she was just trying to pick up a coin she had dropped. Throughout the film the mysterious appearances of the old lady are strategically placed to insinuate a sense of ominous presence. The play with audience expectations is repeated in several subsequent scenes, where ghostly faced young women with all the trappings of a classic female ghost (pale faces, blood-red lips, white dresses) turn out to be humans, to the surprise and relief of both the taxi drivers and the audience. Yau's deconstructive approach to the stock imagery of the scary movie is carefully manipulated in his *Troublesome Night* films to create refreshing, though sporadic, deviations from the formulaic treatment of plot, character and atmosphere in low-budget commercial horror films. Yau's creative dialogue with horror conventions, however, tends to be improvisational rather than schematic, which is a shared predicament of low-budget entertainment films in Hong Kong.

Yau's later *Troublesome Night* films tend to be routine genre exercises, and not without signs of creative fatigue. Instead of sustaining a lively dialogue with generic norms, some later entries became opportunistic gambles on the series' brand name. Nonetheless, Yau managed to leave his directorial imprint on the final instalment, *Troublesome Night 20: Gong Tau* (2007).[12] In the Asian horror tradition, *gong tau* is a familiar device associated with shamanistic practices allegedly originated in Southeast Asia. In the popular cultural imagination, *gong tau* is black magic that casts deadly curses upon its targets. Where *gong tau* is cinematically invoked, it is usually practised or procured by aggrieved women betrayed or abandoned by their lovers. Embittered male–female relations because of illicit affairs or unhappy marriages provide the social anchor for plot development. The denouement, whether open-ended or not, will bring in moral lessons drawn upon the Buddhist notion of karmic retribution. Yau's film is no exception. At the core is a moral lesson that casts the main character in a morally compromised role: Lok-man is a detective whose family is under a deadly *gong tau* curse. His infant son died of multiple injuries of an unknown cause, while his wife, Kar-pi, suffers from debilitating headaches and hallucinations after the tragic incident. Lok-man's own investigation finally leads him back to a secret he has almost forgotten: he had an affair with a stripper called Yili from Mainland China while on official duty in Thailand. Realising that her relationship with Lok-man was a lost cause, Yili committed suicide. Her death prompted her young secret admirer, who happens to be a *gong tau* practitioner, to take revenge. The subplot of hunting down another ex-convict, Lam Chiu, complicates the main action, as Lam is also a *gong tau* master who knows the counter-curse to save Kar-pi. The two plot lines finally converge in the grand finale, when Lok-man connives with Lam to break the curse, on the condition that he will set free Lam, now in police custody. In the final confrontation, the two *gong tau* masters die in a messy combat, hence lifting the curses they respectively have cast on Kar-pi. As the couple make their exit, Lok-man is gripped by a chest convulsion and falls unconscious. The camera cuts to a flashback to a long withheld secret: it was Yili who cast this killing curse on Lok-man three years ago, probably as a precaution against his betrayal. From plot design to the use of generic conventions – from oriental black magic and rituals to the characterisation of the femme fatale and her ally as exotic others – *Gong Tau* fulfils the expectations of a cult film. The composition and structure of the film shows a sophisticated grasp of genre vocabulary to stimulate sensational excitement. *Gong Tau* shuns the comic action and hyperbolic style that has become a trademark of the *Troublesome Night* series; instead, the cinematography and screenplay manage to sustain the psychological tension within and between the main characters through atmospheric suspense. At times the film's awareness of its cult identity is overloaded for the sake of graphic display, where brutality and nudity seem disproportional to diegetic explication. As the final instalment of the series, *Gong Tau* is both a deviation from the *Troublesome Night* formula and also an apt closure, in the sense that in this film we see the contending traits of two generic sources at work: its unambiguous generic lineage, announced in the film title, means the film must adhere to the formulaic treatment of women and/as the cultural other. Yau's characterisation of Kar-pi renders her less an individual than a caricature of the helpless (screaming) victim, and Yili as a monstrous other – hence Southeast Asia as a land of black magic is associated with subversive femininity – is the film's major setback at odds with Yau's own artistic temperament.[13] Yet, the tension between genre expectations and artistic temperament produces interesting results: the film remains critical of Lok-man, whose integrity as husband and law-enforcer is systematically undermined by his shady conduct. Yau's readiness to give up the episodic, comic-horror style of the series in favour of a more coherent storyline, psychological complexity and atmospheric suspense gives the film a transitional quality, one that bespeaks the genre's need of transformation to adapt to contemporary sensibilities, audience tastes and market realities.

Another noteworthy property of the later *Troublesome Night* films is the gradual shift toward overt and out-of-place political jokes and commentaries on the decline in public governance in postcolonial Hong Kong. In *Troublesome Night 5* (2002), for example, the plot revolves around a court mistrial that led to the suicide of a couple. The film clearly belongs to the haphazardly put together run-of-the mill production category; but precisely as such it carries a no-holds-barred attitude, throwing arbitrary and sarcastic remarks on the erosion of basic rights and freedom in Hong Kong since the handover. The inmates' bonding and sense of brotherhood recalls John Woo's gangster ('hero') films of the 1980s; while the ghosts are victims of institutionalised power abuse and the disempowerment of the working class. As the foregoing discussion on Fruit Chan's *Midnight After* has shown, the use of outrageous political in-jokes at the expense of plot coherence obtains a new significance at a time when 'local' films are being marginalised in the commercial cinema. The longest horror series in Hong Kong cinema did struggle to survive in its final phase. Unfortunately, like many of its peers, the series suffered from a drastic decline in quality due to the departure of Yau and overproduction, and finally came to an end under the new market conditions of the mid-2000s.

'Art horror': Allegory and the Pan-Asian Cultural Imaginary

Another category of horror films that made an impact on later works displays a trendier, art-house style with greater transnational appeal. Representative works in this category are Ann Hui's *Visible Secret* series, Peter Chan's *Going Home* (the Hong Kong segment of the pan-Asian omnibus film, *Three*, produced by Chan) and the Pang Brothers' *The Eye* and *The Eye 2*. Different from the exploitative cult film aesthetics of the *Troublesome Night* series, these art horror films adopt a more contemplative, slow-paced, character-driven approach to utilise the allegorical potential of cinematic horror. Cynthia Freeland characterises Hollywood's 'art horror' as 'better films of dreadful horror'. Instead of an over-reliance on gore and special effects, art-dread requires 'a combination of effective narrative with other cinematic features'. Art dread in this definition 'involves an anticipated encounter with something 'profound'– something particularly powerful, grave, and inexorable' (Freeland 2004: 192; 195–6). Horror therefore is less a means to create hyper-sensational excitement or to test the limits of visual extremities for cathartic effects, but a vehicle for metaphorical conjectures, and possibly transcendence and reconciliation, through the encounter with the supernatural.[14]

One of the most senior members of the Hong Kong New Wave, Ann Hui is best known for her docu-drama films, which arguably is a defining quality of Hong Kong's art house cinema of the 1980s. A prolific and versatile director, Hui's opus consists of a wide range of genre films and horror is no exception. Her debut film, *The Secret*, is a thriller based on a real-life murder case in the 1970s. Although the supernatural elements (ancestor worship, supernatural sightings and the eerie apprehension of an avenging female ghost) are mainly used for suspense and criticism of the Chinese tradition and its patriarchal practices, Hui's interest in the supernatural goes beyond social criticism, which can be seen in *The Secret* and her later horror films, *Spooky Bunch* and *Visible Secret (1 & 2)*.

Unlike *The Secret*, in which supernatural horror elements are displaced and dismissed by the detective plot (which symbolises rationality and reason), the world of *Visible Secret* is haunted by ghosts from start to finish, and the world of the supernatural is very much present in everyday life, visibly and invisibly. The story revolves around a fatal traffic accident at a crowded intersection in West Point, one of the oldest districts on

Hong Kong Island and Ann Hui's favourite locale, where a man (name unknown) is beheaded. What actually happened at the time of the accident is not immediately clear. Keeping the scene of the accident off-screen, the camera turns to the shocked expressions of onlookers in a quick succession of shots. Our attention is also drawn to a little girl in the custody of a human trafficker, who earlier on has disembarked from a boat at a nearby pier. As she tries to retrieve an apple from underneath a tramcar, she comes face to face with a human head, whose eyes seem to be gazing into her face. The eye contact scene under the tramcar is followed by a jump cut to a headless man walking haphazardly until he falls over a bicycle, blood spurting out from his opened neck. Many years later, the girl, now a young woman called June, recalls what she saw more than a decade ago.

As in *The Secret* and many of Hui's films, memory lost and recalled has important thematic and schematic functions. In *Visible Secret*, a man was killed during a tram accident one evening. June, a little child then, was traumatised when she saw the victim's head rolling by her feet. Suffering from memory loss, June remains haunted by the headless ghost seeking revenge for his death, but she has no recourse other than remaining on the run. She was picked up and raised by a petty criminal who later became a fake Daoist exorcist. Similar to *Spooky Bunch*, the film belongs to the hybrid form of comic-horror and the narrative develops through the increasing visibility of ghosts, not just to June (who allegedly is gifted with supernatural vision) but to other characters as well, especially her boyfriend Peter. Peter meets June in a disco and finds himself intrigued by her apparently neurotic behaviour. The romance between Peter and June is dotted with ghostly encounters: the headless ghost, a young lady haunting a campsite on Cheung Chau island, a little boy's mother possessed by the ghost of a 'Mainland mistress' and the ghost of the little boy himself right after they have saved his mother. While Hui renders these ghostly encounter scenes with a generous dose of comic action and suspense, these encounters are strategically placed to connect different strands of the film narrative to reveal a predicament shared by both humans and ghosts, that is, the need to answer certain haunting questions, whether in the human or supernatural realm. More importantly, these questions usually arise from the need for reconciliation with one's own past, and sometimes the realisation of the 'truth' reinforces the sense of futility in holding on to one's obsession in and after life. Ann Hui's interest in cinematic horror, therefore, is consistent with her more 'worldly' preoccupation with history, memory and social reality. Arguably the supernatural opens up an alternative imaginative space where Hui's social realist sensibilities speak through an other-worldly medium.

As a veteran member of Hong Kong's commercial cinema, horror is not immune from the forces of globalisation. Since the 1980s many Asian countries have witnessed state-level reforms in film policy to protect and promote the national film industries in the region in face of Hollywood's near-global dominance.[15] In fact horror proved to be an effective means to access the regional market due to its capacity for cross-cultural adaptation and borrowing. Perhaps buzzwords such as 'pan-Asian horror' and Asia Extreme sound more like lacklustre clichés to film audiences after almost two decades of over-circulation in popular and critical writings on Asian cinema. Yet I would like to argue that as a production strategy 'pan-Asian' is an important thread linking Hong Kong horror films over the last two decades. In this connection, it is worth pointing out that Hong Kong film-makers were the first to officially advocate pan-Asian cinema as a production strategy. Peter Chan Ho-sun, together with Teddy Chen and Allan Fung, co-founded Applause Pictures in 2000, announcing on their company website their commitment 'to syndicate financing, promote co-production agreements, encourage the exchange of talent on both sides of the camera, and to expand the regional and global distribution possibilities for the new pan-Asian films.'[16] Between 2002 and 2008 Applause Pictures produced seven horror films out of a total output of thirteen films. Among these are *The Eye* and *The Eye 2*, which made the Pang Brothers a regional brand name of pan-Asian horror. The initial success of small-to-medium-budget horror films proved the commercial viability of pan-Asian horror with a more illustrious line-up of directors and stars: *Three* (2002) consists of three horror shorts, *Going Home* (Peter Chan, Hong Kong), *Mitigum* (Nonzee Nimibutr, Thailand) and *Memories* (Kim Ji-woon, Korea). Its sequel, *Three . . . Extremes* (2004), solicited contributions from Hong Kong's Fruit Chan (*Dumplings*), Japan's Miike Takeshi (*Box*), and South Korea's Park Chan-wook (*Cut*).

The regional outlook of pan-Asian horror tends to be highlighted through casting and certain stylistic markers to highlight cross-cultural properties. Apart from utilising Asian pop stars, the filming locations in *The Eye* and *The Eye 2* cut across Hong Kong, Singapore and Thailand. Where local rituals and supernatural traditions are invoked, 'local flavour' is usually cast in the context of social and cultural critique. For instance, the narratives of both the *Eye* films are focalised on female protagonists. In both films, female agency is privileged in the process of encoding and decoding horror. In *The Eye*, visual perception provides the primary access to the supernatural and is also the key to unlock the secrets of the dead and the living. Foregrounding the female characters as the owners of supernatural vision aligns the audience's point of view with the female protagonist as the centre of consciousness, hence creating a bond between the female visionary and the viewer as we participate in her journey of (self-) discovery.[17]

Chan was perhaps an ideal candidate to launch a pan-Asian film production network: he lived and worked in Thailand before taking up a filmmaking career in Hong Kong. He set up an advertising agency in Thailand for which the Pang Brothers directed their first TV commercials. Like his more established peers, Chan later turned to Hong Kong–China co-productions (*Perhaps Love* (2004); *The Warlords* (2007); *American Dreams in China* (2013)), but Applause's strategy of producing smaller-budget 'quality' films for the regional market has set a precedent for later attempts to seek out alternatives to blockbuster-style Hong Kong–China co-productions, a less-trodden path these days that nonetheless promises greater creative freedom and not necessarily higher commercial risks. These considerations are of particular relevance to the recent revival of Hong Kong horror on local screens (the primary destination of supernatural horror) discussed below.

Relocalising Hong Kong Screens in the Age of the China Market

As mentioned above, making horror films can be risky business in the age of the burgeoning China market, especially films that overtly claim to have a 'real ghost', that is, the presence of a ghostly being or 'spirit' that unambiguously affirms the existence of the supernatural.[18] In other cases, such as the Pang Brothers' *Forest of Death* (2007) and *Diary* (2006), the supernatural is reduced to a form of pathology, such as schizophrenia or extreme psychic states. In these films, the supernatural becomes a plot device to create shock effects, which usually will dissipate as the plot unfolds. Under such circumstances, making a 'real horror film with a real ghost' amounts to a gesture of deviance and commercial suicide. The significance of the return of supernatural horror to local screens therefore lies in its counter-hegemonic character. While horror in general can be an embodiment of the dark side of the human and social psyche, supernatural horror has been a forsaken genre in post-CEPA Hong Kong cinema. In order to gain access to the Mainland market, the supernatural is often an effect of psychosis or schizophrenia. Under these circumstances, the revival of supernatural horror is a self-conscious statement against a market-driven delocalisation and a gesture of deviance that resonates with the city's renewed crisis of 'disappearance' and identity politics.

The sensational pleasure derived from this newfound creative autonomy can be gauged by the generous deployment of out-of-place political jokes and satirical references to unpopular political figures in these films. Scenes that overtly ridicule local political leaders would easily gain crowd following on social media. In *Tales of the Dark*, an episode entitled *Jing Zhe* (directed by Fruit Chan) begins with an ageing Triad boss who procures the service of a spiritual medium, Grannie Zhu, to cast a deadly curse upon his rivals in the gang. The scene utilises the popular local voodoo tradition of 'beating petty villains' to anchor the dialogue between the triad boss 'ZY' (a pun on the initials of Hong Kong's Chief Executive C. Y. Leung, a hardliner who was rumoured to be connected with financial and political scandals since his assumption of duty in 2012) and Grannie Zhu, who half-jokingly tells her client that he is doomed by virtue of his name. This conversation does little to advance the plot, though Grannie Zhu's character and the setting turn out to bear important clues to the unfolding mystery. Meta-textual political and social commentaries in these films have little diegetic function. In terms of comic effect, instead of building up the atmosphere or suspense, they play the role of a generic device, or a hand signal to gain rapport with local audiences.

The alterity and subversiveness of horror as a popular genre, therefore, obtains a new meaning in the context of post-CEPA Hong Kong: apart from formal and cultural encoding generally attributed to film horror, alterity and subversiveness are registered in the form of a self-conscious deviation from the prevailing production norms of commercial filmmaking. Unlike art house and independent films, which tend to seek out niche audiences through festivals and special screening avenues, this type of local horror cinema has to rely on commercial exhibition and distribution channels. Making films primarily for the local market certainly does not make good business sense. As such, the 'less is more' logic of local horror films may well be the first attempt to experiment with a new strategy to relocalise commercial film-making in Hong Kong by, ironically, scaling *down* their commercial ambitions.

Apart from reinvigorating horror as a 'local' genre, Juno Mak's second feature, *Rigor Mortis* (2013) is a recent example of repositioning Hong Kong horror in the pan-Asian film network. The involvement of J-horror maverick, Shimizu Takashi (director of the *Ju-on* series) as producer strengthens the film's generic identity in the eyes of horror fans in the region, while the cast, screenplay and setting are unmistakably Hong Kong (cinema)-inspired. The story takes place in an old and dilapidated working class estate. A newcomer, Chin, finds himself in the company of strange neighbours who appear to be harbouring their own respective secrets, among whom are an old seamstress Auntie Mei, a Daoist monk and neighbourhood eatery boss Yau, and a mysterious woman who appears to be haunting the estate during the night. An ex-kung fu star long past his prime, Chin's main luggage is a set of Chinese vampire costumes, a token from the heyday of his acting career (and Hong Kong's popular cinema). A series of inexplicable events soon unfolds as Chin tries to adapt to the new environment. In *Rigor Mortis*, the run-down housing estate – a familiar setting of Hong Kong's urban cinema – becomes the haunted house par excellence populated by aggrieved spirits and freaky characters. The director generously deploys motifs from both J-horror and Hong Kong vampire movies to create a hybridised visual palette. In the film, the vampire figure is given a twist that references Frankenstein, *Psycho* (1960), and most of all the dark magic of the Chinese vampire movie tradition, whereas the imprint of J-horror aesthetics is unmistakable in the characterisation of the vengeful female ghosts, twin sisters raped and brutally killed by their private tutor. It turns out that the deadliest monster is Uncle Tung, the deceased husband of Auntie Mei. She resorts to traditional Chinese dark magic in the hope of reviving her beloved, but inadvertently turns him into a zombie-like monster. Metaphorically, the Chinese vampire as living dead in *Rigor Mortis* is not without melancholic overtones, evidenced by a 'reality check' at the end in much the same way as other post-CEPA co-productions. After the joint effort of Chin and Yau to destroy the vampire, the final scene takes us back to the beginning to reveal a long-withheld plot device: Chin is seen hanging himself inside his unit. As the suicide scene gradually melts into Chin's dying vision, the supernatural is drained of its ethereal charm. What we have seen therefore is no more than a projection of the ex-kung fu star's play to end all plays, a hallucination before his final exit. This ending may be seen as yet another compromise to accommodate the China market. At another level, if we see *Rigor Mortis* as a film within a film, the meta-textual resonances go deeper than just a commercial compromise.

As a regional co-production film, *Rigor Mortis* is not strictly speaking a 'local' film in the same sense as *The Midnight After* and *Tales of the Dark*. Aesthetically more refined and less given to sensational excesses, the film is closer to the art horror and pan-Asian horror films mentioned above. References to Hong Kong cinema's 'golden age' are rendered diegetically (an ex-kung fu star, a Daoist exorcist and a Chinese vampire), as well as non-diegetically through casting film stars from the 1970s and 1980s to play the main characters. (These efforts to inscribe the historical memory of Hong Kong's film culture in the film's cast, setting and plot is a continuation of a general trend in the local film scene since the mid-1990s, most notably in Stephen Chow's *Kung Fu Hustle* (2004), where aging and overweight ex-kung fu stars take the centre stage of a comic-kung fu blockbuster). Symbolically, the vampire's 'revival' connotes both Chin's

nostalgia for the good old days and also the film's ambition to contempo-
rise the 'Chinese vampire' genre by updating its visual vocabularies and
regional cross-breeding. Enthusiastically received in Hong Kong, *Rigor
Mortis* raises a new possibility of making 'Hong Kong horror films' that
can better negotiate the post-CEPA political and economic realities. The
film's mode of production is typical of the pan-Asian strategy initiated
by Applause Pictures. Yet its 'Asianness' is more concretely anchored
in the local social and cultural milieu. Instead of effacing the local in the
service of the regional, culture-specific elements in *Rigor Mortis* demonstrate how the regional can mobilise the local to reinvigorate a popular
film genre and still be commercially successful inside and outside Hong
Kong.[19] Calling it a 'new' possibility is not to deny the rich heritage of
Hong Kong horror, and Hong Kong cinema at large, which essentially is
the inspiration behind *Rigor Mortis*. Juno Mak himself once commented
at a press interview that *Rigor Mortis* is a story about 'the anxiety of being
forgotten'.[20] As an attempt to relocalise Hong Kong cinema by mobilising
the resources of transnational film-making, *Rigor Mortis* is not without
apprehension of the sustainability of its own approach: how far can the
local go amidst, if not against, the odds of regionalisation, nationalisation
and globalisation? How would these hegemonic forces play out in the local
film culture in the years to come? These thoughts are perhaps haunting
the creative crew of *Rigor Mortis*, and given expression in the thematic
foci, that is, the ultimate question of whether the dead *can* be revived, and
to what end: is it not a freak destined to be disavowed, or, more precisely,
the final fantasy of a nostalgic subject before the light goes out?

Conclusion

This chapter has attempted to trace the footprints of Hong Kong horror
films along the changing social and political landscape of the city in the
last two decades. Through observing the connections and disconnec-
tions registered in a selection of films from the 1990s to the present, the
above discussion has demonstrated how horror in postcolonial cinema
has become a vehicle for political expression while maintaining its function as popular entertainment. The post-CEPA era has witnessed an
important structural shifting of the film industry toward China-oriented
co-productions, which effectively relegates horror films into a negligible
margin in commercial film-making. Using the *Troublesome Night* series as
a precursor to the later developments, the above discussion has outlined
the major shifts from 'pure entertainment' of local horror (which, as
shown, is not without its sociopolitical trappings as a pop culture product)

to a more self-consciously politicised form of film-making practice. This is not to say that all Hong Kong horror films have a political mission; nor are they, as a genre, going against the grain of commercial film-making. The above analysis suggests that cinematic horror in present-day Hong Kong embeds the complexities and anxieties of the city's cultural politics, which borders on a new crisis of disappearance. As popular entertainment, its cult qualities have created a space for deviant practices that challenge not only social propriety (as most horror films do), but also commercial logic. The revival of horror films thus reinstates the local as a still relevant category of meaning; yet, as in the case of *Rigor Mortis*, 'film(ing) horror' also bespeaks the predicament of relocalisation amidst the tension-stricken geopolitics between city and nation.

Notes

1. On 28 September 2014 a mass student-led protest against the Hong Kong Special Administrative Region (SAR) Government's proposed reform of the Chief Executive election mechanism (which effectively ruled out the possibility of universal suffrage in future elections) turned into a large-scale 'Occupied Movement' that would paralyse major business and commercial districts in Hong Kong for nearly three months. It was the largest-scale civic disobedience movement in the history of Hong Kong, with thousands of protestors setting up camps and commune-like settlements along the city's commercial artilleries and public transportation routes for seventy-nine days. As the anti-riot police fired tear gas to disperse the crowds during an initial stand-off outside the government headquarters, thousands of unarmed protestors put on face masks and opened their umbrellas for protection. In the following days, passers-by would parachute their umbrellas from nearby footbridges as a gesture of support. The campaign was hence named the 'Umbrella Movement' (or 'Umbrella Revolution') by the local and international media.
2. The agreement was signed between Hong Kong and Beijing in 2003, in the wake of the SARS epidemic and a mass public protest on 1 July 2003 against the government's proposed anti-subversion law, Article 23, which many feared would threaten freedom of expression.
3. This phrase became a slogan among pro-establishment politicians and media after ex-Hong Kong Chief Executive Tung Chee Hwa's public and policy speeches between 2003 and 2004. In the 2004 policy speech, he used '*beikao neidi, mianxiang shijie*' (leveraging on the Mainland, engaging ourselves globally) as a strategic direction in the post-SARS years: see Tung (2004), available at <www.policyaddress.gov.hk/pa04/eng/p5.htm> (last accessed 4 September 2017). The slogan was later revised to '*Beikao zuguo*' (literally, backed by the Motherland) by official Mainland media and senior members of the pro-establishment political parties: see NPC (2006), available at

<www.npc.gov.cn/npc/oldarchives/dbdh/dbdh/common/zw.jsp@label= wxzlk&id=346535&back=1&pdmc=3380.htm> (last accessed 4 September 2017). Pro-China media adapted this slogan to give it a stronger patriotic accent: '*beikao shijie, mianxiang zuguo*' (leveraging on the world [global economy], engaging ourselves with the Motherland): see Kam (2011), available at <www.npp.org.hk/zh-hk/node/6773> (last accessed 4 September 2017).

4. Fruit Chan's penchant for fantastic excesses in portraying everyday vulgarities is present in his earlier works, such as *Little Cheung* (1999) and *Hollywood Hong Kong* (2001).

5. The crisis consciousness in Hong Kong cinema is discussed in Tony Williams (1997) and Esther Cheung et al. (2004).

6. For a discussion of Asia Extreme and pan-Asian horror, see Nikki Lee (2011) and Patrick Galloway (2006).

7. The *Mr. Vampire* series by director and action star Lam Ching Ying is an iconic symbol of the modern Chinese vampire movies in the 1980s combining horror and comic kung fu action. Low-budget horror films were a favorite vehicle for social commentaries in the hands of veteran action-thriller director Kueh Chi-hung (*Hex* (1980), *Bewitched* (1981) and *The Boxer's Omen* (1983)). Reputed as a cult film director, Kueh's films combine Asian witchcraft with Western-style mystery and revenge in creating a cinema of excess seldom found among his contemporaries.

8. As this volume goes to print, a new Troublesome Night film, *Always Be with You* (2017), also directed by Herman Yau, was released to mark the series' twentieth anniversary.

9. According to some published statistics, the average production cost per film between 1997 and 1999 was HK$2.8–3 million (approx. US$350,000–400,000). The box office records ranged between HK$6.55–2.52 million (approx. US$300,000–800,000), with an average per film revenue of HK$4.08 million (approx. US$520,000). See Shi, Man-hung, 'Opportunities and crises in the turn of the century', in Lee (ed.), *New Perspectives on Hong Kong Media* (in Chinese), Hong Kong: Chinese University Press, 2003: p. 268, n. 13; box office figures reported in *Film Bimonthly*, vol. 491 (February 1998): p. 37.

10. The Closer Economic Partnership Arrangement (CEPA) signed between Hong Kong and Beijing in 2003 formally took effect in 2004. From then on the Hong Kong film industry accelerated its integration with Mainland China followed by systemic relocation of production headquarters over the border. Under CEPA, Hong Kong films enjoy the benefits of domestic productions as long as they satisfy the required ratio (adjusted and relaxed at different stages) of Mainland capital, artists and crews, which effectively means all such films will be co-productions with Mainland partners subject to the more stringent censorship mechanism of the Chinese authorities.

11. Yau directed the first six *Troublesome Night* films between 1997 and 1999, and the last episode, *Gong Tau* (discussed below) in 2007, which concluded the series.

12. Gong Tau has the same Chinese title of a 1975 Shaw Brothers production (entitled *Black Magic* in English), directed by Ho Meng-hua. Also known as *Gong Tau* or *Gong Tau: an Oriental Black Magic*, this film is sometimes treated as a stand-alone work. Some website listings do not include this film in the *Troublesome Night* series. While this ambiguity should be acknowledged, Gong Tau is treated as a *Troublesome Night* film since it has been advertised and titled under this series. As with other Hong Kong-made films, different English (and sometimes even Chinese) film titles are used upon international releases due to commercial and marketing considerations.

13. *Gong Tau* as well as other films in this series is not immune from a taken-for-granted sexism toward women in general, and ethnic minority women in particular, which Yau seeks to address in his social dramas (*From the Queen to the Chief Executive* (2000); *Whispers and Moans* (2007); *SARA* (2015)).

14. Noël Carroll, from a more philosophical angle, distinguishes 'natural horror' (for example an abhorrent real-life event) from 'art horror' (as artistic creation): '[art-horror's] objects . . . are, by definition, impure. This is to be understood in terms of their being anomalous. Obviously, the anomalous nature of these beings is what makes them disturbing, distressing and disgusting. They are violations of our ways of classifying things and such frustrations of a world-picture are bound to be disturbing' (Carroll 1990: 39).

15. The regionalisation of Asia's national film industries since the 1980s and 1990s is discussed in Davis and Yeh (2008), Chapter 1.

16. Available at <www.applausepictures.com/profile/index.html> (last accessed 18 July 2016).

17. For a close analysis of the film, see Lee, 'Universal hybrids: the trans/local production of pan-Asian horror', in Peter Braunein and Andrea Lauser (eds), *Ghost Movies in Southeast Asia*, Leiden: Brill (2016).

18. The supernatural in films is still a sensitive issue in Mainland China today. Film-makers usually resort to 'scientific' clues to rationalise the presence of the supernatural, for example hallucinations, schizophrenia, or dreams, as in *Rigor Mortis* (discussed later in this chapter).

19. The film topped the domestic box office for first-run local productions with a revenue of HK$17 million and was also a top-grossing film in Taiwan on its first week of release. Sources: *Hong Kong Film Industry Info 2013*: 21; Report on *Rigor Mortis*, *chinatimes.com*, available at <www.chinatimes.com/realtimenews/20131111003718-260404> (last accessed 20 July 2016).

20. Report on *Rigor Mortis*, *Apple Daily* (Taiwan), 6 November 2013. Available at <ent.appledaily.com.tw/enews/article/entertainment/20131106/35417 580/> (last accessed 20 July 2016.

References

Applause Pictures, box office figures, *Film Bimonthly*, vol. 491 (February 1998), <www.applausepictures.com/profile/index.html> (last accessed 18 July 2016).

Carroll, Noël (1990), *The Philosophy of Horror, or Paradoxes of the Heart*, London and New York: Routledge.

Cheung, Esther M. K. and Yiu-wai Chu (eds) (2004), *Between Home and World: a Reader in Hong Kong Cinema*, Hong Kong: Oxford University Press (China).

Davis, Darrell William and Emilie Yueh-yu Yeh (2008), *East Asian Screen Industries*, London: British Film Institute.

Freeland, Cynthia (2004), 'Horror and art-dread,' in Stephen Prince (ed.), *The Horror Film*, New Brunswick, NJ: Rutgers University Press, pp. 189–205.

Galloway, Patrick (2006), *Asia Shock: Horror and Dark Cinema from Japan, Korea, Hong Kong and Thailand*, Berkeley: Stonebridge Press.

Kam, Man-fung (2011), 'Beikao shijie, mianxiang zuguo', originally published in *Commercial Daily* (18 October), reposted on New People's Party official website: <www.npp.org.hk/zh-hk/node/6773> (last accessed 15 November 2014).

Lee, Nikki (2011), '"Asia" as regional signifier and transnational genre-branding: the Asian horror omnibus movies *Three* and *Three . . . Extremes*,' in Vivian Lee (ed.), *East Asian Cinemas: Regional Flows and Global Transformations*, Basingstoke: Palgrave Macmillan, pp. 103–17.

Lee, Vivian (2016), 'Universal hybrids: the trans/local production of pan-Asian horror', in Peter Braunlein and Andrea Lauser (eds), *Ghost Movies in Southeast Asia*, Leiden: Brill, pp. 43–60.

Motion Picture Industry Association (2013), *Hong Kong Film Industry Info 2013*, Hong Kong: MPIA.

National People's Congress (2006), 'Rita Fan: leveraging on the Motherland, facing the world'. *NPC online*, 8 March, <www.npc.gov.cn/npc/oldarchives/dbdh/dbdh/common/zw.jsp@label=wxzlk&id=346535&back=1&pdmc=3380.htm> (last accessed 15 November 2014).

Prince, Stephen (2004), 'Introduction', *The Horror Film*, Piscataway, NJ: Rutgers University Press, pp. 1–14.

Report on *Rigor Mortis*, *Apple Daily* (Taiwan), 6 November 2013, <ent.apple daily.com.tw/enews/article/entertainment/20131106/35417580/> (last accessed 20 July 2016).

Report on *Rigor Mortis*, *chinatimes.com*, <www.chinatimes.com/realtime news/20131111003718-260404> (last accessed 20 July 2016).

Shi, Man-hung (2003), 'Opportunities and crises at the turn of the century', in P. S. N. Lee (ed.), *New Perspectives on Hong Kong Media* (in Chinese), Hong Kong: Chinese University Press, p. 149–66.

Tung, Chee Hwa (2004), *Policy Address*, Hong Kong SAR Government, 7 January, <www.policyaddress.gov.hk/pa04/eng/p5.htm> (last accessed 15 November 2014).

Williams, Tony (1997), 'Space, place and spectacle: the crisis cinema of John Woo', *Cinema Journal*, 36:2, pp. 67–84.

Index